I NEVER CALLED IT RAPE

Consulting Editor
Ellen Sweet

I NEVER CALLED IT
RAPE

The *Ms.* Report on
Recognizing, Fighting, and Surviving
Date and Acquaintance Rape

ROBIN WARSHAW

Afterword by Mary P. Koss, Ph.D.

Ms. Foundation/Sarah Lazin Books

1817

HARPER & ROW, PUBLISHERS, New York
Cambridge, Philadelphia, San Francisco
London, Mexico City, São Paulo, Singapore, Sydney

FIRST EDITION

Designer: Joan Greenfield
Copy editor: Libby Kessman

Library of Congress Cataloging-in-Publication Data

Warshaw, Robin.
   I never called it rape.

   "Ms. magazine/Sarah Lazin Books."
   Includes index.
   1. Acquaintance rape—United States—Case studies.   2. Rape victims—United States—Case studies.   3. Rape—United States—Prevention.   I. Koss, Mary P.
I. Ms.   III. Title.
HV6561.W38   1988   362.8'8   87-46180
ISBN 0-06-055126-7   88 89 90 91 92 DT/FG 10 9 8 7 6 5 4 3 2
ISBN 0-06-096276-3 (pbk.)   88 89 90 91 92 DT/FG 10 9 8 7 6 5 4 3 2

CONTENTS

ACKNOWLEDGMENTS   ix

Introduction   1

1: The Reality of Acquaintance Rape   11

2: Women You Know   27

3: Why Date Rape and Acquaintance Rape
   Are So Widespread   35

4: Why Women Are "Safe" Victims   48

5: The Aftereffects of Acquaintance Rape   65

6: Men Who Rape Women They Know   83

7: Gang or "Party" Rapes   99

8. Teenagers and Acquaintance Rape   115

9: Police, Court, and University Responses to
   Acquaintance Rape   127

10: For Women:
    How to Prevent Acquaintance Rape   151

11: For Men: The Benefits of Change   161

12: Whose Responsibility Is It? Parents, Schools,
    Lawmakers, and Acquaintance Rape   168

13: Helping the Acquaintance-Rape Survivor 180

14: What to Do if Acquaintance Rape
Happens to You 185

AFTERWORD: The Methods Used in the *Ms.* Project on
Campus Sexual Assault, by Mary P. Koss, Ph.D. 189

SELECTED BIBLIOGRAPHY 211

RESOURCES 217

INDEX 225

If you have been forced to have sex by a date or an acquaintance, please read this before going any further.

It's hard to believe when rape happens to you, especially when the rapist is a man you know. But understand this: You *have* been raped. It was *not* your fault. And you are *not* alone.

Even if you have never heard of such a thing before, you've just survived the most common type of rape that occurs to women.

And "survived" is the right word. Rape is a life-threatening experience. Don't try to tough it out alone—getting help is not a sign of weakness. In the long run, talking to someone about the rape will give you greater strength and help you recover more quickly and more completely. *Tell someone*—a trusted friend, a close family member, a teacher. Also call a local rape-crisis hot line, women's center, or counseling center. You'll benefit from talking with a professional and such counseling is often free and always confidential.

You may want to turn immediately to Chapter 14, What to Do If Acquaintance Rape Happens to You. When you are ready, you may want to read the rest of this book (and some of the material in the Resources section) for a fuller understanding of acquaintance rape and its aftereffects. Later, you may also want to talk with your female friends and other women about your experience and theirs. Many communities have support groups for rape victims, as do some colleges and universities. These groups can help you regain your equilibrium.

If you were the victim of date rape or acquaintance rape in an incident that occurred years ago but never talked to anyone about it, do so now. Rape-crisis counselors offer their services no matter when your rape occurred. It's important for you to understand your rape experience in order to move on to a happier future.

ACKNOWLEDGMENTS

I'd like to thank several people for the assistance they gave me during the writing of this book: Mary P. Koss, who headed the *Ms.* national research project on acquaintance rape and helped me translate the pounds of statistical data the study produced; Ellen Sweet, my editor at *Ms.* magazine, who was involved in the research project from its inception and offered me solace and guidance when I needed it the most; Sarah Lazin, of Sarah Lazin Books, who coordinated the publishing project and kept me afloat; Janet Goldstein, my editor at Harper & Row, who enthusiastically supported the book; and Carol Mann, my agent, who provided helpful advice.

In addition, I thank the many rape researchers, counselors, college administrators, and antirape workers, women and men, around the country who talked with me and opened their programs to me. I also wish to thank my family and friends for the help they provided throughout and especially Craig R. McCoy, for his love and support.

But the largest share of my thanks goes to the many women who shared their experiences of date rape and acquaintance rape with me, who volunteered to tell their stories in the hopes that, through greater awareness, such rapes might end. They taught me much and I am grateful to them.

INTRODUCTION

In the beginning—that is, the early and mid-1970s—rape awareness meant women learning where to kick and how hard.

America was just starting to acknowledge its rape problem. Rape counseling centers and support groups opened in many cities and towns, and women began talking about their experiences and working in positive ways to fight back against the effects of sexual assault. *Ms.* magazine documented the growth of this organized response and provided a forum for the personal voices of rape victims. The very act of speaking out—on the printed page and at public meetings—was a courageous first step for many women in naming the unnameable and identifying rape as an act of violence and hatred against all women. Although official response was still slow in coming, police and prosecutorial procedures in many states changed to offer more support for victims. Rape laws were rewritten to place a greater emphasis on protecting victims' rights, and some states developed more effective ways to investigate and prosecute rape complaints.

Women joined self-defense classes. They were cautioned to carry whistles, air horns, or simply their car keys gripped firmly in their hands when walking alone, at night, down empty corridors, through parking lots, on elevators. These were the places they were told to fear. There were undoubtedly few women who had not worked out a "what if" scenario of sexual self-defense for themselves.

The crime, the criminal, and the victim of rape all began to come into focus. Women understood that they had to be wary of strange men. They locked the doors of their cars and homes, checked over their shoulders as they walked down the street, learned to react defensively and even aggressively if a suspicious-looking man loitered in the lobby of their apartment building or stood on their porch asking to use the telephone. For many women, becoming aware of the threat of rape meant limiting activities, staying indoors, even pretending to have a husband or boyfriend in the house to provide a threat of force greater than their own. Thus armed—or limited—by their defensive strategies, most women felt they had done as much as they could to prevent an attack.

But as the awareness of rape grew, so too did the understanding of it as a phenomenon that reaches beyond dark hallways and alleys. In September 1982, *Ms.* magazine published an article that offered disturbing evidence of a still hidden type of rape—popularly called "date rape"—that involved men and women who knew each other. Preliminary research indicated that there were more victims of this kind of rape than of what was believed to be more common, rapes by strangers. Scores of responses from readers proved the magazine was on the right track.

To explore that possibility, *Ms.* approached the National Institute for Mental Health for a grant to do a major national study. The Center for the Prevention and Control of Rape teamed the magazine with Mary P. Koss, Ph.D., then a psychology professor at Kent State University in Ohio, who had already conducted research for NIMH in the field. There followed three years of exhaustive work by Koss, her team of researchers, and *Ms.* staff, with surveys administered on 32 college campuses to more than 6,100 undergraduate women and men. The *Ms.* project—the largest scientific investigation ever undertaken on the subject—revealed some disquieting statistics, including this astonishing fact: *One in four female respondents had had an experience that met the legal definition of rape or attempted rape.*

By that point, the phenomenon was starting to be called by the broader term "acquaintance rape," a more accurate label for rapes that occur between people who know each other, whether from dating relationships or otherwise. Indeed, women are being raped by a wide range of men they know: by dates, by friends, by fellow students, by men they know from work or whom they meet at parties, in bars, at religious functions, or in their neighborhoods.

A word about the scope of this book: Incest, "authority rapes" (by doctors and teachers), spousal rape, and the rape of children under age 14 have been excluded from the acquaintance-rape umbrella, although these are subjects that also figure prominently in the overall phenomenon of violence against women. Also, although some rape centers now say that 10 percent of victims reporting to them are male (nearly all from male-against-male rapes), this book addresses male-against-female assaults because those constitute the overwhelming majority of acquaintance rapes and are the types of rape measured in the *Ms.* survey. (Chapter 5, however, contains a section on male victims.)

If the early chapters of this book seem to dwell on establishing the reality of acquaintance rape, that's because acquaintance rape continues to be unknown, ignored, or denied by most people. Indeed, study after study has shown that women who are raped by men they know often don't even identify their experiences as rape. Moreover, most people, male and female, still don't recognize that acquaintance rape is a crime—an admonition that would be unnecessary to make if we were discussing robbery, forgery, arson, embezzlement, or even now, thankfully, stranger rape. It is hoped that *I Never Called It Rape* will help change all that.

The intent here is not only to define and demonstrate the prevalence of acquaintance rape, but to point toward ways to reduce such assault. Acquaintance rape *can* be avoided. Knowledge is power: By the time you finish reading this book, you should be better equipped to prevent acquaintance rape from happening to you or someone you love. This book has been written for women and men, parents, educators, counselors, and those in the legal system. A Resources section has been included to help readers with a variety of interests, from learning more about the dynamics of acquaintance rape to setting up a campus or community program for prevention. In addition, a Technical Afterword by researcher Mary P. Koss explains the scientific methodology of the *Ms.* study.

Although the *Ms.* survey focused on college campuses according to the requirements of the NIMH grant, the editors had always believed the scope of the problem went far beyond university walls. Indeed, while college campuses are petri dishes of date rape and acquaintance rape, due to their demographics, many letters received by *Ms.* offered testimony to the fact that these rapes occur throughout society and affect women both younger and older than the traditional undergraduate. From its inception, the purpose of this book was to draw a fuller picture of acquaintance rape, one that documented how often women—regardless of their ages, ethnicities, schooling, or income—are raped by men they know. Acquaintance rape remains largely hidden because few people identify it for what it is—a crime punishable by law. Because the assault occurs between individuals who know each other, within the context of the often confused personal and sexual relationships between men and women, it's difficult for many people to label it correctly.

But acquaintance rape *is* a crime. And it is no less a crime simply because the perpetrator has a familiar face.

It was a low point in my life. The war in Vietnam, which I, along with hundreds of thousands of other college students, took to the streets to oppose, was becoming more bloody—at home and abroad. In unrelated violence, a friend I loved was murdered that spring by a teenage gang. A few weeks after my friend's murder, I ended a relationship with my boyfriend, whom I will call Carl. Carl and I parted on unpleasant terms—with me wanting a clean break, him wanting another chance. He left town and traveled for a while, with no clear plans.

One day, about two months after our breakup, Carl appeared at my apartment door entreating me to talk to him, to get back together. I told him I wasn't interested in reviving the relationship. He began to shout that he would kill himself if I wouldn't speak with him.

I had loved this man once and felt guilty that I was making him so unhappy. I thought that he really might try to commit suicide. I agreed to go outside to talk with him. Once outside, he insisted that I go with him to a mutual friend's apartment where he was staying. According to Carl, that friend wanted to see me and had planned that we would all have dinner together. We could talk there, he said.

It never occurred to me that Carl was lying. I thought that

maybe our friend could help me convince Carl that the relationship was really over. The friend's apartment was in a part of the city that I wasn't very familiar with. I can still remember climbing up the stairs to the apartment, thinking how glad I was that our friend would be there. I stepped into the apartment, calling out his name. Behind me, I heard the thunk of a door bolt.

I turned and Carl was standing, grinning. He held a large knife he must have retrieved from the kitchen as we walked in. Needless to say, our friend was not in the apartment—Carl had known that when he brought me there. I immediately believed that I could die. If I had any doubts, he removed them moments later by telling me that he was going to kill me.

As the night progressed, he continued to threaten to kill me and himself if I refused to renew our relationship. We talked around and around that subject for hours. He only let me out of his sight to use the bathroom, where I discovered the window had bars across it. I could have yelled out it for help, but I did not. My reasons are contradictory, yet very like the reasons I heard from many of the women I interviewed for this book: I didn't know where I was or who might come; I didn't want to embarrass Carl or myself; I still felt I could talk him out of the situation and I was afraid that my yelling would only make him angrier and put me in more danger.

When, late into the night, he motioned to the bedroom with the knife, I followed. In bed, he draped his arm across me, holding the knife on the far side of the pillow all night. He had intercourse with me at least once, but I think it might have been more than that. It seemed to go on for a long time. I felt like I was in a corner of the room, watching the bed from a distance. Eventually, he fell asleep. I did not move. I did not holler. I did not try to leave. In the morning, Carl walked me back to my apartment. We parted company about a block from my door at my insistence, although now I think he agreed because he didn't want to risk running into my roommates. When I finally got inside, I stripped off my clothes and stood in the shower for an hour. I did not go to work that day.

Several times in the next week or two, Carl intercepted me on the way to my job. My boss, who was also a friend, called the security office so I would have an escort. I had told no one about what happened, but she could tell that I was frightened by Carl's hanging around. After a few more weeks, he was gone, but my fears that he would reappear were not. For months, I dreaded going anywhere he might be—and that was everywhere.

It took me about three years to realize I had been raped. Before that, all I focused on about the assault was the feeling that I could die. Since my attacker had been my boyfriend, with whom I had had sexual intercourse before, I never attached the word "rape" to what happened. Rape, after all, was what vile strangers did to you. Then one day, after a close friend became head of a local rape-crisis group, I was listening to her tell me about some of her group's recent cases. They were all rapes committed by strangers, but the stories evoked a rush of feelings about my own experience. Then I knew: I had been raped.

I'd like to say that naming it helped, but it didn't, not for a long time. The rape contributed to problems I had for the next several years. Eventually, counseling helped overcome the cumulative effect of those years.

Ten years after the episode, I finally felt that I had worked it all through. Of course, I harbored my revenge fantasies—I daydreamed of encountering Carl in a public place and proclaiming him to be a rapist, which, most certainly, he would loudly deny—but I felt that at least I now understood what had happened, although I shared my story with very few people.

It was Christmas Eve and I was home alone when the phone rang. I picked it up and a man said, "I bet you don't know who this is. This is a voice from your past." I recognized Carl's voice immediately, which seemed to flatter him.

He then told me he had been reading the articles I was writing. I felt angry and afraid. Carl obviously knew where I lived and probably still lived in the area, since much of my writing at that time was for local publications. I asked him questions to try to figure out where he was and to determine how much of a danger he posed. He gave me little information about himself. I wanted to hang up, but I wanted to confront him even more. He had attacked me again, this time by telephone, and this would probably be my only chance to strike back. I steadied myself.

"Do you realize that the last time you saw me you raped me?"

There, I had said it to him, just as I always hoped I would. Now I braced myself for the outraged denial that I knew would come. I could feel my whole body tighten, waiting for the blow.

After a long pause, his voice came over the line.

"Yes," he said, and then, after another pause, he added, "but the statute of limitations is up."

I became enraged and warned him never to contact me again or I would call the police. Then I slammed down the phone. I couldn't believe it: I had confronted him and he had admitted that, yes, he *had* raped me.

When I finally calmed down, there was still anger. But most of it was anger at myself. I had really thought I was done with it. But after the phone call I realized that over the years I had still harbored some doubts: How could it be rape if you knew him? If you dated him? If you had had sex with him before?

By answering "yes" to my question, Carl gave a power to my belief in what happened that it had not had before. I was angry and disappointed in myself that his corroboration could mean so much.

That was seven years ago. When *Ms.* editor Ellen Sweet and I first talked about my writing this book, she did not know that I had been raped by a man I knew. I would not tell her that for several months. I needed time to think about the project. What would it be like for me to concentrate my efforts for more than a year on a subject that had already personally caused me pain, confusion, and anger? I realized, too, that my interviewing could dredge up pain for my subjects—much more than I, as a reporter, liked to stir. I am, after all, not a therapist or a rape-crisis counselor. Could I take women back over their experiences without causing more damage? I also knew I would have to write about my own acquaintance-rape experience. I could not ask other women to reveal what I was unwilling to show. As the book's author, I knew I would be asked if I had ever been the victim of such rape. I could not imagine lying about that.

Writing the book would also mean, finally, that I would have to tell my parents I had been raped.

When I decided to go ahead, I talked with and listened to date-rape and acquaintance-rape survivors around the country. To find a fuller range of women who had been raped by men they knew, I purchased advertisements in local newspapers, received some help from rape-crisis workers, and placed a small notice in *Ms.* seeking women willing to talk about their experiences. (It elicited scores of responses.) Some women I interviewed in person, others wrote eloquent narratives. In all, I talked to or heard from more than 150 women. It is these women who are quoted throughout this book. For many of the women I interviewed, it was the first time they had talked with anyone other than a counselor about their incidents. Most said they agreed to talk with me to educate other women and to encourage acquaintance-rape survivors who may be suffering in solitude to seek help. I also spoke with men who were sympathetic and unsympathetic about women's experiences with date and acquaintance rape as well as with male and female sociologists, psychologists, educators and crisis workers who are looking for solutions to the problem.

When I began my research, I thought I understood my own rape experience fully. But, time and again, while working on this book, I realized that I did not. Talking with other women who had been raped by men they knew, I learned much more about what happened to me. Nothing follows a formula, but I discovered how my experience—which I always thought to be one of a kind—was a typical acquaintance rape in many aspects (it was planned by the man, it happened in an isolated location, I didn't identify it as rape because I knew my attacker). Although most acquaintance rapes and date rapes don't involve a weapon as mine did, many of the women I interviewed spoke of how they feared for their lives during their assaults, how they truly believed that they were going to die. The tales of recovery that many women shared with me also helped me examine my own aftermath.

I mention all of this, in part, because it is a fondly held belief among journalists that we come to our subjects with no particular opinion or ax to grind. When we do have a bias, we like to make it clearly known up-front. I know that my having been raped makes a difference—not necessarily to my editors or to the experts I spoke with, but to the women who shared their stories with me. Early on in each interview, I mentioned briefly that I had been raped by a man I knew. Each time, my listener visibly relaxed. That piece of information was powerful enough to remove the ever-present fear among acquaintance-rape survivors—the fear of not being believed.

CHAPTER 1

The Reality of Acquaintance Rape

"I never heard of anybody having that happen to them."
— Lori, raped at 19 by a date

Women raped by men they know—acquaintance rape—is not an aberrant quirk of male-female relations. If you are a woman, your risk of being raped by someone you know is *four times greater* than your risk of being raped by a stranger.

A recent scientific study of acquaintance rape on 32 college campuses conducted by *Ms.* magazine and psychologist Mary P. Koss showed that significant numbers of women are raped on dates or by acquaintances, although most victims never report their attacks.

Ms. SURVEY STATS □ 1 in 4 women surveyed were victims of rape or attempted rape.
□ 84 percent of those raped knew their attacker.
□ 57 percent of the rapes happened on dates.

Those figures make acquaintance rape and date rape more common than left-handedness or heart attacks or alcoholism. These rapes are no recent campus fad or the fantasy of a few jilted females. They are real. And they are happening all around us.

The Extent of "Hidden" Rape

Most states define rape as sexual assault in which a man uses his penis to commit vaginal penetration of a victim against her will, by force or threats of force or when she is physically or mentally unable to give her consent. Many states now also include unwanted anal and oral intercourse in that definition and some have removed gender-specific language to broaden the applicability of rape laws.

In acquaintance rape, the rapist and victim may know each other casually—having met through a common activity, mutual friend, at a party, as neighbors, as students in the same class, at work, on a blind date, or while traveling. Or they may have a closer relationship —as steady dates or former sexual partners. Although largely a hidden phenomenon because it's the least reported type of rape (and rape, in general, is the most underreported crime against a person), many organizations, counselors, and social researchers agree that acquaintance rape is the most prevalent rape crime today.

Only 90,434 rapes were reported to U.S. law enforcement agencies in 1986, a number that is conservatively believed to represent a minority of the actual rapes of all types taking place. Government estimates find that anywhere from three to ten rapes are committed for every one rape reported. And while rapes by strangers are still underreported, rapes by acquaintances are virtually nonreported. Yet, based on intake observations made by staff at various rape-counseling centers (where victims come for treatment, but do not have to file police reports), 70 to 80 percent of all rape crimes are acquaintance rapes.

Those rapes are happening in a social environment in which sexual aggression occurs regularly. Indeed, less than half the college women questioned in the *Ms.* survey reported that they had experienced *no* sexual victimization in their lives thus far (the average age of respondents was 21). Many had experienced more than one episode of unwanted sexual touching, coercion, attempted rape, or rape. Using the data collected in the study (see the Afterword on page 189 for an explanation of how the survey was conducted), the following profile can be drawn of what happens in just one year of "social life" on America's college campuses:

Ms. SURVEY STATS   □ In one year 3,187 women reported suffering:
                    □ 328 rapes (as defined by law)
                    □ 534 attempted rapes (as defined by law)
                    □ 837 episodes of sexual coercion (sexual
                       intercourse obtained through the aggressor's
                       continual arguments or pressure)
                    □ 2,024 experiences of unwanted sexual contact
                       (fondling, kissing, or petting committed against
                       the woman's will)

Over the years, other researchers have documented the phenomenon of acquaintance rape. In 1957, a study conducted by Eugene J. Kanin of Purdue University in West Lafayette, Indiana, showed that 30 percent of women surveyed had suffered attempted or completed forced sexual intercourse while on a high school date. Ten years later, in 1967, while young people donned flowers and beads and talked of love and peace, Kanin found that more than 25 percent of the male college students surveyed had attempted to force sexual intercourse on a woman to the point that she cried or fought back. In 1977, after the blossoming of the women's movement and countless pop-culture attempts to extol the virtues of becoming a "sensitive man," Kanin found that 26 percent of the men he surveyed had tried to force intercourse on a woman and that 25 percent of the women questioned had suffered attempted or completed rape. In other words, two decades had passed since Kanin's first study, yet women were being raped by men they knew as frequently as before.

In 1982, a doctoral student at Auburn University in Auburn, Alabama, found that 25 percent of the undergraduate women surveyed had at least one experience of forced intercourse and that 93 percent of those episodes involved acquaintances. That same year, Auburn psychology professor and acquaintance-rape expert Barry R. Burkhart conducted a study in which 61 percent of the men said they had sexually touched a woman against her will.

Further north, at St. Cloud State University in St. Cloud, Minnesota, research in 1982 showed 29 percent of women surveyed reported being physically or psychologically forced to have sexual intercourse.

In 1984, 20 percent of the female students questioned in a study at the University of South Dakota in Vermillion, South Dakota, said they had been physically forced to have intercourse while on a date. At Brown University in Providence, Rhode Island, 16 percent of the women surveyed reported they were raped by an acquaintance and 11 percent of the men said they had forced sexual intercourse on a woman. And another study coauthored by Auburn's Burkhart showed 15 percent of the male respondents reporting having raped a date.

That same year, the study of acquaintance rape moved beyond the serenity of leafy college quadrangles into the hard reality of the "dangerous" outside world. A random sample survey of 930 women living in San Francisco, conducted by researcher Diana Russell, showed that 44 percent of the women questioned had been victims of rape or attempted rape—and that 88 percent of the rape victims knew their attackers. A Massachusetts Department of Public Health study, released in 1986, showed that two-thirds of the rapes reported at crisis centers were committed by acquaintances.

These numbers stand in stark contrast to what most people think of as rape: that is, a stranger (usually a black, Hispanic, or other minority) jumping out of the bushes at an unsuspecting female, brandishing a weapon, and assaulting her. The truth about rape—that it usually happens between people who know each other and is often committed by "regular" guys—is difficult to accept.

Most people never learn the truth until rape affects them or someone they care about. And many women are so confused by the dichotomy between their acquaintance-rape experience and what they thought rape really was that they are left with an awful new reality: Where once they feared strange men as they were taught to, they now fear strange men *and* all the men they know.

Lori's Story

How can a date be a rape?

The pairing of the word "date," which conjures up an image of fun shared by two companions, with the word "rape," which evokes the total loss of control by one person to the will of another, results in the creation of a new phrase that is nearly impossible for most people to comprehend. To understand how date rape happens, let's look at a classic case.

THE SETUP: It was natural. Normal. Lori's friend Amy wanted to go out with Paul, but felt awkward and shy about going out with him alone. So when Paul's roommate, Eric, suggested that he and Lori join Amy and Paul for a double date, it made sense. "I didn't feel anything for Eric except as a friend," Lori says of her reaction to the plan. "I said, 'Okay, maybe it will make Amy feel better.' "

Agreeing to go out with Eric was no great act of charity on Lori's part. He *was* attractive—tall, good-looking, in his mid-20s and from a wealthy family. Lori, who was 19 at the time, knew Eric and Paul as frequent customers at the popular Tampa Bay restaurant where she worked as a waitress when she was between college semesters.

On the day of the date, Eric called several times to change their plans. Finally, he phoned to say that they would be having a barbecue with several of his friends at the house he and Paul shared. Lori agreed.

> We went to his house and I mentioned something about Paul and Amy and he kind of threw it off, like, "Yeah, yeah." I didn't think anything of it. There we are, fixing steaks, and he was saying, "Well, this is obviously something to help Amy."
>
> He kept making drinks all night long. He kept saying, "Here, have a drink," "Here, drink this." I didn't because I didn't want it. He was just downing them right and left.

THE ATTACK: Unknown to Lori, Amy had canceled her plans to see Paul the day before. Paul told Eric, but Eric never told Lori. As the barbecue party progressed and her friend failed to show up, Lori questioned Eric again. He then lied, telling her that Paul had just called to say he and Amy weren't coming.

> I was thinking to myself, "Well, okay." Not in my wildest dreams would I have thought he was plotting something. Then all of his friends started leaving. I began to think, "Something is wrong, something is going on," but I've been known to overreact to things, so I ignored it.

After his friends left, we're sitting on the couch and he leans over and he kisses me and I'm thinking, "It's a date, it's no big deal." So then we started kissing a little bit more and I'm thinking, "I'm starting to enjoy this, maybe this isn't so bad." Then the phone rang and when he came back I was standing up. He grabbed me from behind and picked me up. He had his hands over my eyes and we were walking through his house. It was really dark and I didn't know where on earth he was taking me. I had never actually walked through his house.

He laid me down [on a bed] and kissed me. . . . He starts taking off my clothes and I said, "Wait — time out! This is not what I want, you know," and he said to me something like this is what I owed him because he made me dinner.

I said, "This is wrong, don't do this. I didn't go out with you with this intent."

He said, "What do you call that on the couch?"

I said, "I call it a kiss, period."

And he said, "Well, I don't."

The two struggled until Eric rolled off her momentarily. Lori jumped up and went into the bathroom. Her plan was to come out in a few minutes and tell him it was time to take her home.

The whole time I'm thinking, "I don't believe this is happening to me." I didn't even have time to walk fully out of the bathroom door when he grabbed me and threw me on the bed and started taking my clothes off. I'm yelling and hitting and pushing on him and he just liked that. He says, "I know you must like this because a lot of women like this kind of thing." Then he says, "This is the adult world. Maybe you ought to grow up some."

I finally got to the point where there was nothing I could do.

Eric pushed his penis into her and, after a few minutes, ejaculated. Lori had had only one other experience with sexual intercourse, about a year before with a longtime boyfriend.

Then Eric just rolled over and I started to get my clothes together. He said, "Don't tell me you didn't like that." I looked at him and said, "No," and by this time I'm crying because I don't know what else to do. I never heard of anybody having that happen to them.

THE AFTERMATH: Finally, Eric took her home.

> In the car he said, "Can I call you tomorrow? Can I see you next weekend?" I just looked at him and he just looked at me and started laughing.
>
> My mom had gone out and I just laid on my bed with the covers up. Everything I could possibly put on I think I put on that night — leg warmers, thermal underwear — everything imaginable in the middle of summer I put on my body. That night I dreamed it was all happening again. I dreamed I was standing there watching him do it.
>
> For two weeks I couldn't talk. People would talk to me and I felt nothing. I felt like a zombie. I couldn't cry, I couldn't smile, I couldn't eat. My mom said, "What's wrong with you? Is something going on?" I said, "Nothing's wrong."
>
> I thought it was my fault. What did I do to make him think he could do something like that? Was I wrong in kissing him? Was I wrong to go out with him, to go over to his house?

After two weeks, she told her mother what happened and they talked about what to do. Lori decided not to report it to the police for fear Eric would blame her. Eric continued to frequent the restaurant where she worked. Several weeks after their date, he cornered her in a hallway near the kitchen.

> He touched me and I said, "Get your hands off me." At first, he thought it was funny. He said, "What's wrong?" then he started pulling me, trying to hug me. I pushed him and said, "Leave me alone," and I was starting to get a little loud. As I was walking away, he said, "Oh, I guess you didn't get enough."
>
> I walked in the kitchen and I picked up this tray full of food. I don't know how it happened, I just dropped the whole tray and it went everywhere. My friend, another waitress, went to the manager and said, "She's not going to be much good to you tonight," so they sent me home.

Lori decided to move to a town about 150 miles away to avoid continued encounters with Eric. There she found work as an office assistant and cashier and enrolled for a few classes at a new college.

Sitting in a darkened restaurant on her lunch break one year after the rape, Lori is still looking for answers.

When I moved here, nobody knew about it. I just figured, this only happened to me. Then my roommate told me it happened to her in Ohio. We talked about it once and that was it. It just upset me too much to talk about it anymore. I mean, she understood, it upset her a lot, too, so we just don't bring it up.

How do other women handle it? I work two jobs and I go to school because I don't want to have to deal with the situation of having somebody ask me on a date. If I go out with a guy, I'm wondering, is he thinking dinner means "I'll get you into bed"?

I'm not going to be stupid enough to put myself in that situation again. I grew out of being naive just like that. This experience grew me up in about two weeks.

The Myths About Acquaintance Rape

Like most women with date-rape or acquaintance-rape experiences, Lori did not report the incident to police and did not, at first, even understand it to be rape. Instead, she felt almost totally isolated and blamed herself for what happened. She changed her life in order to feel physically safe from her attacker. She is now filled with doubts about her own judgment, fears socializing with men, and despairs about her ability to have a "normal" relationship.

But ask a group of college students what they think of a story like Lori's and they might tell you:

- "She deserved it."
- "What did she expect? After all, she went to his house."
- "That's not rape. Rape is when a guy you don't know grabs you and holds a gun to your head."
- "She wasn't a virgin, so no harm was done."
- "He bought her dinner. She owed him."
- "She liked kissing him. What's the big deal if he went farther?"
- "She just 'cried rape' later because she felt guilty about having sex."

Those are the kinds of comments heard recently on all kinds of campuses—Ivy League, state universities, small schools—when date rape was discussed by both male and female undergraduates.

But let's not blame college students alone for their views: Their parents, indeed most of our society, would agree with one or more of those statements.

These are the myths that have formed what we believe to be the truth about women who are raped by men they know. But the actual truth is different indeed. Here are several of the most common myths about acquaintance rape juxtaposed with the reality:

MYTH	REALITY
Rape is committed by crazed strangers.	Most women are raped by "normal" acquaintances.
A woman who gets raped deserves it, especially if she agreed to go to the man's house or ride in his car.	No one, male or female, deserves to be raped. Being in a man's house or car does not mean a woman has agreed to have sex with him.
Women who don't fight back haven't been raped.	You have been raped when you are forced to have sex against your will, whether you fight back or not.
If there's no gun or knife, you haven't been raped.	It's rape whether the rapist uses a weapon or his fists, verbal threats, drugs or alcohol, physical isolation, your own diminished physical or mental state, or simply the weight of his body to overcome you.
It's not really rape if the victim isn't a virgin.	Rape is rape, even if the woman isn't a virgin, even if she willingly had sex with the man before.
If a woman lets a man buy her dinner or pay for a movie or drinks, she owes him sex.	No one owes sex as a payment to anyone else, no matter how expensive the date.
Agreeing to kiss or neck or pet with a man means that a woman has agreed to have intercourse with him.	Everyone has the right to say "no" to sexual activity, regardless of what has preceded it, and to have that "no" respected.

MYTH	REALITY
When men are sexually aroused, they need to have sex or they will get "blue balls." Also, once they get turned on, men can't help themselves from forcing sex on a woman.	Men don't physically need to have sex after becoming aroused any more than women do. Moreover, men are still able to control themselves even after becoming sexually excited.
Women lie about being raped, especially when they accuse men they date or other acquaintances.	Rape really happens—to people you know, by people you know.

Like most of our beliefs, we absorb these myths as we grow up: from the people around us, from the books we read, from the movies and television programs we watch, even from the way products are sold to us in advertisements.

Because of the myths, the reality of acquaintance rape is largely ignored. On college campuses, when a woman is raped in a dormitory or fraternity house by another student, university officials announce new plans for better lighting in the parking lots and expanded hours for escort services—positive safety precautions that have nothing to do with stopping acquaintance rape. The few women who report their date rapes (and whose cases are accepted for prosecution) are usually met with skepticism and disbelief from jurors and judges when they testify about being raped by a man they knew or chose to be with in a social setting.

No wonder that while many rape-prevention activists would like to see more prosecutions for acquaintance-rape cases, many admit privately that they counsel women not to press charges because of the difficulty of convincing jurors—whose views are shaped by the myths—that a rape has really taken place.

Rape Is Rape

Rape that occurs on dates or between people who know each other should not be seen as some sort of misguided sexual adventure: Rape is violence, not seduction. In stranger rape *and* acquaintance rape, the aggressor makes a decision to force his victim to submit to what he wants. The rapist believes he is entitled to force sexual intercourse from a woman and he sees interpersonal violence (be it simply holding the woman down with his body or brandishing a gun) as an acceptable way to achieve his goal.

"All rape is an exercise in power," writes Susan Brownmiller in her landmark book *Against Our Will: Men, Women and Rape.* Specifically, Brownmiller and others argue, rape is an exercise in the imbalance of power that exists between most men and women, a relationship that has forged the social order from ancient times on.

Today, that relationship continues. Many men are socialized to be sexually aggressive—to score, as it were, regardless of how. Many women are socialized to submit to men's wills, especially those men deemed desirable by society at large. Maintaining such roles helps set the stage for acquaintance rape.

But despite their socialization, most men are not rapists. That is the good news.

The bad news, of course, is that so many are.

Ms. SURVEY STAT □ 1 in 12 of the male students surveyed had committed acts that met the legal definitions of rape or attempted rape.

Blaming the Acquaintance-Rape Victim

Without question, many date rapes and acquaintance rapes could have been prevented by the woman—if she hadn't trusted a seemingly nice guy, if she hadn't gotten drunk, if she had acted earlier on the "bad feeling" that many victims later report they felt but ignored because they didn't want to seem rude, unfriendly, or immature. But acknowledging that in some cases the woman might have prevented the rape by making a different decision does not make her responsible for the crime. Says a counselor for an Oregon rape-crisis agency: "We have a saying here: 'Bad judgment is not a rapeable offense.' "

As a society, we don't blame the victims of most crimes as we do acquaintance-rape survivors. A mugging victim is not believed to "deserve it" for wearing a watch or carrying a pocketbook on the street. Likewise, a company is not "asking for it" when its profits are embezzled; a store owner is not to blame for handing over the cash drawer when threatened. These crimes occur because the perpetrator decides to commit them.

Acquaintance rape is no different. There are ways to reduce the odds, but, like all crimes, there is no way to be certain that it will not happen to you.

Yet acquaintance-rape victims are seen as responsible for the attacks, often more responsible than their assailants. "Date rape threatens the assumption that if you're good, good things happen to you. Most of us believe that bad things don't happen out of the blue," says psychologist Koss, chief investigator of the *Ms.* study, now affiliated with the department of psychiatry at the University of Arizona Medical School in Tucson, Arizona. Society, in general, is so disturbed by the idea that a "regular guy" could do such a thing —and, to be sure, many "regular guys" are made uncomfortable by a concept that views their actions as a crime—that they would rather believe that something is wrong with the woman making such an outlandish claim: She is lying, she has emotional problems, she hates men, she is covering up her own promiscuous behavior. In fact, the research in the *Ms.* survey shows that women who have been raped by men they know are not appreciably different in any personal traits or behaviors than women who are not raped.

Should we ask women not to trust men who seem perfectly nice? Should we tell them not to go to parties or on dates? Should we tell them not to drink? Should we tell them not to feel sexual? Certainly not. *It is not the victim who causes the rape.*

But many persist in believing just that. An April 1987 letter to syndicated columnist Ann Landers from a woman who had been raped by two different men she dated reportedly drew heavy negative reader mail after Landers responded supportively to the woman. "Too bad you didn't file charges against those creeps," Landers wrote. "I urge you to go for counseling immediately to rid yourself of the feeling of guilt and rage. You must get it through your head that you were not to blame."

So far, so good, but not for long. Three months later, Landers published a letter from an irate female reader who noted that the victim said she and the first man had "necked up a storm" before he raped her. Perhaps the raped woman hadn't intended to have intercourse, the reader said, "but she certainly must accept responsibility for encouraging the guy and making him think she was a willing partner. The trouble starts when she changes her mind after his passions are out of control. Then it's too late."

Landers bought this specious argument—a variant on the old "men can't help themselves" nonsense. In her reply to the follow-up letter she wrote, "Now I'm convinced that I must rethink my position and go back to telling women, 'If you don't want a complete sexual experience, keep a lively conversation going and his hands off you.' "

In other words, if you get raped, it's your own fault.

Date Rape and Acquaintance Rape on College Campuses

Despite philosophical and political changes brought about by the women's movement, dating relationships between men and women are still often marked by passivity on the woman's part and aggression on the man's. Nowhere are these two seen in stronger contrast than among teenagers and young adults who often, out of their own fears, insecurity, and ignorance, adopt the worst sex-role stereotypes. Such an environment fosters a continuum of sexual victimization—from unwanted sexual touching to psychologically coerced sex to rape—that is tolerated as normal. "Because sexually coercive behavior is so common in our male-female interactions, rape by an acquaintance may not be perceived as rape," says Py Bateman, director of Alternatives to Fear, a Seattle rape-education organization.

Indeed, we speak of "the battle of the sexes" and, for many, it is just that. In their teens, many boys are counseled by their friends and older males to practice the "4Fs" when dealing with women: "Find 'em; feel 'em; fuck 'em; forget 'em." On the other hand, many girls, who have been admonished to "save it" for Mr. Right, want sexual intercourse to take place in the context of a relationship with some continuity attached to it. Kurt Weis and Sandra S. Borges, researchers at the University of California at Berkeley, pointed out in a 1973 paper that dating places individuals with these highly socialized but differing expectations into an ambiguous situation in which there is maximum privacy.

That is, dating can easily lead to rape.

Not surprising, then, that the risk of rape is four times higher for women aged 16 to 24, the prime dating age, than for any other population group. Approximately half of all men arrested for rape are also 24 years old or younger. Since 26 percent of all 18- to 24-year-olds in the United States attend college, those institutions have become focal points for studying date rape and acquaintance rape, such as the *Ms.* research.

Ms. SURVEY STAT □ For both men and women, the average age when a rape incident occurred (either as perpetrator or victim) was 18½ years old.

Going to college often means going away from home, out from under parental control and protection and into a world of seemingly unlimited freedoms. The imperative to party and date, although strong in high school, burgeons in this environment. Alcohol is readily available and often used in stultifying amounts, encouraged by a college world that practically demands heavy drinking as proof of having fun. Marijuana, cocaine, LSD, methamphetamines, and other drugs are also often easy to obtain.

Up until the 1970s, colleges adopted a "substitute parent" attitude toward their students, complete with curfews (often more strict for females than males), liquor bans, and stringent disciplinary punishments. In that era, students were punished for violating the three-feet-on-the-floor rules during coed visiting hours in dormitories or for being caught with alcohol on college property. Although those regulations did not prevent acquaintance rape, they undoubtedly kept down the number of incidents by making women's dorms havens of no-men-allowed safety.

Such regulations were swept out of most schools during the Vietnam War era. Today, many campuses have coed dorms, with men and women often housed in alternating rooms on the same floor, with socializing unchecked by curfews or meaningful controls on alcohol and drugs. Yet, say campus crisis counselors, many parents still believe that they have properly prepared their children for college by helping them open local bank accounts and making sure they have enough underwear to last until the first trip home. By ignoring the realities of social pressures at college on male and female students—and the often catastrophic effects of those pressures—parents help perpetuate the awareness vacuum in which date rape and acquaintance rape continue to happen with regularity.

"What's changed for females is the illusion that they have control and they don't," says Claire P. Walsh, program director of the Sexual Assault Recovery Service at the University of Florida in Gainesville. "They know that they can go into chemical engineering or medical school and they've got their whole life planned, they're on a roll. They transfer that feeling of control into social situations and that's the illusion."

When looking at the statistical results of the *Ms.* survey, it's important to remember that many of these young people still have years of socializing and dating ahead of them, years in which they may encounter still more acquaintance rape. Students, parents of college students, and college administrators should be concerned. But many are not, lulled by the same myths that pervade our society at large: Rape is not committed by people you know, against "good" girls, in "safe" places like university campuses.

The Other Victims of Acquaintance Rape

Date rape and acquaintance rape aren't confined to the college population, however. Interviews conducted across the country showed that women both younger and older than university students are frequently acquaintance-rape victims as well.

A significant number of teenage girls suffer date rape as their first or nearly first experience of sexual intercourse (see Chapter 8, page 115) and most tell no one about their attacks. Consider Nora, a high school junior, who was raped by a date as they watched TV in his parents' house or Jenny, 16, who was raped after she drank too much at a party. Even before a girl officially begins dating, she may be raped by a schoolmate or friend.

Then there are the older women, the "hidden" population of "hidden" rape victims—women who are over 30 years old when their rapes occur. Most are socially experienced, yet unprepared for their attacks nonetheless. Many are recently divorced and just beginning to try the dating waters again; some are married; others have never married. They include women like Helene, a Colorado woman who was 37 and the mother of a 10-year-old when she was raped by a man on their third date, and Rae, who was 45 when she was raped by a man she knew after inviting him to her Oklahoma home for coffee.

"I Never Called It Rape"

Ms. SURVEY STAT   □ Only 27 percent of the women whose sexual assault met the legal definition of rape thought of themselves as rape victims.

Because of her personal relationship with the attacker, however casual, it often takes a woman longer to perceive an action as rape when it involves a man she knows than it does when a stranger assaults her. For her to acknowledge her experience as rape would be to recognize the extent to which her trust was violated and her ability to control her own life destroyed.

Indeed, regardless of their age or background, many women interviewed for this book told no one about their rapes, never confronted their attackers, and never named their assaults as rape until months or years later.

CHAPTER 2

Women You Know

"Acquaintance rape was an unknown thing — at least in my world it was."

— Paula, raped by a co-worker when she was 22

Look around the factory, office, or shop where you work, the classroom where you study, the place where you worship. Select any four women at random.

Now consider this: At least one of those women has probably had a rape or rape attempt committed against her by a man she knew.

You won't be able to tell which one she is; acquaintance-rape victims aren't different from other women. Yet in cases of date rape and acquaintance rape, outsiders often search for some flaw in the victim to explain the attack. Women especially often need to find a *reason* why the rape happened to a certain woman and why it could not happen to them.

But there are no hard and fast reasons. Witness the experiences of these four very different women, who represent the four most common categories of acquaintance-rape victims: teenagers, college students, young single working women, and older women.

Jill: A Teenager

Jill lives in a cottage in the fog-shrouded foothills of Washington state near where she grew up. Now 25, she works hard all day at her secretarial job and then comes home to help her 8-year-old son

Donny with his homework. Jill loves her son, but she tries to block the memory of why she became a mother at such a young age: Donny is the result of a date rape that happened when Jill was 16, during the summer between her junior and senior year in high school.

She was on an outing with several male and female friends to a lake when she met the man who would later rape her.

> We asked him to come over and sit with us. Later on, I gave him my phone number and he called me up to take me out. He was really cute, but he was older.

His seeming maturity (he was in his early 20s) made him attractive, as did his sandy-colored beard and hair and the fact that he was a carpenter, not a high schooler. But Jill worried about what her parents would think. She still didn't date much, although, unknown to her mother and father, she had had one experience of sexual intercourse with a steady boyfriend her own age several months before.

The day of the date arrived and the sandy-haired man rode up to Jill's house on a motorcycle. She climbed aboard and they drove further into the countryside, to a secluded spot near a river.

> We were talking, it was just like a date, you know, when he pulled a gun out of the bag on the back of his motorcycle and started playing with it. I don't like guns. My parents don't have guns. I said, "Oh, gee, that's not loaded, is it?" and he said, "Oh, yeah."
> I was very scared.

Jill's date laid the gun down on the blanket they were sharing. He then put his arm around her and started kissing her, but just briefly. He almost immediately proceeded to have intercourse with her.

> I remember at the time I thought, "Just go along, it doesn't matter." I didn't want to take any chances. I just wanted to get home and get out of that situation.

Like date rapists then and now, the handsome carpenter never thought about birth control or the possibility of sexually transmitting disease to his victim. He drove her home and Jill was grounded for being late; she went to her room vowing to tell no one.

She made good on that vow for several months, until her pregnancy forced her to confide in a friend. Jill wanted to have an abortion until the medical procedure that would be used was explained to her. That, coupled with her parents' feelings against abortion, led her to decide to remain pregnant and keep the child. Always a good student, Jill went through her senior year pregnant and maintained an A average. She went to graduation with her son in her arms and her dreams of going to art school set aside; instead, she faced the reality of supporting a child.

Rachel: A College Student

Rachel blends in easily with the attractive young crowd filling a downtown Boston street on a mild spring afternoon. Her spiky short brown hair is the arty fashion of the season; her big hoop earrings mimic the large roundness of her eyes. She comes from an intelligent and loving family. Her father is a lawyer; her mother teaches.

Rachel was raped during her freshman year in college. She has never told her parents.

> I was at a big university. We had coed dorms, with two hallways on each floor being girls and two hallways were guys. This guy was a football player, about six foot five and 265 pounds. I knew he lived down the hall from me, but I didn't really know him. I thought he was an attractive guy. He was a junior.
>
> There was a party on our floor with all the guys and girls from our floor. There were kegs and stuff. The drinking age was 18, but even though I wasn't quite 18 they let me into the party. We had already been drinking a lot and we got to the party and this guy [the football player] was talking to me.

Rachel was flattered by the attention.

> He wasn't drinking, but he was feeding me alcohol. He asked me to come back to his room — it was right down the hall from where all of us were. I was just so out of it, I said, "Sure." I had no idea. I didn't think he'd hurt me.

> I thought there would be other people there. I thought it was just like, "Let's get out of this party." When we got to his room and I saw there was nobody there, I didn't think I could do anything about it.
>
> We started kissing and then he started taking off my clothes. I kept telling him to stop and I was crying. I was scared of him and thought he was going to hurt me. . . . He had a hand over my face. I was five foot two and weighed 110 pounds. I didn't have any choice.

The assault lasted about half an hour. When it was over, Rachel went to her own room, just down the hall. She went to sleep praying that she wasn't pregnant.

> I just wanted to block it out. I felt ashamed because it happened. I just felt dirty, violated. I thought it was my fault. It wasn't like he did something to me, it was like I let him do something to me, so I felt very bad about myself.
>
> He came to my room the next day and wanted to go out with me. He felt that was the normal thing to do, I guess.

Rachel turned him down, but offered no explanation. She also did not report the rape.

> Who would believe me? He was a really good football player. No one would have believed me if I said anything. I wouldn't have dreamed of saying anything.

Rachel's perception about not being believed would prove prescient. Later that year, her residence hall adviser (an older student) was raped by another athlete who came into her room as she lay in bed in a drunken stupor after a party. A university disciplinary board decided that since the woman was unconscious, the action could only be considered sexual misconduct, not rape. The male student received a light reprimand.

Four years later, Rachel finally began to tell people about the rape. Her friends, men and women, have been sympathetic and supportive. One friend even related her own date-rape experience. Talking about it has helped in Rachel's recovery, helped her believe in herself again. "I made some stupid choices, but him hurting me is not my fault," she says.

You know, you're away from home for the first time and you want to go wild. You don't know what you're getting into. You just don't think people are going to hurt you.

I just had no concept that anyone would do something like that to me.

Paula: A Young Single Working Woman

Paula is a social service professional who lives in the South with her young daughter. When she was 22, she worked as a hospital ward clerk at a Virginia medical facility. For several weeks, one of the young doctors, a resident specializing in the care of cancer patients, had been pressuring her to go out with him. "He had kind of a reputation (for dating a lot of women) around the hospital," she says. "I was aware of that, which is probably why I resisted seeing him for so long." But he was tall, good-looking, and successful, traits which probably had much to do with his popularity. "He had been bugging me for maybe two months, saying, 'I just want you to come over for dinner. Nothing's going to happen.' I mean, he made a really big production out of assuring me of that," she says.

Paula had recently broken up with her boyfriend. The doctor's fiancée lived out of town. After talking with him several times, she decided that he was just trying to be friendly.

I thought how nice it would be to spend a platonic evening with a sympathetic ear. The first couple of hours were just that — good conversation, a wonderful meal, and a bottle of wine. He lived in a nice apartment with expensive furniture.

After we finished eating, I felt ready to go. He pleaded with me to stay a bit longer. He had some pot he wanted to share and told me that it would relax me and lift my spirits.

Paula had smoked marijuana before, but never anything this potent. Looking back now, she believes it was medical-strength marijuana, the kind that is sometimes given by prescription to chemotherapy patients to ease their pain.

I got real delusional. I felt like I was having hallucinations. I remember his face and it seemed disconnected from his body. It was distorted. I can remember losing muscular control.

Her date, however, was having no such problem. He took off her clothes and dragged her up some stairs to a bedroom.

I started to cry. It was the only coping mechanism I had. I remember saying, "No, no, no," and crying profusely.

I remember feeling like it was never going to stop. He was able to maintain an erection for a long time without coming. I remember thinking, "Oh, I can't stand this anymore. Either I have to die or he has to stop." It got to the point where the crying wasn't working; nothing was working. I was feeling like I was going to burst if he didn't stop doing these things to me because it was oral sex and he tried anal sex. He was forcing me to have oral sex and I said something like, "I'm going to throw up," and I think that's what spurred him to finish.

He finished and that's when I was really in shock. I was in denial and disbelief up to that point, but when it was over with, I was very much in shock and really quite unable to maneuver around much. I think he must have helped me get dressed and sort of dragged me to the door. His demeanor was real sheepish.

I remember somehow getting in my car, somehow driving home. I have no idea how I got home, none whatsoever. I'm lucky I didn't kill somebody on the road.

Paula went home and told her sister-in-law, who immediately wanted to go back and confront the man. Instead, Paula made her promise that she wouldn't tell anyone. Several days later, Paula saw the doctor at work; she glared ferociously at him, but said nothing.

Acquaintance rape was an unknown thing, at least in my world it was, so the anger at him was in the form of "You lied to me. You tricked me. You conned me." I was aware of that, but I was totally unaware that what he had done to me was a crime. I had no idea I could report it to the police. I had no idea I could charge him with anything.

A month later I moved more than a thousand miles away and lived with my folks for a while. I couldn't stand my father to touch me; I didn't even like to be real close to him. I just didn't want any bodily contact at all.

> I cut off all my hair. I did not want to be attractive to men. I started
> wearing real androgynous clothes — nothing tight, nothing revealing —
> and reduced my makeup to almost nil. I just wanted to look neutered
> for a while because that felt safer.

It was several years before Paula started dating again, years filled
with anger and distrust and sexual problems. As for the man who
assaulted her, she did not speak to him before she quit her job and
left town. But she has thought about him since.

> At the time, it never crossed my mind that he would do this again and
> again. Now I am acutely aware that he probably used the same plan
> of action to rape a lot of women.

Deborah: An Older Woman

Deborah had been married for 15 years when she and her husband
separated. Among her friends at the time was a man named Alex.

> Alex and I had been good friends for about five years. We were both
> involved in community activities for children, mainly softball.
>   During the first four months [of the separation], Alex and I became
> closer. He helped me tremendously mentally. One thing led to another
> and we became sexually intimate. That lasted approximately six weeks.

Deborah, who was 34 at the time, and her husband decided to try to
make their marriage work again. Alex was not happy with her decision. After six months, she and her husband again separated. Alex
was ready to begin their relationship again, but she told him she
needed time alone. One night, drunk and angry, Alex confronted
her outside a restaurant near their California hometown. He threw
her against a wall and started to choke her. She kneed him in the
crotch, broke free, and ran inside where a female friend was waiting.
Alex jumped in his car and drove off.

> My friend and I left. She wanted me to spend the night with her
> because she was afraid for me. I told her I'd be okay and went on
> home.
>   At 4:00 A.M., I woke up with a start. Alex was standing over me,

just staring. I told him if he didn't leave, I would call the police. He made no response. I picked up the phone, he grabbed it, ripped it out of the wall, and came after me. He started hitting me, throwing me, and became verbally abusive.

At one point I grabbed a ceramic bowl and hit him on the head with it as hard as I could. He didn't even flinch. Blood was everywhere.

Finally he got me pinned down on the bed. There was no fight left in me.

Then, as sometimes happens in rapes, Alex lost his erection although he had partially penetrated Deborah. He screamed at her and began hitting her again. He told her to lie still on the bed. When she moved, he would hit her. Finally, he got dressed and left, without ejaculating. He had been there for two hours.

There was enough evidence that I didn't have to press charges — the D.A. did. Alex was arrested that morning . . . on charges of rape, burglary, assault, and destruction of telephone equipment. At the preliminary hearing he plea-bargained to assault with attempt to rape. He pleaded guilty and got four years. He's now in state prison.

My year anniversary [of the rape] is coming up, but I feel I'll do fine. I have a lot of family and friend support. The only exception is my ex-husband. He says I got what I deserved.

CHAPTER 3

Why Date Rape and Acquaintance Rape Are So Widespread

"When she finally says, 'No,' he simply may not listen, or he may convince himself that she is just 'playing hard to get' and that she really means 'Yes'."
— student Erik Johnke describing how dating rituals may lead to rape

Rapes between men and women who know each other are happening in big cities, small towns, and rural areas. They occur among all ethnic and religious groups, regardless of education or wealth. Many of these rapes are rooted in the social behavior men and women learn.

The story of Donna and Eli shows how adherence to such roles can escalate into rape. Donna was 18 and Eli was 20 when they met at a party and became interested in each other. Once they were alone, Donna knew what limits she wanted to place on their sexual activity and she voiced them, but not very clearly or assertively. Eli chose not to hear or interpreted her resistance (both verbal and, ultimately, physical) to mean something else. He decided to use force to get what he wanted.

The following is part of a report Donna gave to university police at her Illinois college:

I went to a party about 9:00 P.M. on Friday. My friends accompanied me to the party. When we arrived, we started to drink. We mingled and talked with our friends and met some new people. Among these new people was Eli.

All I had to drink all night were two beers, so I was totally sober. We were in a group of friends talking and I noticed him. He had on a blue hooded sweatshirt with white print on the front and Levi's jeans. His friend introduced us and I began to talk about school and our hometowns.

Sometime around midnight, one of Donna's friends left the party. The other stayed with her.

About 12:45 A.M., Eli asked me if I wanted to come over to his house and talk for a while. I talked to my friend and she wanted to go home, so he got his two friends who he was with and I got my friend and we all left together. Eli's friend drove my friend to our dorm and then we proceeded to his house. We all went into the house and Eli and I went into the TV room.

He turned the TV on, changed channels, and then turned and kissed me. His friend came in and began to talk to us for a while. When his friend left, Eli asked me to go upstairs. I said to him, "I don't want to do that. We are here to talk, I thought." His response to me was, "We don't have to do anything you don't want to do."

The next thing I said was, "I don't want to do anything. I don't even know you." He said that was fine and we would just talk. We got up and went upstairs.

They went into Eli's room, which, like college students' rooms everywhere, held not much more than a bed and a bicycle, with clothes strewn around.

He motioned for me to sit down on his bed and he turned around and locked three locks on his door, and then sat down next to me. Immediately he started kissing me and I pulled away. He said again, "We don't have to do anything you don't want to do," and again I said, "I don't want to do anything." He ignored my statement and started forcing himself on me.

He laid me out on the bed and got on top of me and started kissing me. I pushed away and verbally said no to him. He ignored me and kept on.

He kept asking me to spend the night and the first couple of times I ignored him, but finally I had to answer. I said, "No, I have to do lots of things tomorrow and I should go home." He kept pleading with me and finally he stopped asking me. I thought at that point I would be able to leave soon.

I was wrong. He got up and began removing his clothes and then he forcibly removed my pants and put his body between my legs. At this point I was still pinned down and I couldn't move. He was lying on me and begged me to have sex with him. I verbally said, "No," and I also had my hands on my pelvic bones with my palms up, pushing him away.

I forcibly pushed away like this for a while until he began to become more forceful to me. I didn't want to get hurt, so I began to ease up from pushing, but I was still verbally saying no. At this point he had intercourse with me.

As he forced himself inside me, I tried to push away and to get him to stop, but he wouldn't. I began to cry and he asked me what was wrong. I said, "I don't want this. I don't even know you." Next he asked me, "Have you ever done this before?" and I never answered him. He then said, "Come on, can't we have some fun?"

Finally he stopped and rolled off me and laid beside me with a firm grip on me. He looked in my eyes and said, "I'm sorry." He then took my hand and wanted me to fondle him, but I refused. He then started masturbating with himself to the point of ejaculation. Next he began to fondle me and then placed himself on top of me again. Once more he pleaded to have sex with me. I refused many times, but nothing helped. I was still crying, but he ignored it totally. He then had intercourse with me again against my will.

He finally got off me and took his arms away and laid beside me. Again, he said, "I am sorry, Donna." I said I had to leave and by this time it was 7:30 A.M. He said okay and got up and went to he bathroom.

While Eli was gone, Donna got dressed. He returned and drove her back to her dormitory.

> When we got to the dorm, he kissed me and said, "Call me sometime."
> I immediately got out of the car and went to my room.

In tears, she told her roommate what had happened. Her roommate took her to the student health center and then they went to a hospital for a rape examination. Donna decided not to press criminal charges against Eli, but brought the case before a university judicial board, comprised of a college administrator, a professor, and two students. After a three-hour hearing, the board found Eli in violation of the school's behavioral conduct code. But although the college code called for suspension as the punishment for rape for a first-time offender, he was merely put on probation and ordered to write a paper on sexual assault.

Analyze Donna's story for a moment. After saying "no" several times to Eli's entreaties for sex and recognizing that her wishes were being ignored, she told him, "I have to do lots of things tomorrow and I should go home." Why didn't she just tell him flat out to let her up or insist that she wanted to go home? Why didn't she scream? Why didn't she bite him? Why didn't she pound on the locked door and try to get away? Granted, none of these options might have saved her from being raped, but Donna would never have thought of them then. That's because she was handicapped from the start by the way men and women are taught to interact with each other.

Dating Rituals

This interaction comes into sharpest focus in traditional dating behavior where the male initiates the date by asking the woman out, with him paying all of the expenses or buying the liquor, food, or entertainment. When this happens, the man may expect sexual activity or intercourse, with or without a serious attachment between himself and the woman; she, on the other hand, may want intimacy only after a relationship has developed over a period of time. Even when the woman wants sex without a developed relationship, she may put up a protest because she has been trained that only "bad girls" have sex willingly. Her date, on the other hand, has learned from seeing such behavior (or from the advice of other men) that women often say no when they mean yes.

If the male is nonaggressive sexually, there's no problem. But if he is aggressive, the female enters into a contest with him—either because she really doesn't want to have sex with him or because she feels she must put up some resistance to maintain a good reputation. Dating then becomes a game which each side tries to win. And date rape may be the result.

Listen to Erik Johnke, one of a group of male students at Haverford College, near Philadelphia, who sought to open other young men's eyes to acquaintance rape. In his 1987 senior thesis, Johnke described, with the clear vision of an insider, the often imperceptible gender-role transactions that go on between a man and a woman on a date.

> The man is taught to look upon his actions on a date as a carefully constructed strategy for gaining the most territory. Every action is evaluated in terms of the final goal—intercourse. He continually pushes to see "how far he can get." Every time she [his date] submits to his will, he has "advanced" and every time she does not he has suffered a "retreat." Since he already sees her as the opponent, and the date as a game or a battle, he anticipates resistance. He knows that "good girls don't," and so she will probably say "no." But he has learned to separate himself from her and her interests. He is more concerned with winning the game. Instead of trying to communicate with her, he attempts to pressure her into saying "yes."
>
> Every time she submits to his will, he sees it as a small victory (getting the date, buying her a drink, getting a kiss, or fondling her breasts). He plays upon her indecisiveness, using it as an opportunity to tell her "what she really wants," which is, in fact, what he wants. If her behavior is inconsistent, he tells her that she is "fickle" or "a tease." If he is disinterested in her desires and he believes that she is inconsistent, he is likely to ignore her even when she does express her desires directly. When she finally says, "no," he simply may not listen, or he may convince himself that she is just "playing hard to get" and that she really means "yes." With such a miserable failure in communication, a man can rape a woman even when she is resisting vocally and physically, and still believe that it was not rape.

And so the game is afoot from the outset of many traditional dates, with the man pressing his attempts at seduction and the woman keeping a check on how sexually involved the couple will become. This balance might be maintained for a long time in a way that is satisfactory to both people. But if the man moves from trying to cajole the woman into sexual activity to forcing her to comply by raping her, he may encounter what seems to him little resistance. That's because the woman's socialization has most likely taught her that she must not express her own wishes forcefully, that she should not hurt other people's feelings or reject them, that she should be quiet, polite, and never make a scene. And, as a girl, she has also learned not to be physical.

"I never considered punching him or doing something really drastic," says Abby of the acquaintance who raped her. "I guess I was a 'nice girl' and you didn't do that, even if somebody was being un-nice to you."

Interpersonal Violence

All it takes to solidify the aggressor/victim relationship of the dating couple is the addition of a belief in using violence to deal with personal conflict. Studies show that may not be a great leap.

A Minnesota survey of 202 male and female college students revealed that, in dating relationships:

- nearly 13 percent had either slapped their date or been slapped
- 14 percent were pushed or did the pushing
- 4 percent were punched or did the punching
- 3.5 percent were struck with an object or did the striking
- 1.5 percent were choked or did the choking
- 1 percent were assaulted with a weapon or committed such an assault

Study author James M. Makepeace, a sociology professor at the College of St. Benedict/St. John's University, St. Joseph, Minnesota, notes that "if the 4-percent incidence of assault with closed fists (punching) is typical, then 800 of the students on a 20,000-student campus would have experienced this form of violence" in a social-sexual relationship. Overall, the report showed that more than one in five students had direct experience of dating violence.

The same strong evidence of violence in dating couples has been found elsewhere. A University of South Dakota study showed that 10 percent of the undergraduate women questioned had been physically abused in one or more relationships. Still other researchers have seen a corollary between cultural depictions of violence against women, such as in some movies, and an increased desensitization to such violence, indirectly resulting in acceptance of it off the screen, even among dating partners.

Communication

Miscommunication contributes to the factual and perceptual fogs that cloud acquaintance-rape incidents. This miscommunication may occur because men and women often interpret behavior cues and even direct conversation differently. In general, men give a more sexual reading to behavior and conversation than women do. In a 1982 study conducted by Antonia Abbey of Northwestern University in Evanston, Illinois, male and female subjects watched a male and female actor talk to each other, and the males rated the female actor as being more seductive and promiscuous than did the women. Another study, this one with high school students in California, showed that males consistently rated various dating behaviors, types of dress, and dating activities as signals for sex more often than females did.

Male and female subjects in a 1983 research project read scenarios about college students who went on dates, then evaluated whether the date participants wanted sex from each other. Regardless of who had initiated the date, who had paid for it, or where the couple went, the male students were more likely than their female counterparts to think that the woman in the scenario wanted sex from the man she was with. "It seems likely that a man might misinterpret a woman's behavior and think that she is more interested in him than she really is," writes the study's author, Charlene

L. Muehlenhard of Texas A&M University, College Station, Texas. Indeed, many men only ask a woman out after they've decided that they'd like to have sex with her, whereas many women view dates, especially the first few dates, as opportunities to socialize and learn more about the man.

Some people hope that improving the woman's ability to clearly communicate what she wants will naturally lead the man to understand how to proceed. Although the "deafness" of some males involved in acquaintance rapes may, in part, be due to not being told in a decisive way what the woman wants, many men simply discount what a woman is saying or reinterpret it to fit what they want to hear. They have been raised to believe that women will always resist sex to avoid the appearance of being promiscuous (and, indeed, some do), will always say "no" when they really mean "yes," and always want men to dominate them and show that they are in control. Further, many men have been conditioned to simply ignore women—whether those women are responding positively to sexual interactions or pushing, fighting, kicking, crying, or otherwise resisting them.

When it comes to sexual relations, saying "no" is often meaningless when the words are spoken by a female.

Belief in the "Justifiable" Rape

The result of these conflicts in communication—the socialized "deafness" of men toward women and the likelihood that a man will interpret a situation to have stronger sexual overtones than a woman will—leads to the belief among many men (and some women) in "justifiable rape," somewhat along the lines of "justifiable homicide." In "justifiable rape," the victim's behavior is seen as being responsible for triggering the man's action. Although there is no legal concept as there is in "justifiable homicide," the idea of "justifiable rape" influences the opinions of everyone from the rape victim's own family to the jury who may sit in judgment of her attacker.

Recent studies show that men believe date rape is more justifiable if one of these circumstances occurs:

- the woman invites the man out on the date
- the man pays for the date
- she dresses "suggestively"
- they go to his place rather than to a movie
- she drinks alcohol or does drugs

Men with traditional attitudes toward women rate these situations as justifying rape significantly more often than do men who hold nontraditional attitudes.

The research also shows that many times men will feel "led on" while women will not have the slightest clue that their actions are being interpreted as sexual. In a 1967 study by Purdue's Eugene Kanin, sexually aggressive college men said they believed their aggression was justified if the woman was "a tease." A 1979 survey of California high school boys showed 54 percent thought rape was justifiable if the girl "leads a boy on."

In a study exploring correlations between people who rated rape as justifiable under certain circumstances and people who actually were involved in sexually aggressive incidents, Texas A&M's Muehlenhard found that men were much more likely than women to say that the woman had hinted beforehand that she wanted the man to ask her out. When she looked at just those subjects whose dates involved sexual aggression, Muehlenhard saw this difference in high relief: 60 percent of men reported that the woman had hinted she was interested in dating him; only 16 percent of the women said they had so hinted. Those men clearly felt "led on" by the women who refused them sex, a feeling which many of them may have regarded as justification for committing rape.

The Role of Alcohol and Drugs

It's impossible to consider why acquaintance rape is so widespread without mentioning the correlation between drug and alcohol use and sexual assault.

Although it is certainly possible to drink alcohol without becom-

---

Ms. SURVEY STAT □ About 75 percent of the men and at least 55 percent of the women involved in acquaintance rapes had been drinking or taking drugs just before the attack.

---

ing intoxicated, in many social settings—particularly those involving teenagers and young adults—getting drunk is the point of drinking. And because there is really no drug-taking corollary to drinking just one glass of beer, using drugs like marijuana, hashish, cocaine, crack, methamphetamines, LSD, angel dust, and heroin almost always means becoming intoxicated or "high," although the depth of that intoxication may vary from drug to drug.

As has been seen in federal highway safety tests, alcohol begins to affect people in negative ways long before they believe they are actually drunk. Alcohol and drugs distort reality, cloud judgment, and slow reactions, causing men and women to expose themselves to dangers or disregard social constraints that might otherwise influence them.

When intoxicated, a woman's perceptions about what is happening around her and to her become blurred. Her ability to resist an attack is lessened as her verbal and physical response mechanisms become sedated. She may rely on other people to take care of her, to see that she gets home safely, and to protect her from harm. Some men purposely "feed" a woman alcohol or drugs before forcing her to have sex to reduce her defenses. That's what happened to Patty, who was joined at a restaurant dinner with two female friends by a man she knew casually, a man who would rape her later that night.

We proceeded to drink a lot, but, looking back, I notice he didn't drink a lot, just the women did. After a couple of hours, we decided we were going to go in town and go dancing and he said, "Why don't you ride with me?" I said, "Okay, fine." We started smoking weed in his pickup on the way back into town and, again, looking back, I notice he didn't have any. But he kept piling this weed down me.

By the time we got to the place where we were going, I couldn't think. I mean, I didn't hardly know who I was, let alone was I able to make a decision about anything. So we got out and . . . he said to me, "Come on, we're going to go up to my place." Well, I didn't want to go, but I did not have the capability to say, "No, I don't want to do that."

Moreover, women who have become obviously drunk or high on their own often become targets for individual men or groups of men scouting for a victim. And the fact that a woman is drinking, even if she's not drunk, is often believed by men to be a justification for rape (since "good girls" aren't supposed to drink). It also makes police and prosecutors less inclined to press charges in acquaintance and date rapes.

An intoxicated man may become more sexually aggressive, more violent and less interested in what the woman wants than when he's sober. And many men who commit acquaintance rape excuse their acts because they were drunk or under the influence of drugs.

Social Cultures That Support Rape and Violence

Rape-supportive attitudes occur in abundance among men who rape, yet these attitudes are also held by a wide cross section of society. In a 1977 study of 598 Minnesota adults conducted by Martha R. Burt of The Urban Institute in Washington, D.C., more than half agreed with the statements that: "A woman who goes to the home or apartment of a man on the first date implies she is willing to have sex" and "In the majority of rapes, the victim was promiscuous or had a bad reputation." More than half those adults also believed that 50 percent or more of reported rapes are reported only because the woman was trying to get back at a man she was angry with or to cover up an out-of-wedlock pregnancy.

Research shows, though, that while women often believe these myths, many more men believe them, with far greater intensity. Because men often associate with friends and peers who also hold these beliefs, they are reinforced in their ideas that women are responsible for rape, that rape is only committed by mentally ill strangers, and that women lie about being raped.

A survey of 400 undergraduate students (200 male/200 female) conducted by Nona J. Barnett of the University of Miami School of Law and Hubert S. Feild of Auburn University showed the following attitudes on rape:

STATEMENT	PERCENTAGE OF MEN AGREEING	PERCENTAGE OF WOMEN AGREEING
In most cases, when a woman was raped, she was asking for it.	17	4
If a woman is going to be raped, she might as well relax and enjoy it.	17	7
Women provoke rape by their appearance or behavior.	59	38
A woman should be responsible for preventing her victimization in a rape.	41	27
The degree of a woman's resistance should be the major factor in determining if a rape has occurred.	40	18
In order to protect the male, it should be difficult to prove that a rape has occurred.	40	15
It would do some women some good to get raped.	32	8

Such beliefs help form a social reality among many people that is antifemale and rape supportive. Often those beliefs will spill out in a public way. In April 1987, about 200 marchers, many of them women, walked to protest Princeton University's handling of a sexual harassment complaint brought by a female student against a male student. As the protestors passed in front of several all-male collegiate eating clubs, they had cups of beer hurled at them and were met with cries of, "Go get raped!"

Some dismiss acquaintance rape as just a case of boys being boys —that is, men exuberantly displaying the natural male sexual imperative to rape when aroused. Nothing could be farther from the truth of what is "natural." As anthropologist Peggy Reeves Sanday of the University of Pennsylvania in Philadelphia explained in a cross-cultural study of rape: "It is important to understand that violence is socially and not biologically programmed. Rape is not an integral part of male nature, but the means by which men programmed for violence express their sexual selves. Men who are conditioned to respect the female virtues of growth and the sacredness of life do not violate women."

Toward Reducing Acquaintance Rape

How do we eliminate acquaintance rape? Certainly not by ending dating, but by redefining it and the other social interactions between men and women—how we relate as parents, siblings, friends, peers, co-workers. That means teaching young children long before they begin to date to break the model of aggression/passivity that marks male/female relations: by promoting constructive, nonviolent ways to deal with personal conflict and anger as well as by teaching young people the responsible use of alcohol, the dangers of drugs, and rejection of the myths that contribute to belief in "justifiable" rape.

Says researcher Burt, "Only by promoting the idea of sex as a mutually undertaken, freely chosen, fully conscious interaction . . . can society create an atmosphere free of the threat of rape."

CHAPTER 4

Why Women Are "Safe" Victims

 tacks and stacks of research papers from social scientists across the country attest to the fact that sexual assault is a common experience for women. How common is it?

Ms. SURVEY STATS **Of the 3,187 female college students questioned:**
- □ **15.3 percent had been raped**
- □ **11.8 percent were victims of attempted rape**
- □ **11.2 percent had experienced sexual coercion**
- □ **14.5 percent had been touched sexually against their will**

All the students who participated in the *Ms.* study were in randomly selected classes at campuses that reflected a cross section of regions and cultures (see Afterword) and the survey was administered by clinical psychologists. Only 45.6 percent of the young women polled by the study had *never* experienced sexual victimization.

It's important to note that although the purpose of the *Ms.* survey was to determine the frequency of acquaintance rape, the word "rape" did not appear in any of the descriptions of aggression or victimization contained in the 71-page questionnaire. The reason was simple: Many women and most men involved in acquaintance rape don't label it as rape. To ask, "Have you ever been raped?" or "Have you ever raped anyone?" would have greatly—and falsely—reduced the number of affirmative responses. Instead, clearly worded descriptions of activities that met the most common legal definitions of rape were used to classify respondents' experiences.

Who were the women identified as victims? On the whole, they were no different than the nonvictims in personality and family-background characteristics. However, the rape victims were somewhat more likely to have been the recipients of physical violence in their homes, to have lived without their mothers for a period of time, and to have run away from home. Forty-one percent of the women who were raped were virgins at the time of their attacks.

How did the rapes occur? Nearly all (95 percent) involved only one rapist. Most of the women (84 percent) knew the men who attacked them, with more than half the assaults happening on dates. On the average, consensual sexual intimacy to the point of petting above the waist had occurred some time before. Nonetheless, most of the raped women reported that they had made it "quite clear" to the men involved that they did not want to have sexual intercourse with them.

Most of the rapes happened off campus and were as likely to occur in the woman's home or car as in the man's. Women said that 73 percent of their attackers were under the influence of drugs or alcohol and 55 percent said they themselves were intoxicated. The average amount of force used by the men was rated as moderate, usually twisting the victim's arm or holding her down. Only 9 percent of the women said their rapists hit them; 5 percent were threatened with weapons. Most (84 percent) tried unsuccessfully to reason with the men and many (70 percent) put up some form of physical resistance.

Nonetheless, these women were raped, at a rate far exceeding the national crime statistical average of 37.5 rapes per 100,000 inhabitants. But very few of the rapes uncovered by the *Ms.* study were counted in those federal records, because very few of the women involved officially reported their experiences.

Ms. SURVEY STATS   □ 42 percent of the rape victims told no one about
                          their assaults.
                     □ Only 5 percent reported their rapes to the police.
                     □ Only 5 percent sought help at rape-crisis centers.

The *Ms.* Study found three chief characteristics that kept women
from identifying what happened to them as rape or from reporting
it to authorities:

□   when the rape took place between dating partners
□   when prior consensual sexual intimacy occurred between the
    rapist and victim
□   when minimal violence was involved

In interviews for this book with women of various ages and backgrounds, other reasons for not calling it rape or keeping silent about
an attack emerged: Women didn't want to get men they knew in
trouble; they were embarrassed about the details of the rape (leaving
a bar with a man, taking drugs, etc.) and felt they would be blamed
for what occurred, or they simply felt the men involved had too
much social status for their stories to be believed.

No wonder acquaintance rape continues to be a largely hidden
phenomenon.

What Makes a "Safe" Victim?

Women raped by men they are dating or whom they know are what
sociologists and psychologists sometimes call "safe" victims—
"safe," that is, for the rapists. These women are ideal candidates for
victimization because they are unlikely to report their rapes or offer
serious resistance.

Various researchers have tried to theorize why some women
become rape victims and others don't. *Ms.* study researcher Mary
Koss sought to determine if there were predictive factors associated
with acquaintance rapes. Koss grouped information gathered from
victims in three blocks: experiences such as family violence, child-

hood sexual experiences, and age of first sexual intercourse; social-psychological characteristics such as rape-supportive beliefs; and other variables such as alcohol and drug use. She then compared those findings with the most commonly held theories about rape victimization, with the following results:

□ Theory #1—*Victim precipitation*—asserts that certain personality characteristics such as having a "bad" reputation or stereotyped gender behavior such as passivity in women predicts the likelihood of being raped.

Ms. study finding: Acquaintance-rape victims showed no significant personality differences from women who were not raped. In fact, analysis showed these women actually were more socially poised, forceful, and confident than nonvictims.

□ Theory #2—*Social control*—postulates that women are vulnerable to rape because they accept rape-supportive beliefs. (This is seen as a corollary to the fact that men who rape score high in their adherence to rape-supportive statements.)

Ms. study finding: Acquaintance-rape victims do not believe more strongly in myths about rape than nonvictimized women.

□ Theory #3—*Situational model*—suggests that rape is more likely to occur in certain environments (isolated areas, the male's territory) after particular behavior by the victim and perpetrator (drinking, previous sexual contact). These factors may increase a woman's "exposure" risk to rape by putting her in situations in which she meets more men and is more likely to become drunk.

Ms. study finding: Raped women showed somewhat more liberal sexual values (they believe intercourse may be appropriate if a couple is dating regularly rather than only if the couple is formally engaged or married), a slightly higher number of sexual partners and somewhat higher alcohol use.

Although situational factors contribute to greater exposure to the risk of acquaintance rape, they are not sufficient to explain why so many women are raped by men they know. Consider that 41 percent of the rape victims in the *Ms.* study were virgins and 45 percent were sober. It becomes clear, then, that no one theoretical model fits when it comes to explaining why women experience acquaintance rape.

The Story of a "Safe" Victim

Carol sits at her kitchen table in an affluent New Jersey suburb. Her toddler son is upstairs napping, a clothes washer chugs in the laundry room, and her answering machine is switched on, taking messages for her at-home business. At 33, she has her life happily in order.

But she is talking about a different Carol—an 18-year-old college freshman whose dating and sexual experiences were limited. That Carol was home from college for midwinter break when she received a call from a boy she knew, inviting her to join him, his girl friend (Carol's friend Terri), and his roommate at a New Year's Eve party at the boys' fraternity house. She would, in effect, be the roommate's date.

> He was some nice boy from the next suburb over from me. I had known his cousin in high school. He was this perfectly acceptable person that you could bring home and not be ashamed to be dating.

She agreed to join them. At the party, the fraternity members concocted a punch, using wine and a little fruit juice. Carol had never drunk alcohol before.

> The night wore on and I was drinking this punch—it was great, delicious. I had no idea what it was doing to me and I ended up rip-roaring drunk.
>
> We went back to the guys' apartment and my friend Terri went too. It never occurred to me that anything was going to be going on. We were just going to be sleeping there. I had actually spent the night with men, but never had sex with them, as strange as that may seem. We just slept together.

But just sleeping together is not what Carol's date had in mind. After they got into bed, he started kissing her, then escalated his sexual attention. Despite her repeated, "No, no, no" and her physically pushing him away, he used the advantage of his six-foot-three body to overpower her five-foot frame.

> I just realized I had no choice. I didn't feel that I could hurt him. It was unpleasant . . . a really painful experience.
>
> He drove me home to my parents' house the next day. We didn't say anything on the entire ride. I think he was embarrassed.
>
> I felt raped, but I didn't realize I had been raped. I felt I had been an unwilling participant and that the woman was always guilty until it had been proved that she had been knocked unconscious or doped and mutilated before being raped and then murdered.
>
> It didn't occur to me that it was okay to hurt him, to kick him in the balls, or punch him in the eye. Good girls don't do that. You sort of just lie back and let this happen and then you deal with the consequences.

How Women Are Taught to Be "Safe" Victims

The average woman, when faced with an impending acquaintance rape, is unable to use the full force of her real power to fight back. That's because, like Carol, she was raised not to believe in that power or to think that she had the right to assert it, especially against a socially acceptable man. Most girls are still being brought up to think like this. They are taught directly and indirectly (by parents, teachers, playmates, and pop culture role models) to be passive, weak, and opinionless. They are expected to remain in this state—that is, childlike—even after they mature and become young adults and women. They are expected to be fearful and inhibited and are not encouraged to develop independence and self-reliance. Rather, they learn to look to men for their physical and economic protection.

Girls quickly learn from this socialization that as women they will grant men sexual favors in exchange for these protections, preferably with the permanence of marriage attached. As discussed in Chapter 3, this reduces dating, which precedes marriage, to a transaction in which the man tries to get a little bit more sexually from the woman than she is willing to give. The woman's reluctance may be built not on a lack of sexual desire (in the case of a man she may be attracted to), but on the training which has taught her to protect her sexuality because it represents her "market value." Girls learn to control the dispensing of their sexual "favors" so that they do not appear to give in too quickly and therefore end up with a reduced worth.

Girls are thus taught what is basically a good lesson—that sexuality should occur within the context of a loving relationship—for a bad reason—that is, because as defenseless women they need men to support and protect them. Sex is understood to be the medium of exchange they will use to secure that protection.

Such conditioning helps produce "safe" victims—women who react with denial, dissociation, self-blame, and rejection of their own misgivings as acquaintance rape threatens, who cannot fight back during the rape or report it to the police afterwards, and who, often, become victims again later.

Victim Reaction #1: Denial

Most women raped by an acquaintance recall denying to themselves that a rape was happening even as the situation was worsening. Disbelief and denial by the victim often occur even in the face of the most excruciating evidence: violence, forceful isolation, restraint, verbal abuse, and, of course, the man's disregard of any negative reaction by the woman. This denial by the victim is rooted in the simple fact that she knows her attacker. If her assailant was a stranger, she'd have little difficulty in identifying what was happening. Instead, she believes that if she just talks to the man and tries to dissuade him, he'll become reasonable. She searches frantically for some explanation of what the man's behavior means—any explanation that does not include calling what's happening rape.

Jodie, for example, had spent a lonely year at a new school. In that time, however, she had become friends with one male student, with whom she had had sex twice. They decided not to continue their sexual relationship, but remained friendly. By late spring, Jodie was dating the man's best friend, seemingly with no ill feelings. When the first man invited her to his place for a drink to celebrate his new job, she thought nothing was odd about it: It was how friends reacted to each other's good news. Once there, though, he began to reach for her in a sexual way and Jodie decided to leave. That was when he attacked her, forcing her into his bedroom and throwing her against a wall.

> All I could think was that he really wasn't going to do it. . . . He'd said that I was his friend. I was also interested in someone else, someone he had known and been friends with for years.

Regardless of all those good reasons not to rape her, the man did.

For many women, denial works as a way to protect themselves against the pain of what they're experiencing, in much the same way that children who are abused bury their experiences deep inside. Indeed, several of the women interviewed for this book spoke of how they repressed their acquaintance-rape episodes for years until a conversation, a news article, or another emotionally disturbing event brought the reality of the rape rushing back at them.

Bonnie was raped on her family's farm in Iowa by a man she had been dating for three weeks. It was her first experience with sexual intercourse. She felt "incredibly violated," but she told no one. Five years later, a stranger broke into Bonnie's apartment and sexually assaulted her and a roommate. That experience she talked about freely. But she never identified her first sexual experience as rape, not even after she participated in a rape-victim support group following her rape by the stranger. Then she read an article on acquaintance rape, nine years after the incident in her apartment and 14 years after her date rape. "It was like being freed, like a tremendous insight," she says. "Things fell into place and started making sense. That allowed me to talk about it for the first time."

Victim Reaction #2: Dissociation

Along with disbelief and denial comes a phase during the actual rape when the woman may feel physically and mentally removed from what is happening. This dissociation may slow down or block her ability to respond to what's happening. As with denial, dissociation is a protective reaction that helps the victim survive the experience by not feeling it completely. Some women remember most clearly the part of the rape that happened during the time in which they felt dissociated, as if they were watching a movie about the rape rather than experiencing it firsthand.

Maggie was punched and dragged through several rooms of the house where she was staying by a man whom she had dated several times and then stopped seeing. They fought until he dragged her into the bedroom and threw her on the bed.

> I left my body at that point. I was over next to the bed, watching this happen. So there's a period of time where my memory of the rape is real different than my other memories of the rape . . . I wasn't in my body. I dissociated from the helplessness. I was standing next to me and there was just this shell on the bed.
>
> There wasn't a feeling of dispassion or not caring, there was a feeling of flatness. I was just there.
>
> When I repicture the room, I don't picture it from the bed. I picture it from the side of the bed. That's where I was watching from.

Victim Reaction #3: Self-Blame

Acquaintance-rape victims feel betrayed by their own judgment because men that they know, men to whom they have often been attracted, men they have sometimes chosen, have turned on them in such a terrible way. The feelings of self-blame begin as the woman recognizes her inability to make the man stop. Immediately after the rape, self-blame leads many women to try to shut the episode out of their minds, not reporting it to police and not even turning to close friends for comfort, for fear that others will blame them just as they blame themselves.

There are multiple reasons for these feelings of self-blame. Women who willingly accepted drinks or drugs from the man before the rape, or who became drunk or stoned on their own, fault themselves for being too debilitated to figure out what was going on.

Even when the woman hasn't been drinking or taking drugs, she's likely to blame herself for an acquaintance rape. Nina was 20 and had been home from the hospital for two weeks after undergoing major surgery that had removed one ovary and left her with only a partially functioning second one. The incisions were still healing when she agreed to go to a local club with friends. It was a welcome break from being cooped up in her apartment.

At the club, Larry, who had been one of the most popular boys in high school, came by her table and asked Nina where she had been hiding lately. Nina told him she had been in the hospital. When he pressed her for details, citing his interest as a paramedic, she briefly described her recent operation. Larry then invited Nina back to his house for a party celebrating his roommate's birthday. He drove to a house out in the Illinois countryside. Nina soon became tired. When others started leaving the party, she asked Larry to drive her home.

> He told me he was too tired to drive, that there were extra bedrooms upstairs and would I mind just sleeping over and he'd take me back in the morning. Normally I would have been suspicious, but because he knew all the details of my surgery, I knew that he must realize that sex was out of the question. I was exhausted, so I told him to just show me where I could sleep. By this time, all the guests had left and his roommate had gone to bed.

When they went upstairs, Larry wanted sex. Astonished, Nina told him she couldn't even if she wanted to because of her surgery.

> He turned into a monster. He grabbed me and yanked down my slacks, exposing my abdomen and the ugly incision and said, "It's no big deal."
>
> I fought him at first and told him to stop. Then he said I'd better not scream for his roommate because his roommate had the hots for me and knew what was going on and would just join in. That was hard for me to believe, but then so was what was happening.
>
> I stopped fighting and began begging when I realized that one good punch to the stomach might start me hermorrhaging and either ruin the small chance I still had left to have children or I might bleed to death.

After he ejaculated, Larry fell asleep. Nina crept downstairs and was so shook up that she had to call directory information to get the number for her own apartment. Her roommate picked her up, then drove Nina to the hospital. There a police detective asked her what had happened.

> I was afraid to tell him the story because there were so many places in it where I felt I could be judged and that I was naive and stupid. I was really blaming myself.
>
> Why did I go with him? Why didn't I drive my own car? Why didn't I scream for his roommate? Why didn't I know that he was this kind of guy?

Like a good "safe" victim, Nina decided not to press charges against Larry. She felt she wasn't emotionally strong enough to endure a trial.

Victim Reaction #4: Ignoring the "Little Voice"

Somewhere inside of most women, no matter how thoroughly socialized they are to respond to others' needs, lives a creature of the self, an independent force—however small—that can sense danger and send out a warning signal. Most women have learned to discount this "bad feeling" over the years. After all, their inner self may be urging them to be careful, but their socialized self believes in giving people the benefit of the doubt. Young girls learn to "go along," to defer to a boy's wishes in part because a good girl doesn't disappoint people. She's supposed to be nice regardless of her own feelings.

Regardless of her own feelings.

Time and again during the interviews for this book, women spoke about how, before their rapes, they disregarded their own feelings, inner signals that were telling them something was wrong with the guy, the place, the situation. A few women turned down the man's invitations for a date several times because of "a bad feeling" about him. Unfortunately, later they relented.

Some of the soon-to-be-rapists gave verbal clues about their attitudes of hostility and aggression toward women, clues that their eventual victims decided to ignore. "When we went out to his car (after an evening dancing), I opened my own car door," Meryl says. "After he started up the car, he almost exploded at me, 'You'll never open up your own car door again when you're with me!' " Meryl decided to ignore the outburst since she had already decided never to go out with the man again. When they arrived at her house, he raped her. Tonya's date, who would later try to rape her, also made remarks that she decided to overlook. "At dinner, when I tried to express some opinions, he said, 'You're too cute to be talking about such things.' . . . [later] he admired my necklace, asking, 'What did you do to deserve that?' "

Often there are no clear clues from the man. The "bad feeling" that women talk about comes solely from within, seemingly triggered by nothing.

Vera had known Steven for years. Their families belonged to the same church and lived in the same community. Vera became a professional singer and Steven a professional trumpet player; when she was 18, they played with the same band.

Vera was 20 and out of work when she ran into Steven one day. He said the band he was with was auditioning singers the next day —was she interested? Of course she was. He said he'd call to get directions to her place in order to give her a lift.

> I don't know why . . . but from the moment he said he would take me to the audition, I felt dread. He hadn't acted or spoken strangely, yet I was scared. A voice, quietly at first, began to whisper, "Don't go!" By the following day I had a massive headache, and this voice was shouting, "DON'T GO!"
>
> I have had experiences of intuition before, but this was actually frightening, it was so strong, and did not seem to be the same as intuition. . . . I was so scared, I decided that when Steven called, I would tell him I wasn't interested. Once that decision was made, I began to feel a little better.

Two hours before the audition, and without a phone call, Steven and a friend of his showed up at Vera's front door.

> "How did you find out where I lived?" I asked. [Now how am I going to tell him I'm taking a pass, I thought.]
>
> "Oh, I have my ways," Steven said. "Listen, I know it's early, but I have a couple of things to do and your place was on the way. Are you ready to go?"

By this time the voice (inside) was pleading and screaming, "DON'T GO!" I thought to myself, "You must be paranoid, Vera. Why would you be afraid of Steven? You've known him for years. You need a job. Go to the audition."

The moment I decided to go, I heard, clearly and with great sadness, the voice say, "Oh no. Oh no." And then it faded away.

On the way to the audition, Steven said he had to stop at his apartment and wouldn't Vera join him and his friend for some coffee? They went inside, but the friend quickly disappeared on an errand. Steven then raped Vera.

Victim Reaction #5: Not Fighting Back

After being raped, many victims are angry with themselves for not fighting back harder, even though, at the time of the rape, most report feeling afraid for their lives. With the calm vision of retrospect, they think of ways they could have fought off the attack, screamed for help, or escaped. They often replay their mental videotapes of the episode, trying to give it a different ending. Says Imani, who was raped by a date in her brother's Philadelphia home while she was baby-sitting: "I would like to believe that night, had my nephews not been there, it would have been a fight to the finish."

Some women talk about how the rape occurred at a low point in their lives—after a breakup or divorce, being away from home for the first time, losing a job—during a time when they were feeling powerless and suffering from low self-esteem. For these women, the thought of fighting back is particularly fleeting since they do not feel in control of much in their lives.

But not fighting back—or even raising an alarm—is a well-ingrained female tradition. In general, girls are raised to care about other people, to sacrifice their own concerns for what other people want. These are not necessarily bad things to learn. But when a woman applies these "female" characteristics in an acquaintance-rape situation, they serve only to harm her. Barry Burkhart, a psychologist and date-rape expert from Auburn University, reports that one victim, raped in a man's room at a fraternity house, when asked why she hadn't screamed during the attack said that she didn't want to embarrass the man in front of his fraternity brothers.

For nearly all women, not fighting back is rooted in plain old physical fear. The reality is that men are stronger than women. Most women walk around knowing that just about any male over the age of 14 could physically overpower them if he wanted to. The threat of violence from a man, even just an angry glare or a muttered obscenity, is enough to make most women feel afraid. When that threat comes in an isolated location, even from someone they know, it is terrifying.

Nonetheless, acquaintance-rape victims try many forms of resistance. Analysis of the *Ms.* study data shows that of the women who were raped by men they knew, 83 percent tried to reason or plead with their attacker, 77 percent turned cold in hopes of repelling him, 70 percent physically struggled, 11 percent screamed for help, and 11 percent tried running away.

Many acquaintance rapes are accomplished by the man simply using the weight of his body to hold the woman down. Wrestlers and boxers know that being equally matched in weight to your opponent is the only way to have a fair fight. An edge of 10 pounds is a lot between professional fighters. With the average man weighing 40 to 50 pounds more than the average woman, the "fight" in a date rape is likely to be no contest from the start. And many men know how to fight, having been encouraged to punch or wrestle their way through quarrels as they were growing up. Many women, however, have never struck anyone, in anger or play. And they are afraid to start with someone who is bigger, stronger, and acting violently and abusively.

Meryl, who weighs 105 pounds, yelled when her date attacked her in her home. She also put up a physical struggle, but only for a short while.

He said he would hurt me if I didn't quit fighting him. I knew I was going to be raped, and I decided I could make the choice of being raped, or being raped and beat up or perhaps worse. . . . The upper-most thought in my mind was that my son would come home and find his mother dead and how traumatic that would be for him. I decided my best chance for survival was to "play along" with this guy.

To a certain degree, women overestimate men's strength and that fear incapacitates them. It *is* possible for a woman to fight off a man, but she needs to be prepared—practically and emotionally—for that possibility in advance.

Victim Reaction #6: Not Reporting the Attack

Many women do not want to undergo police or medical scrutiny immediately following a rape and therefore don't report their experiences. This group includes the vast majority of acquaintance-rape survivors. They think the police won't believe their stories, will blame them, or not consider the episode rape. In short, they expect the police to react the way much of society will react—with disbelief and recriminations.

Those fears by date-rape and acquaintance-rape victims are hardly unfounded. Police and prosecutors may simply tell the woman that the circumstances preclude being able to make a rape charge stick. After Nina was raped, she says, "The detective told me that since I had also been drinking and had gone with the man willingly, and because I knew him, that it was unlikely the State's Attorney would charge him with rape. But he [the detective] said he would charge him with aggravated battery." Sometimes police attitudes move from indifference to outright rejection of the woman's story. Anna recalls, "One evening, this detective, whom I had counted on to conduct an impartial and intelligent investigation, called and said I was a liar and accused me of 'making it' with my attacker at the party. I was devastated!"

Most women raped by men they know don't bother going to the police. And so they remain "safe" victims, indeed. Helene, raped at 37 by a date, knew the police in her Colorado town would be unsympathetic—she had seen them deal with other victims when she worked as a rape-crisis counselor. "They would have thought I was stupid," she says, "that it was just a date that 'got out of hand.' "

Victim Reaction #7: Becoming a Victim Again

Among the most disturbing figures to emerge from the *Ms.* study are these:

Ms. SURVEY STATS   □ 42 percent of the women who were raped said they had sex again with the men who assaulted them.
                     □ 55 percent of the men who raped said they had sex again with their victims.

What could explain the phenomenon of women having sex with their attackers after a rape? The answer lies in the confusion that date-rape and acquaintance-rape victims feel about their rapes. Because most don't know what to call what happened to them, they fall back on typically self-blaming female explanations: "I must have misunderstood him," "I didn't make myself clear," "I'm wrong for feeling bad about this. He must really like me, because he asked me out again."

Because the rape victim doesn't believe that what has happened to her is rape, she sometimes decides to give her attacker another chance. After all, he's nice-looking, has a good job or belongs to the right fraternity, and everyone else seems to think he's a great guy.

What happens? Often, the same thing: He rapes her again. That's when most women bail out of continuing to see the men involved. In the *Ms.* survey, women who were raped had a mean average of 2.02 episodes; men who committed rape said they had done the behavior to the same woman a mean average of 2.29 times.

Sometimes a woman sees the man who raped her again in order to turn the rape into an experience of sexual intercourse that happened in the context of an ongoing relationship and, therefore, to make it acceptable. For example, after being raped by a man she had dated for three weeks, Bonnie then had intercourse with him (she had been a virgin at the time of the rape). She explains her action as an attempt to "sort of legitimize what happened." That attempt didn't work and they stopped dating soon afterward. Researchers Weis and Borges note that in the case of rape by a former boyfriend, the man may be trying to "establish old rights" and force the woman back into a relationship or make her suffer for rejecting him. The woman may then feel tied to the man because of their "shared 'guilty secret.'"

Ruth eventually married the man who raped her on their second date after she had passed out from too much drinking.

> In my naiveté, I thought that he truly did care for me and I blamed myself for what happened. I wish I had known about date rape then; maybe I wouldn't have felt like I was such a tramp, that it was my fault. Unfortunately, I believed he cared about me and married him six months later. We were married for 10 years. I found out after the divorce that he had tried this (getting a woman drunk and then trying to rape her) on both of my sisters too.

It's likely that most of these women would not have gone out with their rapists again if they had been able to correctly label their experiences as rape in the first place. Indeed, the women interviewed for this book who clearly identified their assaults as rapes when they occurred did not have sex with their attackers again.

But most women don't have that realization and are easily set up for revictimization. That helps contribute to the saddest statistic of all to emerge from the study, a statistic that shows the power of date rape and acquaintance rape to strip a woman's belief in her ability to control her own life:

Ms. SURVEY STAT □ **41 percent of the raped women said they expect to be raped again.**

CHAPTER 5

The Aftereffects of Acquaintance Rape

□ ──────────────────────────────────── □

"I felt as if my whole world had been kicked out from under me."
— Georgette, raped by a man who lived in her dorm

Many people would like to believe that because date rape and acquaintance rape usually involve little "real" violence —such as brutal beatings or the use or threatened use of weapons—victims are likely to be less profoundly traumatized than women raped by strangers. In fact, the opposite may be true. According to Bonnie L. Katz and Martha R. Burt, researchers with The Urban Institute in Washington, D.C., acquaintance-rape victims rate themselves less recovered than do stranger-rape victims for up to three years following their rape experiences. One explanation for such results, says Andrea Parrot, a date-rape expert from Cornell University in Ithaca, New York, may be that since an acquaintance-rape victim often represses recognition of her experience, she may carry the effects of the assault for a longer time than a stranger-rape victim who may seek counseling or other support help more quickly.

In any rape, a woman feels invaded and violated, her comfortable reality shattered because she has not been able to control her own physical safety. Yet a woman raped by a stranger can often hold on to a sense—even if it is very fragile—that the people she knows provide a zone of protection and support. Her experience as a victim may be validated by the sympathetic reactions of the people close to her.

For a woman raped by a man she knows, this zone is often missing. Like a stranger-rape victim, her confidence in the world has been upended; unlike a stranger-rape victim, few people will offer her sympathy due to social myths about acquaintance rape, the tendency to blame the victim, and her own likelihood to keep silent about the rape.

Psychologists and rape-crisis counselors know that talking about an attack helps the woman understand her post-rape reactions and steers her toward recovery. Although women raped by strangers are often reluctant to discuss their experiences, many do reach out for help from professionals, friends, and relatives. But women raped by acquaintances are most likely to tell no one, thereby blocking the road to recovery. Indeed, because so many of these women don't understand that they have been raped, they do not even internally deal with what has happened to them.

A comparison of women identified as rape survivors by the *Ms.* study found that those raped by men they knew reported the same levels of psychological impact as those raped by strangers. The two groups also scored the same in the clarity with which they communicated their nonconsent, the degree of resistance they offered, and their feelings of anger and depression during the assault. In both groups, the effects of rape were profound, reflecting feelings of diminished self-worth, heightened fear and anxiety as well as depressed expectations for the future.

Ms. SURVEY STATS □ Whether they acknowledged their experience as rape or not, 30 percent of the women identified in the study as rape victims contemplated suicide after the incident
□ 31 percent sought psychotherapy
□ 22 percent took self-defense courses
□ 82 percent said the experience had permanently changed them

---

Alice's story demonstrates the similarity between the aftereffects of rape by a stranger and rape by an acquaintance. Recently, Alice, who is 30, was raped by an unknown man who broke into her California home, woke her, and threatened her with a knife. Twelve years ago, as an 18-year-old, Alice was raped by a boy she worked with. "I went through several months of very deep depression after the first rape," she says. "My symptoms were very similar to the ones I have this time around. I overate, gained weight, and spent a lot of nights crying. This time I'm seeing a doctor and taking an antidepressant—that time (after the first rape) I often seriously considered suicide."

If Alice's experiences had happened in reverse order, things might have been different. Women who have been raped by strangers and later find themselves in rape-threatening situations with men they know say that they are able to quickly identify what is happening as rape because it "feels like what happened before." Thus alerted, they sometimes are able to get away.

Emotional Consequences of Acquaintance Rape

Georgette was 18, a freshman at a state university in North Carolina. Mel was one of the resident assistants in her dormitory, an older student employed as an on-site adviser and watchdog. About 2:00 A.M., Georgette was standing outside the dorm. She had been drinking a little at a party but was not drunk. Mel approached and, in her words, "started making advances." After she repeatedly told him no, he grabbed her arm and dragged her inside to his room. They fought, but it did Georgette little good. She now remembers the physical pain of the rape and the shadows that played on the wall during their struggle. But the pain that was to follow was even greater.

> I didn't tell anyone. In fact, I wouldn't even admit it to myself until about four months later when the guilt and fear that had been eating at me became too much to hide and I came very close to a complete

nervous breakdown. I tried to kill myself, but fortunately I chickened out at the last minute.

There's no way to describe what was going on inside me. I was losing control and I'd never been so terrified and helpless in my life. I felt as if my whole world had been kicked out from under me and I had been left to drift all alone in the darkness. I had horrible nightmares in which I relived the rape and others which were even worse. I was terrified of being with people and terrified of being alone. I couldn't concentrate on anything and began failing several classes. Deciding what to wear in the morning was enough to make me panic and cry uncontrollably. I was convinced I was going crazy, and I'm still convinced I almost did.

Georgette has accurately described what the American Psychiatric Association in 1980 identified as posttraumatic stress disorder. This syndrome is evident in survivors of both stranger and acquaintance rapes. It manifests itself in a wide range of emotion and behavior. The victim may react openly to her experience or she may control her response, appearing outwardly calm and composed. Regardless, she may be experiencing a generalized sense of fear or a specific fear of death, anger, guilt, depression, a fear of men, anxiety, humiliation, embarrassment, shame, or self-blame. She may feel one or more of these, at varying times and intensities, accompanied by radical mood swings. She may consider suicide. Having just survived a life-threatening experience, she may also feel euphoric for a brief time. She might be unable to concentrate or set her mind to perform simple tasks or, conversely, she may be fixated on one thought, such as the assault itself or the fear of encountering the rapist again. The woman may be jumpy or edgy, suffer shakiness, trembling, rapid pulse, or hot and cold flashes. She also may have trouble sleeping, lose the desire to eat, and suffer various medical complaints, some of which might be specifically related to the assault.

For many of the acquaintance-rape victims interviewed for this book, the first emotional reaction to their experience after they were free from the rapist was the feeling that they would never get clean again. Vera, the professional singer raped by a longtime friend, recalls, "The first thing I did was take a shower. A hot one. Then a bath. A really hot one. Then another shower. Another bath. I couldn't get clean. I couldn't get his smell, his touch, his semen, his skin, away from me."

Emma, now 31, was raped at age 17 by a boy who lived on her dormitory floor at a New York state university. Like Vera, she too went through the washing ritual.

> I locked the door and I cried. Then I went into the bathroom and I took a bath and I took a shower and another bath and another shower. It wasn't until I was drying myself off that I caught a look at myself in the mirror and realized that my whole upper body, my neck, my chest, was covered with marks — hickeys. I was repulsed. I was so disgusted. I felt dirty and violated. I didn't want to leave the bathroom, so I just sat on the floor with my towel around me, crying.

Additionally, some women may suffer other immediate emotional impacts of the rape. Women who endured a previous trauma (serious illness, psychological problem) may have a compounded reaction to the rape—one that includes symptoms of the rape as well as symptoms of the earlier trauma. Women who were sexually victimized as children or adults but who had not resolved their feelings about those incidents may now suffer a strong reaction to the earlier victimizations as well as to the present one.

The behavior of some victims may change for months or even years. They may have uncharacteristic personality shifts: Women who were careful and controlled in their sexual activity now may become undiscerning about whom they sleep with and under what circumstances; outgoing women may become withdrawn; women who once attended closely to their appearance now may dress themselves with the deliberate intention of going unnoticed. Women who work or go to school with the men who raped them may quit their jobs or change colleges. Some rape survivors move or get new unlisted telephone numbers in order to feel safe. Some may become more dependent on their families. Women who loved running or taking long walks give up these activities. All of these changes may go on in such a quiet, deliberate manner that they seem imperceptible to others.

Susan was a 23-year-old reporter in Iowa, accustomed to working late into the evening and then going out for beers with her co-workers. One night, one of the male reporters offered to see her home for her protection. He walked her to her door and then asked to use the bathroom. When he emerged, his pants were undone. He hit her, raising a black eye. They fought and he raped her. "I thought exactly what we all thought then: 'You slut, you must have led him on.' I blamed myself for having a drink with him. I thought I must have appeared to have been teasing him at work," Susan says. Her reaction to the assault? "I stopped going out for a drink with the other reporters. I studied harder." Probably all that her co-workers noticed was that Susan had become less fun to be around.

Sometimes the fears become debilitating. The raped woman may become afraid of being in crowds or of being alone (or both). She may become distrustful of even close friends or paranoid about the motives of strangers. Triggers related to the rape—a song that may have been playing during the assault, the smell of the liquor the man was drinking or his cologne, just seeing someone resembling him—may make her feel anxious and afraid.

These fears are especially understandable given the unique nature of date rape and acquaintance rape. Both the woman's personal world and the world at large are now seen as threatening: There is nowhere that is safe, no one who may be trusted. Without positive support, the victim may begin to rebuild her life based on the new (and erroneous) knowledge that she is worthless, helpless, and alone.

For some women who have been raped by men they know, rape-trauma syndrome does not emerge until years later, much the way that posttraumatic stress disorders have been shown to emerge a decade or more after the fighting ended for Vietnam veterans. "I put such a tight lid on all my feelings that I didn't have to deal with any feelings. They were all buried very, very deep," says Connie, a 35-year-old Illinois woman who was raped at 19 by a man she met at a local hangout.

> Those feelings — anger, rage, and guilt — remained suppressed and buried for nearly 16 years. But then, just this year, the lid flew off, and suddenly I was experiencing all those horrible emotions and fears. I actually had genuine anxiety attacks with physical symptoms.
>
> It took me several months to figure out that I was going to have to

deal with what had happened so long ago. Those 16 years had allowed those feelings to magnify, to fester, to boil. I was a real basket case. Finally, fearing an emotional breakdown, I decided to seek professional help. Within the last few months, I've been learning to deal with a lot. I'm changing my attitude and my perspective about myself. I'm even learning to like myself for the first time in 16 years.

But I'm still angry that such a single mindless act of violence against a woman can cause such havoc.

Physical Consequences of Acquaintance Rape: Injury, Pregnancy, Abortion

Of all the aftereffects of acquaintance rape, the ones women usually attend to most quickly are the "real" ones—physical problems related to the rape. Such was the case with Wendy. When Wendy's date finally stopped raping her, there was blood all over the bed in his apartment. [A woman may bleed after rape, even when she isn't a hymen-intact virgin or menstruating, due to the roughness of the man, her own physical resistance, or lack of lubrication.] She continued to bleed after she went home; it worsened the next day. Finally, she went to the college infirmary.

They cleaned me up, stuffed a huge wad of gauze up inside my vagina, and told me to come back the next day. They also prescribed what they called a "morning-after pill," which turned out to be DES [diethylstilbestrol, a synthetic estrogen, now less frequently prescribed due to its correlation with cancer in the children of women who used it].

I went back in the morning and they removed the gauze. The bleeding had stopped. I took those awful pills for five days. It was utter agony. Although I was sick and nauseous the whole time, I did not want to be pregnant.

A few days after the pills were all gone, I got very sick. My stomach hurt so bad I could not eat, sleep, or drink. After a week of torture and several trips to the infirmary, someone found the problem. I had an ulcer and had to be hospitalized for a week.

Like Wendy, the women who go for medical help after an acquaintance rape are often worried about pregnancy. Some are also concerned about the possibility that they might have contracted a sexually transmitted disease. Despite the recent media attention to AIDS and campus involvement in AIDS-prevention programs, there seems to be no great worry among assaultive males that they might become infected with the disease during the rape. In part, that may be due to the myth that AIDS only affects homosexual men. Also, since many young rape victims are virgins, the men who rape them are somewhat assured of the "safety" of the encounter. An acquaintance rapist also usually shows no interest in protecting the woman from an unwanted pregnancy, a concern he might have if he and the woman were having consensual sex, as the few men who are apprehended claim.

For women, pregnancy as the result of a date rape can be a riveting fear. Their hopes of telling no one about the assault may disappear as the unmistakable signs of pregnancy increase. On occasion, those signs may be misleading, the result of other elements of rape-trauma syndrome. Emma a 17-year-old virgin at the time she was raped, had a "hysterical" pregnancy, complete with weight gain and nausea following her attack. She didn't get her period for three months. "I was really terrified," she says. Finally, she confided in her dorm director, who took a sample of Emma's urine for pregnancy testing. The results came back negative. The next day, Emma got her period.

The stories don't always turn out that way. At 21, Caitlin was in her senior year at college. She came from a strict Irish Catholic New England family. She was not a virgin, but was accustomed to setting sexual limits with men and having them respected. Over Christmas break, she started dating a man she knew from high school. He raped her on their third date after she refused to have sex with him. Caitlin went home in shock.

About two weeks later, she started feeling bloated. She went to a doctor who treated her for an intestinal virus. When she didn't improve, Caitlin told an older female friend, who urged her to have a pregnancy test. It was positive. Caitlin went to a local Planned Parenthood clinic and had an abortion.

I think I had a harder time dealing with the abortion decision in the beginning than I did with the actual incident itself. It took me a long time. I'm Catholic and I had to go to confession about it.

I told my parents about it six months later. . . . My father's never really brought it up [since] except in terms of, "Have you been to confession yet?" For a long time, for two years, that's all I heard, "Have you been to confession?"

I don't really want to get into it anymore with anyone. There's no need for anybody else to really know about it. It just makes me feel sad when I talk about it.

Sexual Consequences of Acquaintance Rape

The fears that most women experience after date rape or acquaintance rape are often focused on men and sex. Despite being, perhaps, the source of pleasure and joy before, both of these now may evoke dread, anger, or disgust in the rape victim's mind.

Rape survivors in general often have difficulty with sex after their attacks. Acquaintance-rape victims may have an even more difficult time due to the new loss of trust in men who are close to them. "I felt there was danger everywhere because I realized that any man, any time, could and would hurt me or even kill me," says Anna, who was raped at 32 by a man she met at an adult education class.

Many victims experience sexual difficulties caused by physical injuries or emotional worries about their partners' reactions. They suffer a range of sex-related problems—the inability to relax, diminished arousal, sexual disinterest or discomfort—which may last for as little as a few days or as long as several years. Kim, a Maryland woman, was raped by a date five years ago while she was a foreign exchange student. "Three years after the rape, I had a one-night stand. It was the first time I had any physical contact with any man [after the rape]," she says. "Three years and five months after being raped, I was able to make love with my current boyfriend."

Patty repressed the memory of her acquaintance rape for four years. The sexual consequences of her experience didn't appear until after she started examining what had happened to her. "Last fall, when I really started processing it, I had nightmares all the time. I would be sitting doing nothing and having flashbacks," she says. "Every time my husband would touch me, I would see this other man's face. Sex was out of the question, just totally. Somehow, we made it through."

Most women do make it through, although not totally unscathed. Rachel, for example, has had few long-term problems with men or sex, but she will not go out with tall or big men (her rapist was a varsity football player) and she feels panicky if a man holds her down playfully during sex. Some women choose not to have sex for a while. Others begin to have sex more often than before. In that latter group are often found many prerape virgins who feel "devalued" by their experience: Since someone took what they were taught to protect, they feel they now have nothing left that's worth protecting. For these women, who are just beginning their sexual lives, the effects of being raped by a man they know may be profound. Some walk away from the experience believing that their rape experience is what sex is supposed to be. Others walk away wondering whether sex is anything they are ever going to want.

Leona was raised in a fundamentalist Christian home. By age 29 she had still never had a date, so she decided to use a dating service. Through it she met a Los Angeles police officer and they began dating. Mostly their dates consisted of her going to his house and getting into bed for an hour. "I didn't know how else to act," she says. "I was afraid if I didn't, he wouldn't like me anymore."

After several months, Leona decided to move and not give the man her new address. Four months later, he appeared on her doorstep, telling her he had used his police connections to find her. He walked through the door, wearing his guns, forced Leona to the floor, and had her perform oral sex on him, something she had never done. Fearing that he would shoot her or that the guns would go off accidentally, she didn't struggle.

Leona remained celibate for three years after that assault, then met a man she lived with for two years whom she describes as "very, very, very gentle and kind and very slow and very patient." That man died. Now Leona lives with a close woman friend.

I have not dated. I'm working now on my choice of not having sex or being in a sexual relationship with anybody. I'm not sure what sexuality is about for me. I live with a person right now who I love a whole lot. We are not physical with each other, but I imagine if there were anybody that I would be in a relationship with, it would be her.

At some levels, I can see myself living out in the middle of the desert and for the rest of my life not being with anybody. I was really hurt by the trust issue [in relation to the man who raped her].

The "trust issue" has shaped Irene's life too. She was raped by a date at age 18 and again by her brother-in-law five years later. "I have never been married nor do I intend to," she says. "I guess I feel that, since I cannot trust men, I could never put my future in a man's hands, never trust a man for my security. . . . I am currently involved with a married man and for the nine years previous to this relationship, I was involved with women as sexual partners."

Some women feel guilty or repulsed by the sex acts they were forced to commit during rape and may resist participating in them in a consensual relationship. Also, since some women experience involuntary orgasm during rape, their feelings of self-blame and guilt may be compounded by a sense of sexual self-betrayal.

Many acquaintance-rape survivors wonder whether they will ever have a loving relationship with a man again. Among the women interviewed for this book, those who had several good relationships with men before the rape seem better able to see a bright future than do younger or less experienced women. "One thing I'll never get over is my distrust of men," says Alice, who was an 18-year-old virgin when she was raped by a boy who worked with her in a fast-food restaurant. "I may not seem fair to deny all men the benefit of the doubt, but I have to. The costs are too high if I make a mistake the other way."

The Consequences of Telling Boyfriends and Husbands

It is always difficult for a woman to tell her boyfriend or husband about her acquaintance-rape experience. When she does, the readjustment to their prerape sexual and emotional life may prove rocky. It may be impossible for her male partner to see what has happened as rape. He may blame her. He may feel angry and confused about the rape and agonized that he was unable to protect her, even though he wasn't nearby. He may feel that someone else has robbed what is "his" and, if the rapist is someone he knows, he may feel shown up or cuckolded. He may be anxious to have sex again, to ascertain that everything is still "normal," or he may be unable to have sex with the woman.

Many times, the questions and doubts raised by an acquaintance rape cause the end of a relationship. When Jodie told her college boyfriend that she had been raped by his best friend, he was quiet for a long time. When she got up to leave, he told her she should spend the night in his room, that he wouldn't touch her.

> During the night, I woke up to find him on top of me. At first I thought [the rapist] was back and I panicked. My boyfriend said that he was just trying to get me "used to things" again, so that I wouldn't be frigid for the rest of my life. I was too drained to fight or argue, so I let him. My mind was completely blank during it. I felt nothing.
>
> The next day I took my last exam, packed up my things, and left. I broke up with my boyfriend over the summer.

Women in long-term relationships may assume support from their partners that is not there. Even when a woman tries to resume a feeling of emotional closeness or sexual activity, the man still may be unable to deal with the rape. Holly, raped two years ago by a man she met in an Oregon bar, was hopeful that her boyfriend, Al, would react well when she told him about the attack. After all, she knew that Al's former wife had been raped by an acquaintance while they were still married. She believed he would understand what she was feeling.

When Holly told Al about the rape, he telephoned her attacker to confront him. The man freely admitted having forced her to have sex against her will. But Al became angry with Holly when the rapist told him that, after the rape, they had passed a police car and Holly had not screamed for help.

He really keyed in on that . . . and was real weird that night and real mean.

I thought — now or never — we've got to get sexual with each other again or he's really going to think he's losing out on something. So we got sexual and things seemed pretty normal. We went on for three or four more weeks and then broke up.

He says now it had nothing to do with the rape. I don't believe that. I never believed that. I will always think this guy [the rapist] cost me the relationship. Since then I've never really been close to anybody for a long term. Al was the love of my life.

For women who hid their date-rape episodes deep inside and who have just begun to examine them, there's still the problem of telling male partners, even loving ones. Although the rape may have occurred years before, these men experience many of the same confused emotions as men faced with handling the news of a recent attack. Bonnie, a 34-year-old Cambridge, Massachusetts, woman, waited several months after realizing that she had been raped at age 20 before telling her husband. "His initial reaction was very comforting and supportive and very surprised," she says. "Then, over a little bit of time, he was sort of angry, sort of scared that I hadn't told him before. That we'd been together as long as we have and that I couldn't talk to him about it."

Aftereffects on Friendships and Family Relations

At a time when women most need friends and family around them, they often find those sources of emotional support and comfort shut to them. The reason is simple: Acquaintance-rape victims aren't believed or are blamed for what happened, even by those who are close to them.

Caitlin told her roommate about her rape after she found out that she was pregnant. "She said, 'I can't believe he did that' . . . because he was such a popular guy in high school and had so many girls who would readily have gone to bed with him. She said I shouldn't be feeling like this," Caitlin recalls. "It kind of took validity away from what I thought I felt and what my gut feelings were."

Sometimes friends, particularly women friends, need to distance themselves from the victim in order to feel safe. Consider what she's telling them: A "respectable" man, very possibly someone they know and like, is sexually violent. That's too much for many women to acknowledge since it implies that they too could be in danger. Bettina was raped 20 years ago while a student in Ann Arbor, Michigan. "A week or so later, I told my friend what happened because she knew Chris and Joe [the two men involved] and I felt she should know," she says. "Her response was denial that they could have done such a thing. That shut me up. I reasoned that if a friend would not believe me, there was no point in reporting it to police or anyone else."

Sometimes friends treat the rape lightly, as if it were a sexual escapade. "No big deal," they tell the victim. Indeed, virgins are often congratulated and told, "Well, it's about time!" as if they should celebrate having finally gotten rid of their great burden, regardless of how that unburdening occurred. Alice, a virgin and a teenager at the time of her rape, remembers her friend's reaction the morning after. "She thought it was funny and about time. It bothered her that I was so square," she says.

The most logical place for acquaintance-rape survivors to seek support is from their families, but they often don't find it there. In part, that's because parents and other relatives often reflect religious, cultural, and social values that are unsympathetic to rape victims. "I told my mother what had happened . . . and to this day, I wish I had never told her," says Wendy, who was date raped in college. "In her mind, her 'little girl' was ruined. I am afraid I thought the same thing. After all, I was now 'ruined goods.' Unfortunately, she later told my father who said he was 'disappointed'."

Sex is never an easy topic between children and parents. In addition, conflicts with parents over independence and choice of partners may have also arisen before the rape. For such a woman to tell her parents about being raped by a man she knows—perhaps one she selected over their objections—would only open her to attack. Divorced or separated women often have also had prior family conflicts. "I knew my parents would not be the most supportive in the world," says Holly, "because they were not pleased I was separated. They were not pleased that I was dating or going out." It was only after she decided to press charges against the man who raped her that Holly told her mother what happened.

> The first thing I can remember her saying was, "Well, Holly, I don't know what you expected . . ." and that just crushed me. I wanted someone to say, "We still love you, it's okay."
> I said, "Mom, you know, I wish I was having the fun you think I'm having."

Some families with strong religious beliefs may see the rape as something the woman brought on herself and the man, much as Eve was blamed for Adam's expulsion from the Garden of Eden. If the woman is an unmarried nonvirgin, many religions and family members may believe that she got what she deserved.

Most of the women interviewed for this book did not tell their families about their acquaintance-rape incidents. Some fear doing so now for the pain it would bring, both the pain of learning about the rape and of learning that the woman kept quiet about it. "I think it would hurt my parents deeply to know that I had a terrible experience like this and chose to deal with it alone," says Jodie.

Fortunately, there are a few positive stories. In the weeks after her date rape, Lori, a normally outgoing 19-year-old, was acting unnaturally silent and depressed. Her mother kept asking her what was wrong and Lori kept insisting that she was fine. One night, Lori's mother and her mother's close friend took Lori out for dinner. During the meal, the friend launched into a story about the time she went out with a man who raped her.

> My mom just looked at me and said, "Is that what happened to you? Is that what's wrong?"
> I just said, "Yeah."
> She asked me to tell her about it and I did.

Later, her mother gave her an article about date rape to read. "I read it and then I understood what it was and what had happened to me," Lori says.

Confronting the Rapist and Other Postrape Fantasies

Facing the rapist and denouncing him is a fantasy harbored by many acquaintance-rape survivors and born out of the anger they feel. Many hope to put the demons of guilt and self-blame to rest by finally laying responsibility where it belongs. Often that fantasy involves confronting the man in a social or business setting, where he is known and well respected. Says Paula, raped by a doctor with whom she worked, "I wanted to publicly humiliate him by screaming at him in the [hospital] hallway, with all the other doctors and nurses around. I had that fantasy for years, of somehow publicly humiliating him or telling his chief of staff."

Of course, many acquaintance-rape victims *do* encounter their attacker later because the man is often from the same community. Donna went to the campus police at her Illinois college and filed charges against the male student who raped her. Because he was not removed from school, she ran into him several times afterward. "He would just look at me and try to scare me, kind of glare and smile," she says. "One time he physically ran into me at a Hardee's [restaurant]. We had already had eye contact, so he knew I was there. Later, I turned around and he was right behind me. That was very icky." But facing him down eventually helped Donna. She went to a party and discovered, after she arrived, that the man was there. She stayed for a short time and then left, feeling as if she proved— at least to herself and him—that he couldn't scare her away. "It was bad to see him, but it was good to see him, because it helped me get past some things," she says.

Some men wisely disappear, leaving their victims unable to "gain closure," as the psychologists refer to it, through confrontation. Fantasizing about that confrontation, therefore, becomes an aspect of recovery that helps the woman work off feelings of anger as well as understand what has happened. It took Carol 10 years to "cycle through" the aftereffects of being raped as an 18-year-old virgin. She has her speech ready in case she ever runs into the man who assaulted her. "I think I would really light into him and tell him, 'This is what you did to me. Maybe you'll never feel bad about that, maybe you date raped other women and don't have any remorse, but you probably have ruined 50 years of living for five women.' It probably wouldn't affect him, but I think it would help me to say that."

Alice's fantasy: She daydreams about women carrying government-issued Uzi semiautomatic weapons to use against men who show "the slightest hint of violence or condescension." Leona did more than daydream: One night she went and urinated on her attacker's front lawn.

Sometimes a substitute experience provides the woman with another outlet for her feelings. Patty participated in a session in which rape survivors confronted convicted rapists in a therapeutic setting.

> When I turned off the car to walk in there, I was shaking. I thought, "What have you done now? You're going to have to go bare your soul." But I wanted to do this.
>
> We walked in and those men were terrified of us. It was bizarre. It was real evidence that we had power and they didn't. They were spilling their coffee, they wouldn't look at us . . . they were very nervous.
>
> We sat down and they had to face us and tell their first names and what crimes they had committed. That's all they were allowed to say. They couldn't ask us questions. They had to sit and listen to us. It lasted about four hours and it was really intense.

The Long Road to Recovery

The exact process of recovering and healing from acquaintance rape is still something of a mystery. It is as personal as each woman and her story. The most potential damage lies in not recognizing the rape as rape, but instead burying it. This is what hundreds of thousands of women have done. Many of them have not as yet faced their experience and called it by name.

Fran, now 33, was 17 when she was raped by a staff member she was attracted to at the camp where she worked. She was rebuffed when she tried to talk about the rape with the camp director's wife and later with her mother.

Nine years passed. Often, in intimate situations, I would shake uncontrollably. Sometimes I would cry after sex was over; once or twice, I became nauseous. For a long time, pain was always there, despite the reality of my own desires and the gentleness of caring partners.

When she found herself irrationally disliking a new employee at work, Fran realized it was because he looked like her attacker.

I was shocked when I understood that he made me think of [the rapist] and of the rape. I was very angry. And because I was angry, I thought that I was free.

After two more years, I felt sufficiently detached from my experience to consider volunteering to do crisis intervention counseling with rape survivors. But at the training seminar, when a film was shown of a simulated rape, I had to look away. It was too real for me.

I flashed back to that summer night and to the girl that I had been. From my new vantage point, I was able to see how my ability to trust had been stunted and that my healthy curiosity had been twisted by guilt and fear. And with this recognition, I realized that there was still one more thing that I had to do.

And so I began, at last, to grieve for all that I had lost.

CHAPTER 6

Men Who Rape Women They Know

"Both of the guys were Joe Average types. . . . Nothing about their exterior packaging spelled RAPIST."
— Karen, who was raped on two separate occasions by men she knew

R ape is not natural to men. If it were, most men would be rapists and they are not. Nonetheless, the answers given by the male college students who participated in the *Ms.* study delineate a sobering incidence of sexual aggression and assault in a predominantly middle-class, educated population.

As was done for the women surveyed, the word "rape" was not used in questions asked of the men about their sexual behavior; instead, descriptions of specific acts were given (for example, "Have you ever engaged in sexual intercourse with a woman when she didn't want to by threatening or using some degree of physical force?"). The final tally:

Ms. SURVEY STATS In the year prior to the survey, 2,971 college men reported that they had committed:
- 187 rapes;
- 157 attempted rapes;
- 327 episodes of sexual coercion;
- 854 incidents of unwanted sexual contact.

About 8 percent of the men surveyed had raped or attempted to rape a woman sometime since the age of 14. Of those questioned, 75 percent said they had never forced any unwanted sexual act on a woman.

The rapists differed from the nonassaultive males in several ways. They drank one to two times a week and became drunk one to three times a month—more than the rates for nonrapists—and were more likely to describe their family backgrounds as quite strict, with family violence (parents hitting children or each other) occurring once or twice a month.

Sexual values also differed. The rapists said they talked daily with their friends about "how a particular woman would be in bed" and they rated as "very frequently" how often they read *Playboy, Penthouse, Chic, Club, Forum, Gallery, Genesis, Oui,* or *Hustler* magazines. The men who raped also said they approved of sexual intercourse under any circumstances, regardless of how long the man and woman have known each other. They were, on the average, just over 15 years old when they first had intercourse, compared with nonaggressors, who were 17.

The study showed that men who committed rape were more likely to believe rape-supportive myths. They also saw women as adversaries, endorsed sex role stereotypes, saw rape prevention as women's responsibility, and considered the mingling of aggression with sexuality as normal.

Just as the women reported how their rapes occurred, the men answered questions about the rapes in which they participated. On some points, there was agreement between the two groups. Most of the men knew the women they raped (85 percent) and more than half of the assaults occurred on dates. Most happened off campus and most of the men (74 percent) had been using drugs or alcohol beforehand. The rapes were reported to police in only 2 percent of the incidents described by the men.

But the profiles of rape drawn by rapists and rape victims diverged on many important features:

CHARACTERISTIC OF RAPE	MEN'S VERSION	WOMEN'S VERSION
More than one attacker	16%	5%
Rapist hit victim	3%	9%
Woman took drugs or drank beforehand	75%	55%
Degree of petting before	below waist	above waist
Amount of force man used	mild	moderate
Victim tried to reason verbally with man	36%	84%
Victim physically struggled	12%	70%
Incident definitely was rape	1%	27%

It wasn't expected that male and female responses would be exactly equivalent, of course, since the men in the study were not necessarily the aggressors in the specific victimizations described by the women. However, the disparities above, especially in the last four items, are more likely caused by the men's inability to perceive situations as being forceful that women find quite threatening and a male inclination to interpret female resistance as being less serious than it is. Moreover, while the women reported feeling fear, anger, and depression after their assaults, men said they experienced some feelings of pride.

Though acquaintance rapists often hold different attitudes than men who do not rape, to all appearances the two types of men may look the same. In a college setting, they may be sitting side by side in lecture halls and fraternity houses, on athletic teams and student government councils. In the "real" world, both types of men may hold good jobs and be well liked, even admired, by their peers. In most ways, the two groups of men are more similar than they are different.

Just a Regular Guy

Karen, now a lawyer living on the West Coast, was a senior at a prestigious East Coast women's college when she was raped by a man she had met through friends on campus. Several years later, during her last year in law school, she was raped by another man she knew. Now, more than 10 years past her rapes, Karen realizes how unlike the stereotype of rapists her assailants were.

Both of the guys were Joe Average types. The first was reasonably attractive; the second, less so. Both were intelligent and articulate. Nothing about their exterior packaging spelled RAPIST. Neither one of them, especially in the free climate of the 1970s, needed to rape women in order to have sex.

But date rapists and acquaintance rapists are often more than just "Joe Average" guys. Tonya describes her attacker as "tall, good-looking, built, and charming." She met him at a club. A friend who was with her pronounced him "gorgeous." The man called several days later to make a date for the upcoming weekend. "I was feeling a bit of an ego boost," Tonya says, "since he seemed really taken with me, and my sister and friend told me how lucky I was." Later, Tonya had to vigorously fight off a rape attempt during her date with the "gorgeous" man.

It could be suggested that acquaintance rapists just take on the trappings of normalcy, that they've learned to project themselves to be "regular" guys as a cover-up. But research shows that's not the case. Acquaintance rapists *are* regular guys. Nowhere is that more evident than in a study of 71 self-disclosed date rapists conducted by Eugene Kanin of Purdue University. The subjects, all white undergraduate students, volunteered themselves for study as possible rapists. The episodes in which they were involved all included sexual penetration accompanied by the applied or threatened use of force against a nonconsenting female.

The men were mostly from middle-class backgrounds and had had little contact with police. "With respect to prior criminal activity . . . these men look like 'typical' college students," Kanin reports. "There is a scattering of vandalism, petty theft, and the usual proliferation of alcohol-marijuana and traffic violations. There is no conspicuous history of violence. . . . Impulsive behavior and criminal tendencies which have been reported for convicted rapists are strikingly absent." Only six of the 71 men had been reported to police by the women they raped and, in all cases, the women later decided not to prosecute. All of the rapists said they had planned or hoped for a seduction to result from their encounter.

There were differences between the date rapists and a control group of men used in the study: The rapists were more likely to falsely profess love and to get engaged or get a woman drunk in order to have sex with her. They also had more orgasms than did the controls: 1.5 per week versus .8 per month. Yet the men who exhibited, in Kanin's words, "sexually predatory behavior" were significantly more likely than the control group to rate their sexual achievements as unsatisfactory.

Only six of the rapists saw themselves as deserving (but not wanting) imprisonment. Two-thirds said that the fault for the incident was with their victims because of the women's behavior. Some of the rapists focused on other circumstances that they believed justified their raping—such as how drunk they were or how sexually excited.

Kanin concluded that the date rapists were "products of a highly erotic-oriented peer group socialization which started during the junior high and high school years." This socialization, he said, continued into college as the men sought out new peer groups to support and enhance their earlier learned values. "Sexual conquest, as a result," Kanin stated, "becomes intimately associated with their feelings of worth."

Methods Used by Acquaintance Rapists

Although most men who rape women they know don't identify themselves as rapists, there is a strong element of "setting up" the situation. As has been mentioned in earlier chapters, the location of the rape is often isolated, chosen because it is out of earshot or view of other people. Even when the rape occurs in the victim's home, it usually happens when the man knows that roommates or children are away and he and the victim are likely to be undisturbed.

Lydia's story began at a potluck dinner for a group of nursing and medical students who had recently arrived in New York City. Lydia liked one of the men she met there, so when he invited her to dinner, she accepted. On their date, they talked about their lives before coming to the city. The man talked about a friend who was a doctor at a hospital on Long Island and how much he missed him. "It seemed like a spur of the moment idea at the time, but he said, 'Why don't we drive out tonight and surprise him?' " Lydia says. "I went along with the idea, providing we didn't stay too long, as I had a baby-sitting job the next day."

They drove out to see the friend who, curiously, disappeared shortly after their arrival. Lydia and her date were left in the friend's apartment.

A decision was made to head back early the next morning rather than that night. I was to sleep on the couch; my date would sleep in his friend's room.

As soon as I began drifting off to sleep, he was all over me, wanting sex. When I said no, he went back to bed in the other room. But he kept coming back, over and over, just as I had dozed off, so that I would be totally disoriented at first.

He became physically violent as the evening went on and he couldn't get me to change my mind. He would pinch and slap me — I lost a contact lens — and he ripped my clothes trying to get them off. . . . It went on all night. Each time he became more threatening and violent.

No one would have heard if I had yelled. And if I had left — we were in the middle of Long Island in the middle of the night and I had no money or any idea of how to get back to New York City alone. Nor did I have friends or family there to turn to for help.

With the escalation of violence and the change in his personality, I began to fear for my life.

Lydia managed to keep her attacker from penetrating her. At dawn, when perhaps he tired of the assault, he drove her into the city. Looking back, she says now, "It wasn't a spur-of-the-moment idea for him, but well orchestrated, with his friend in collusion."

The man who attacked Lydia showed typical date rapist behavior and methods. To allay the woman's worries, acquaintance rapists often lie about other people being present at the location where they want to go. Sometimes other people *are* in collusion with the rapist, as Lydia suspects was the case in her attack. Rapists also often invent errands in order to stop somewhere secluded or feign an emergency to get their victims to go with them.

Abby, for example, had dinner one night with a co-worker from a Philadelphia advertising agency. The man started drinking at the restaurant bar and soon seemed completely debilitated. "I'd never seen anybody get this drunk—sloppy, falling-down-off-the-stool drunk. I couldn't believe my eyes," she says. "I felt a responsibility to get him safely home. I had people help me get him into his car."

She drove the man to his townhouse and half dragged him up the steps. He roused himself enough to unlock a security gate and she staggered in with him. "I asked if he was okay," she says, "at which point he sprang upon me, completely undrunk." They struggled, but Abby's co-worker overpowered and then raped her.

Some men who rape women they know threaten them with physical harm. These threats are often not carried out: They don't have to be, since a large percentage of women will capitulate on verbal threats alone. "I felt physically threatened because of his anger . . . although he didn't have a knife or gun," says Kim, who was raped at 20 by a man she was dating. "He kept attacking me verbally, saying some really strange things. It was almost as though I, as a person, wasn't there for him. I was just a body he felt like intruding upon."

Some acquaintance rapists actually do injure their victims. Anna was 32, about the same age as her new date. They had been to a party and he had been drinking; when they left, he told her he needed to stop at his house for coffee before driving her home. Inside his home, Anna kept her coat on. When the man told her to take it off, she declined.

> Then he menacingly told me to take it off. . . . It was then that I realized with unbelieving horror that he was going to rape me.
>
> He began to undress. I thought to myself, "How much can it hurt to be hit? If I stand my ground, maybe he will back down even if he does hit me." He was standing close to me, stripped to his shorts.
>
> Suddenly his hands came up and he was hitting me on both sides of my head. His final blow lifted me off my feet, into the air, and sent me flying backward over the edge of the water bed, crashing into the TV stand with my head as I began to fall toward the floor.

In those few seconds my whole life changed. . . . I learned about violence, I learned about pain — and that I wasn't strong enough to withstand it.

He pinned my body to the floor with his and told me that if he had to hit me again I would be very, very sorry. That he would hurt me more than I could imagine. I got up slowly, my head aching, totally defeated. . . . I had two young children at home and I wanted to live. More than anything, I didn't want him to kill me.

The man was eventually prosecuted for raping Anna and was sentenced to five years' probation.

On the other hand, a significant percentage of date rapists don't physically harm the women they rape, but just ignore their protests. Another sizable group use the greater weight of their bodies to pin the women down, restrain them from escape, and force them into positions in which they may be sexually assaulted. In the *Ms.* survey, 64 percent of the men who raped were reported by their victims as simply holding the women down or using light physical aggression, such as arm twisting, to achieve their goal.

Men's Perceptions and Behavior After Acquaintance Rape

How some men behave after committing rape against women they know often contradicts the hostility and aggression that their victims have just experienced. Some acquaintance rapists become oddly tender immediately afterward and try to dress the women or cover them. Some gallantly insist on walking or driving their victims home, telling the women that it's dangerous for them to be out alone. Others profess love and talk about having an ongoing relationship. Another type kisses their victims good-bye and says they will call them again soon. (And some do call, apparently raring to go out on another "date.") In short, many men fail to perceive what has just happened as rape.

Ms. SURVEY STAT □ 84 percent of the men who committed rape said that what they did was *definitely* not rape.

Denise and April agree that sometimes a man's perceptions about a rape incident is the polar opposite of a woman's. Denise was raped in the mid-1970s by a "friend of a friend" in her own apartment. He ignored her protests, pinned her to the bed with his body, and choked her. When he fell asleep after ejaculating, she escaped and drove to a friend's house. The two women returned to Denise's the following morning. The man was gone.

> He left me a note with one of those smile faces drawn on it. The note read: "Denise, I woke up and you were gone. Catch ya later! Have a nice day! Bob"
>
> Minutes later, the phone rang. The voice belonged to a cheerful Bob. I think I called him a bastard or a fucker and I told him not to ever call me again, and then hung up. He called back, sounding surprised, asking, "Hey, what's the matter?"

April, too, was raped by a man who showed no evidence of understanding what had happened. He was a recent acquaintance who offered to help her move into a new apartment. They had never dated or had any sexual relationship. He pushed her onto the floor, slammed her headfirst into a corner, and they struggled until he raped her. "The penetration was very violent," she says. "When it was all over, he asked me if I usually fight so much during sex. I don't think it ever occurred to him that he had raped me."

Sometimes, recognizing their actions as rape, acquaintance rapists launch a preemptive strike against the possibility that their victims will tell someone. Such a man may brag to his friends about having "gotten" the woman in order to quickly make it public knowledge that she willingly had sex with him. That's what the man who raped Nina did—and when she reported the incident to police he sent her a letter from his attorney claiming that he would sue her for defamation of character. "I couldn't believe it!" Nina says. "Finally I got terribly angry for the first time and began blaming him instead of myself for what happened, and began recovering." Nina called the man's lawyer. When she told him the story of the rape, he apologized and said he wouldn't proceed with the case.

Women sometimes encounter their rapists again after the rape, and the men display a range of emotions from innocence to guilt to malevolence. Trisha was raped at 17 by a high school friend and continued to run into him at school and social events. "After about three months, he spoke to me," she says. "He said, 'I'm sorry, really sorry.' I just walked away. I didn't want to say a thing."

Maggie's rapist lived in her hometown and literally stalked her after she pressed charges. He would drive by her on the street and say menacing things, call her a "bitch," or, even more unnerving, just laugh. He would follow her in his car when she was out driving or trail her through the local mall. Once he even sat outside an office where she was interviewing for a job. Finally, the district attorney spoke to the man's lawyer and some of the harassment stopped. The man was eventually acquitted of the rape charges.

How Men Are Taught to Rape

"Rape is not some form of psychopathology that afflicts a very small number of men," says acquaintance-rape educator Py Bateman. "In fact, rape is not that different from what we see as socially acceptable or socially laudable male behavior."

What differentiates men who rape women they know from men who do not is, in part, how much they believe the dogma of what most boys learn it means to be male—"macho" in the worst sense of the word. Some researchers describe this variable as the "hypermasculinity" factor. Others have dubbed the men who embody this behavior "male zealots."

Nearly all men are exposed to this sexual indoctrination, but fortunately only some truly adhere to it. These beliefs are chiefly promulgated by other men: fathers, uncles, grandfathers, coaches, youth group leaders, friends, fraternity brothers, even pop stars. Boys are taught through verbal and nonverbal cues to be self-centered and single-minded about sex, to view women as objects from whom sex is taken, not as equal partners with wishes and desires of their own. Boys learn that they must initiate sexual activity, that they may meet with reluctance from girls, but if they just persist, cajole, and refuse to let up, that ultimately they will get what they want. They view their relationships with women as adversarial challenges and learn to use both their physical and social power to overcome these smaller, less important people.

This is what most boys—not just future rapists—learn about being sexual. Little or no mention is made of sex as an interaction between two people who are mutually participating and enjoying it. And few boys have the benefit of learning what good sexual relations are by the example of the men around them.

Recent research by Virginia Greendlinger of Williams College in Williamstown, Massachusetts, and Donn Byrne of the State University of New York-Albany showed a strong adherence to male sexual socialization values among the 114 undergraduate men surveyed. In the study, the men were asked whether they agreed or disagreed with a series of statements about sex roles and sexuality. A few of the findings:

STATEMENT	PERCENTAGE AGREEING
I prefer relatively small women.	93.7
I like to dominate a woman.	91.3
I enjoy the conquest part of sex.	86.1
Some women look like they're just asking to be raped.	83.5
I get excited when a woman struggles over sex.	63.5
It would be exciting to use force to subdue a woman.	61.7

These ways of viewing sex and women are reinforced vividly through various methods of expression. Consider the language that many men use. In his book, *Men On Rape*, a collection of interviews with men (most of them nonrapists) about sexual violence, Timothy Beneke explores how men's language about sex is often couched in terms that frame sex as an achievement of a valued commodity: that is, gaining possession of a woman. For example:

Sex as achievement:
- "I'd like to make it with her."
- "I hope I score tonight."
- "I could teach her a thing or two."
- "I really put it to her!"

Woman as commodity:

□ "She wouldn't give me any."
□ "I bet I could get her if I tried."
□ "She was the best piece of ass I ever had."
□ "How would you like a little bit of that?"

Beneke goes on to explain that men's language often further objectifies women by reducing them to the status of children, animals,
or, most simply, sexual organs: "Hey, baby!"; "Let's see if we can
shoot some beaver"; "She's a cunt."

This language, Beneke believes, expresses some of the forces that
contribute to the making of an acquaintance rapist. Sex becomes
synonymous only with gaining personal gratification; any interaction with the partner is unimportant and even undesirable (since it
offers the potential for nonachievement of the man's goal). "If men
go out on dates with the idea that sex is achievement of possession
of a valued commodity," writes Beneke, "the woman's consent is
likely to be of peripheral concern."

Most men have used this language at some time. Many ultimately reject the attitudes it expresses as they develop feelings of
empathy, compassion, and love. Nonetheless, for most men, the
imprint of such sexual socialization remains. "Not every man is a
rapist," Beneke writes, "but every man who grows up in America
and learns American English learns all too much to think like a
rapist, to structure his experience of women and sex in terms of
status, hostility, control, and dominance."

Cassie, who was raped one summer by a patron she knew from
the bar where she worked, remembers the language the man used
during the assault.

> As he was tugging away at my slacks, he kept saying, "I want some,"
> and when I said I didn't want to, he repeated, insisting, "I want some!"
> and continued about the business of taking what he wanted.
>
> It was clear that by saying, "I want some," he was sending a
> message to me that he thought that he had the right to take whatever
> he wanted. . . . I was a commodity, a substance, as indicated by his
> use of the word "some."

Language not only leads men to objectify women but to objectify—
and so dissociate themselves from—their own sexual organs. The

man's penis becomes his "tool" and often he might even give it a name. It thus becomes a creature of its own, with a mind of its own, so the man is absolved of responsibility for its actions. This concept meshes with the popular myth of the male sexual imperative: that is, that once he is sexually aroused, a man cannot stop himself from forcing sex on a woman. Such a belief provides a handy rationalization for a man to use to coerce a woman into having sex ("See what you've done to me? Now we've *gotta* do it."). Moreover, the dissociation of the man from his penis and the myth that he can't be held responsible once he has been turned on makes many date rapes the woman's fault, in the man's view, for arousing him and his "friend." (Belief in these myths isn't limited to men. Studies of male and female college students have shown that both groups believe that sex is a biological drive for men but not for women.)

Reinforcing the effect of language on promulgating hypermasculine sexual behavior are the messages transmitted through popular culture such as movies and television. These messages often mix aggression, force, and sex. In the film *Gone With the Wind* (based on a book written by a woman), Rhett Butler and Scarlett O'Hara are seen drinking and fighting, displaying much anger toward each other. Suddenly, he lifts her off her feet, carries her up that dramatic staircase, and (presumably) to bed. "What happens the next morning?" asks rape educator Bateman. "She's got a big smile on her face!" Proof positive that women really want it, especially if you knock them around a little bit and then physically overpower them.

Bateman also likes to cite a scene from the movie *Saturday Night Fever* as reinforcing the belief that women's wishes should be ignored. In that scene, star John Travolta has just offered to walk the woman of his dreams home (and, hopefully, into an intimate encounter), but she refuses. So he starts to walk away, in the direction of his house, as she turns to walk toward hers. She crosses the street, then turns back to him and calls out, "You shouldn't have asked. You should've just done it." The message to men, Bateman says, is, "If you ask, you're gonna lose an opportunity."

Such scenarios are not dated relics. There are dozens and dozens of recent examples. In 1987, the television program *Moonlighting,* supposedly written for a bright and hip audience, focused on the sexual tension between its lead characters, Maddie Hayes and David

Addison, played by the very appealing Cybill Shepherd and Bruce Willis. For two years, *Moonlighting* fans had watched as Maddie and David danced around the issue of getting together sexually, even though everyone knew they wanted to. Finally, the much-awaited night of consummation arrived: ABC even ballyhooed it in TV ads for days in advance. "What happened is they had a fight," Bateman says. "She calls him a bastard and slaps him across the face. He calls her a bitch. And then it's onto the floor, breaking furniture, sweeping vases of flowers off. It was scary. My heart was pounding. I was extremely depressed and distressed." The yuppie lovers battled angrily for several minutes before collapsing into sexual ecstasy. And out in TV viewerland, millions of boys and men saw that this is what women —even smart, independent women like Maddie—really want.

Every now and then there are glimmers of change. A 1988 *Cagney and Lacey* episode realistically dealt with date rape as a widespread phenomenon: The rapist was a successful businessman and the victim was a strong, independent, female cop.

Scenes in movies and TV that reflect acceptance of violence and force in sexual relationships relate directly to acquaintance rape. In a study of 201 college men, Auburn University's Karen Rapaport and Barry Burkhart found that by measuring subjects' attitudes toward the use of aggression in a sexual context, they could predict men who raped as well as those who engaged in sexually coercive behavior. The variables used in the study measured to what extent the men viewed women as manipulative and nontrustworthy, to what degree they approved of using force to gain gratification, and to what extent they saw certain sexual situations as deserving the use of force.

The study revealed some illuminating data about how prevalent sexual touching and other activities—committed against the woman's will—are among college men:

ACTION COMMITTED AGAINST WOMAN'S WISHES	PERCENTAGE OF MEN WHO HAD DONE IT
Kissed her	53
Placed hand on her knee	61
Placed hand on her breast	60
Placed hand on her thigh or crotch	58

Removed or disarranged her outer clothing	42
Removed or disarranged her underwear	32
Touched her genitals	37
Had intercourse	15

Another study, conducted by Alfred B. Heilbrun, Jr., a psychology professor at Emory University in Atlanta, and Maura P. Loftus, a graduate student in psychology at Auburn University, investigated the role of sadism in the sexual aggression of male college students. To test this, subjects were shown 36 photographic slides of women's faces expressing happiness, surprise, anger, fear, disgust, and sadness and then asked to rate the sexual attractiveness of each. They also filled out a questionnaire which measured their levels of sexual aggression.

Heilbrun and Loftus found that 30 percent of the men rated the faces of women displaying emotional distress to be more sexually attractive than the faces showing pleasure. Of those men, 60 percent had committed repeated episodes of sexual aggression. Only 29 percent of the men who found the faces of happy women to be more sexually attractive had engaged in sexually aggressive acts.

Clearly, many men admire the tenets of hypermasculinity regardless of being exposed to moral and ethical forces to the contrary. Indeed, in 1986, UCLA researcher Neil Malamuth reported that 30 percent of the men he questioned said they would commit rape if they knew there was no chance of being caught. When the survey question changed the word "rape" to the phrase "force a woman into having sex"—again with the stipulation that the man would not be caught—more than 50 percent said they would do it.

Male Victims

Perhaps the first question that pops up from the audience at workshops on date rape is, "Don't women rape men too?" Behind that question is the natural defensiveness many men feel about the subject of rape, especially acquaintance rape. (Women often ask this question too, perhaps out of compassion for the discomfort the men in the workshop are feeling.)

The truth is, men *are* rape victims. Some experts estimate that 10 percent of the victims coming to rape-crisis centers are male even though men are far less likely to seek help after being raped than women. *But almost all male rape victims have been raped by other men.*

However, women do rape, as is known from child sexual-abuse cases. And a few women have raped men, as it is possible to stimulate even a terrified man into having an erection or rape him anally with an object. But the number of women who rape men is infinitesimally small.

The frequent asking of the question, though, demonstrates a certain need on the part of men to believe that women do commit rape and that it happens frequently. Indeed, during acquaintance-rape workshops, college men can often be heard chuckling about how much they wish it would happen to them. That's because they enjoy grade-B movie fantasies of what being assaulted would be like: Perhaps a squad of voluptuous cheerleaders might take them to be their sex prisoners.

Nothing could be further from reality. When men are raped, they are raped by other men, regardless of whether the victim or the assailant(s) are heterosexual or homosexual. It is a frightening, painful, emotionally scarring experience—in short, very like what happens to women who are raped. Men are often brutally beaten during the course of their attacks. They are raped by strangers who assault them on the street, break into their homes, or pick them up hitchhiking. Like women, they are also raped by acquaintances and, in the case of homosexual men, by dates. (Of course, also like women, men are raped as children by relatives, baby-sitters, and other adults.)

Unfortunately, it's often only after men are raped that they begin to understand what so many women have experienced. In a May 1985 *Boston* magazine article by Fred Krueger, a heterosexual man talks about his changed view after being raped by a man while hitchhiking:

> Men can't pretend any longer that rape doesn't concern them, because it does. . . . just because you're a man doesn't mean it can't happen to you. If you're a living human being, you can be raped.

CHAPTER 7

Gang or "Party" Rapes

"One of them was inside of me and I'm yelling, 'Get out of me! Get the hell out of me!' The other one was kneeling at my head, holding me down and kissing me and turning my head. . . . Then they switched."
— Elaine, recalling her rape by two men she knew

E laine is 20 years past her rape experience, yet she knows herself well enough to retrieve a box of tissues before sitting down to talk about it. She lives in a group of wooden townhouses now, on a New England military base with her husband and three children. But when she was raped, she was 22 and living in Chicago with her parents.

At the time, Elaine's life had pretty much come unraveled. She had fallen in love with a man and become pregnant by him. He refused to marry her. She dropped out of college and went away to have the child, a girl. Elaine reluctantly gave the baby up for adoption and came home. When her former boyfriend called, asking if she had had a baby, she denied it.

Several weeks after her return, a man she had known in high school, Tom, called to ask if she wanted to go on a double date with him, his friend, and his friend's date. Elaine did not know at the time that Tom and his friend were pals with her former boyfriend.

The plan was that they would go to a local carnival, first picking up Tom's friend's date at the restaurant where she worked. When Elaine and the two men arrived at the restaurant, the friend went inside, only to emerge a few seconds later saying that the woman had gone home sick. "I'm sorry about this," Tom said to Elaine and she replied, "What are you sorry about? It's not your fault if the girl's sick."

So the three of them went on to the carnival, rode the rides, and then went to a bar where the men drank several beers and Elaine had a soda. The men bought a six-pack to take out and Tom said, "I know a really neat cemetery near here. I understand you like cemeteries. Let's go." Elaine remembers:

> I looked at him and I said, "Oh my God, I *love* cemeteries. I love old gravestones." I didn't think, "How does he know that?" He knew it because my old boyfriend had told him.
>
> So we go to this cemetery, this huge enormous cemetery, and there's nobody there. It's the middle of the night. We're driving along in the car and Tom says to me, "I'm sorry about this," and I said, "What are you sorry about? I love cemeteries." They had this six-pack and we each had a beer and we were walking around looking at gravestones and I'm loving it.
>
> Then Tom says again, "I'm sorry about all this, Elaine," and I said, "I don't know what you're talking about."
>
> All of a sudden, I'm laying on my back with my shirt pushed up and my pants pulled down and one of them was inside of me and I'm yelling, "Get out of me! Get the hell out of me!" The other one was kneeling at my head, holding me down and kissing me and turning my head and I was yelling, "Get out of me! Get out of me!" Then they switched and the other guy raped me. Then they both walked away and Tom says, "I'm sorry about all this," and I finally knew what he was talking about.

Later, when Elaine found out that the two men were friends of her former boyfriend, she realized that she had been set up for the multiple attack. "My feeling is part of what happened was that he was trying to find out if I'd had a baby and they [the rapists] could tell by the condition of my vaginal area. And part was how he revenged himself against me for refusing to tell him." In the car headed back home after the assault, one of the men told Elaine how angry he was that a child he had fathered by another woman was being raised by that woman's new husband. "In a way, he was getting his anger out at me too," she says.

I went home and nobody was home. I went upstairs to my room and it was dark. I went to bed. I woke up the next morning and I was still in my clothing. I pulled down my underwear and there was grass — they had mowed the lawn in the cemetery that day — and then I believed it had happened.

I was traumatized . . . sort of numb about the whole rape. If I hadn't pulled my pants down and seen the grass, I probably would not have believed it happened. I would have thought it was a dream because it was so out of the ken of my life. I would never have believed that anyone could do anything like that to you.

The Dynamics of Gang Rape

Gang acquaintance rape is a very real phenomenon, markedly different from individual acquaintance rape. Chief among those differences is the use of the rape as a reinforcing mechanism for membership in the group of men. In *Against Our Will,* Susan Brownmiller writes: "When men rape in pairs or gangs, the sheer physical advantage of their position is clear-cut and unquestionable. No simple conquest of man over woman, group rape is the conquest of men over Woman."

Men who rape in groups might never commit rape alone. As they participate in gang rape, they experience a special bonding with each other, a unity of purpose that comes from the pride they feel in reducing their victim to nothing more than a collective vessel for their "masculinity." Through the rape, they also prove their sexual ability to other group members and underscore their status. Often, the group's leader is the first man to rape the woman; his underlings then follow. Sometimes the woman may have had consensual sex with one member of the group and afterward that man invites the others to take their turns.

Ms. SURVEY STAT □ 16 percent of the male students who committed rape and 10 percent of those who attempted a rape took part in episodes involving more than one attacker.

Gang acquaintance rape has often been tacitly condoned by a society that still believes that boys must "sow their wild oats" before settling down into adulthood. Naturally, if they sow these "oats" with their friends, the notion that such activity is "normal" is preserved. "Boys gang-rape for each other, in a kind of frenzied machismo, to prove themselves, to show off, to be part of a gang or, at best, out of fear of being ostracized if they don't," writes rape expert Helen Benedict in her book *Recovery: How to Survive Sexual Assault for Women, Men, Teenagers, and Their Friends and Families.* "Group rape has traditionally been considered *less* perverted than solitary rape because of the assumption that gang-raping someone is some kind of proof of masculinity, a sort of rite of passage." Refusing to join in a gang rape might cause a group member to become excluded from the group or have his sexuality questioned.

Gang rape also carries with it an added dose of humiliation of the victim that may be absent in single-assailant acquaintance rapes. Even when members of the group do not all participate directly, some may watch the rapes or take photographs or simply know "what's going on in the other room" and do nothing to stop it. Indeed, members usually don't want to stop the rape because it enhances the group's good opinion of itself. The humiliation of the victim continues after a gang acquaintance rape as the group members brag to others who know the woman about their "achievement." And the woman feels horribly betrayed by men she may have to continue to see in her everyday life. (Dominance and humiliation are also reasons that a gang of men might rape a man.)

As cited by researchers Patricia Rozee-Koker of the George Peabody College of Vanderbilt University in Nashville, Tennessee, and Glenda C. Polk of the College of Nursing, University of North Dakota, Grand Forks, North Dakota, characteristics that are twice as likely to occur in gang rape than in individual rape include: insult; forced fellatio; pulling, biting, and burning the breasts; urinating on the victim; putting semen on her body and demanding manual masturbation or masturbating in her presence. Moreover, the amount of aggression and degradation increases as each man takes "his turn."

Of course, participants in a gang acquaintance rape rarely think of it as rape. The woman is a "nymphomaniac," they will tell others later, who willingly engaged in what was nothing more than a spirited group sex adventure. But anthropologist Nancy Scheper-Hughes of the University of California at Berkeley says that a "gang-bang," as the rapists may call the incident, is "not group sex, not kinky sex." Even for the few women who might participate with seeming willingness, such an episode is so basically coercive and degrading that it is akin to rape.

More often than not in gang acquaintance rapes (sometimes called "party" rapes because of their frequent locale), the group has carefully selected its victim. Sometimes she is chosen for her vulnerability or because she was sexual with a group member. On college campuses, she may be a newly arrived freshman student who may have few friends. The victim may be unpopular, unattractive, or simply naive and therefore easily flattered by the attention suddenly lavished on her before the assault begins. She is often drunk or high on drugs—in many cases, she is nearly or totally incapacitated and unable to understand or voice consent or resistance, let alone physically fight or escape from a group of stronger people.

Whatever the woman's condition, the gang will stick to its story —the woman had sex with them because she wanted to—and if the matter gets to court it will be her word against theirs. The "bonds of brotherhood" dictate that even group members who regret the episode will support the group version of what happened when questioned by authorities. "One of the ironies of group acquaintance rape is that the defense witnesses outnumber the complainant-victim," said Jerome H. Skolnick, a professor of law at the University of California at Berkeley, shortly after a much-publicized recent gang rape on that campus.

The groups of men most likely to engage in gang acquaintance rape are those which express hostility and aggression toward women in other aspects of their group's culture. By dominating and over-powering one woman, then, these groups reassert their basic beliefs. While these groups may be very loosely organized—such as the two friends who raped Elaine, possibly on behalf of another man—they may also have a definite structure and identity such as fraternities, athletic teams, all-male living groups (men who live in the same dorm or are roommates in apartments or houses), motorcycle and street gangs. While the latter two groups have criminal connotations that may warn women away from them, the members of the other groups are often socially successful and even admired within their communities.

Fraternities

Undoubtedly more *one-on-one* date rapes and acquaintance rapes occur in fraternity houses than do *gang* acquaintance rapes, but it is the gang rapes that attract headlines and that the general public associates most with fraternity men. Consider these events which occurred in just the last few years:

□ *San Diego State University:* Three or more members of Pi Kappa Alpha fraternity are accused of raping an 18-year-old Delta Gamma sorority pledge at a party. The local district attorney finds not enough evidence to prosecute, but university officials, after questioning 45 witnesses over a 22-hour period, conclude that an attack occurred. The fraternity is dismissed from campus for at least five years and 30 fraternity members are charged with violating the school's conduct code.

□ *University of Florida:* Six Pi Lambda Phi fraternity members are accused of raping a 17-year-old female freshman student who had been at the fraternity house for a rush party for the group's "little sister" program. ("Little sisters" are females affiliated with, but not members of, the fraternity. They often do the behind-the-scenes work at the frat's parties and fund raisers and provide a reliable supply of women for social events.) The university finds the fraternity guilty of hazing and imposes two years of disciplinary sanctions against it, abolishes its "little sister" program, and institutes a live-in house parent requirement.

□ *University of Pennsylvania:* Nine members of Alpha Tau Omega fraternity are accused of raping a 22-year-old senior woman who was drunk and tripping on LSD. The fraternity is banned from campus for three years and two of the men involved are suspended. The men agree to perform community service, read literature on sexual aggression, and participate in a discussion group about the material. There was no criminal prosecution in the case.

- *University of Iowa:* Three fraternity members plead guilty to charges of assault causing bodily injury against a 20-year-old female student who said they raped her in a campus dormitory.

- *University of New Hampshire:* Three sophomore men, two of them fraternity brothers, are accused of raping a drunk female student in a dorm room. After four nights of testimony, a university judicial board finds the three innocent of sexual assault, but suspends two of the men for one semester for "disrespect to others." In criminal court, two of the men pleaded guilty to a misdemeanor charge of sexual assault; they received 60 days in jail, were placed on probation for two years, and ordered to perform 120 hours of community service. Charges were dropped against the third man.

- *Franklin and Marshall College:* Six members of the Phi Sigma Kappa fraternity are accused of raping a female student from another college in their fraternity house during a party. College administrators revoke the fraternity's charter after investigating the incident.

- *University of Virginia:* A 17-year-old freshman female tells the campus newspaper of going to a fraternity party on campus, becoming heavily intoxicated, then being restrained, stripped, and raped by several brothers. She decides not to press charges.

In 1985, the Association of American Colleges' Project on the Status and Education of Women reported that it had found more than 50 incidents of gang rape on U.S. campuses, most occurring at fraternity parties. These 50 cases represent only a small fraction of the collegiate gang rapes actually occurring. "On some campuses, we heard reports of gang rapes happening every week at parties," said Julie K. Ehrhart, who coauthored the study with Bernice R. Sandler. "This behavior is far more common than anyone suspected."

Why do fraternities provide such a good growing medium for gang rape? The culture of many fraternities instills in members a group ethos which objectifies and debases women through language and physical aggression, which lauds heavy drinking and other drug use, and which reinforces group loyalty through united behavior—

especially antisocial and sometimes illegal behavior. Yet on many campuses, fraternities equal social life; there is little else to do *other* than attend fraternity parties where people regularly drink until they vomit or black out and then recover and drink some more, where reports of "trains" (the slang expression for gang rapes, so called because the men line up like cars on a train) are common and where status depends on how long and how hard you party and whether you manage to "score" sexually.

These cultural characteristics are found in fraternity houses from coast to coast. In 1986, San Diego State University had this to say about the fraternity environment in which a gang rape occurred: "Overall, the hearing board found Pi Kappa Alpha Fraternity guilty *as an organization* [emphasis mine] of physical abuse, lewd, inde- cent, and obscene behavior, abusive behavior and hazing, alcoholic beverage violations including the failure to provide for the safety of any guest exhibiting intoxication and obstructing the University's disciplinary process by intentionally destroying evidence related to the incident." And at Cornell University in 1987, the Phi Gamma Delta fraternity was stripped of university recognition—thereby ending all chapter activities and closing the fraternity house for four years—for what university spokesman David Stewart called "a pat- tern of behavior" that spurred two separate university investigations and a grand jury probe into allegations of sexual abuse, house mis- management, and the illegal use of alcohol by fraternity members.

Fraternity members themselves are often unapologetic for being part of an environment that demands loyalty to a belief system that often objectifies and denigrates women. Listen to this description of life in a fraternity house from a frat member at a large New England state university:

> I'll say this, at a fraternity, I'd be a liar if I didn't tell you that just the atmosphere of fraternity or any group of guys in general is they promote how many girls can you have sex with, how many different girls can you have sex with. I hear it every day. At Friday morning breakfast [fraternities on his campus have big parties Thursday night], guys all have stories.
>
> I'd say that 90 percent of the guys I live with are probably aggres- sive.... You gotta understand that in a fraternity, all the guys are

there for common goals, ideals, aspirations. So you get a group of guys who are all thinking the same. Guys will turn on you in a second if you say one thing [to disagree with the group]. After all the things you have to do to get initiated into the house, you better have the same ideals and stuff and same feelings as the other guys. Because I know in our house, especially, guys are pretty tight. Basically, they're all the same type guys.

Questioner: And one common goal is "scoring"?

Well, yeah, basically. There's individuals for who it's not, but, overall, I'd say yeah.

Writing in *Ms.* magazine in 1985, Andrew Merton, an outspoken critic of college fraternities, said, "For many adolescent males just out of high school, the transition to college represents a first step in a struggle for a kind of 'manhood' from which women are viewed as objects of conquest—worthy, but decidedly inferior adversaries. The idea of women as equals is strange and inconvenient at best, terrifying at worst. Unfortunately, most colleges and universities provide refuges ideally suited to reinforce these prejudices: fraternities."

Antiwomen sentiments are in open evidence at many fraternities. Recruiting posters seen during fraternity "rush" season often feature naked women, women in bondage, or, simply, selected women's body parts to convey the unwritten message: "Join us and get laid." Party themes are often sexual, and members seek to gain group approval by publicly convincing women to "go upstairs" with them.

Fraternity rituals, skits, even publications often have obscene, antifemale content. After a gang rape was reported to have happened in their house, members of Alpha Tau Omega at the University of Pennsylvania posted minutes of a house meeting. Under the previous week's "Highlights" was reported: "Things are looking up for the ATO sisters program. A prospective leader for the group [the rape victim] spent some time interviewing several Taus. . . . Possible names for the little sisters include . . . 'The ATO Express' [reference to the "train" which had occurred]." Under "Service" awards, one member had written: "We serviced [the rape victim]." At the University of Florida, the Beta Theta Pi fraternity published a magazine which featured a chart depicting how many beers it took to seduce each of the group's "little sisters," as well as other sexist and racist material. The university slapped the group with a one-year suspension after examining the publication.

Fraternity special events are also dangerous times for women. Imani met her rapist during his fraternity's annual outing in Atlantic City; the attack occurred several days later. But since her rape, she has talked to several women who were raped at the Atlantic City event itself. "There are a lot of women who go down [to the fraternity event] and they are sexually assaulted," she says. "I didn't find this out until I began to meet and talk about rape with other women and I found out there were other victims. I think it's part of the package."

The most obvious and pervasive expression of the sexually aggressive culture which operates in many fraternity houses may be heard in the language of members. In a 1984 issue of the student newspaper at Colgate University in Hamilton, New York, a school where one fraternity reportedly has a pool table named for the first woman sexually conquered on it, five women wrote about fraternity language and how it breeds attitudes that condone rape. Information from that article, added to material gathered from other campuses, provides a lexicon of fraternity row slang that may be summed up this way:

New meat [recently arrived freshman or transfer women] are invited to *cattledrives* or *hogfests* [both terms for parties] depending on how good they look in the *pigbook* [new student directory]. At the party, a woman may be *landsharked* [a frat member kneels on the floor behind the woman and bites her on her rear end] or *bagged* [a group of frat brothers corner her in a room, hiding their faces under bags, drop their pants and underwear, waggle their penises at her, shout insults and threats, and offer to *gang-bang* (group rape) her]. She may also be subjected to the *flying blue max,* in which she is grabbed and passed above the heads of a group of men. A *rude hogger award* may be given to the fraternity member who has sex with the woman deemed most ugly by the other frat members. Sometimes women from local women's colleges are driven in for fraternity parties, expeditions known as *fucktrucks.*

While fraternity brothers *score*, the women they score against, often called *ho's* (slang for "whores") by the members, are said to have gotten *boned*. At one Maine school, fraternity members participate in *ledging*: That's where, in the words of one woman graduate, "a fraternity member invites all his brothers to watch his conquest of a naive freshman woman, and then she hears about it for months afterward." The name "ledging" for this practice refers to the woman's being driven to the point of suicide by the harassment.

"Words have the power to dehumanize," *Ms.* writer Andrew Merton told a national meeting of the Fraternity Executives Association. "When we think of human beings not as human beings, but as Huns, Nips, Gooks, or Slopes, it makes it easier to kill them. And when we think of women by using dehumanizing descriptives, we tend to forget that they are, in fact, full-fledged human beings. And once we forget that, we can abuse them."

Then there are the catcalls that come from the porches of fraternity houses as a female walks by. Sometimes those unwanted comments are accompanied by scorecards being raised by the gathered frat members, rating the woman on a scale of 1 to 10. And sometimes there's physical aggression—unwanted pinching, fondling ("copping a feel"), or blocking the woman's way in the street or hallway. Fraternity members often view this behavior as a type of sport, competing with each other to sharpen their skills at it. Sometimes they might target a particular woman for the group's own reasons. At Central Michigan University in Mount Pleasant, Michigan, for example, several fraternity brothers were accused of harassing and intimidating a female sorority member who was prosecuting their chapter president for rape.

In this culture, the myth of the "gang bang" or "train" thrives. One of the University of Pennsylvania fraternity brothers accused of gang-raping a drunk and drug-intoxicated female student told *Philadelphia Inquirer Magazine* reporter Mark Bowden that his seeing several of his frat brothers have sex with the woman "didn't seem that odd to me. Because of the stories I've heard from other fraternities and from guys in the house and from the movies you see on TV. We have this (Cable) TV in the house, and there's soft porn on every midnight. All the guys watch it and talk about it and stuff, and it [the assault] didn't seem that odd because it's something that you see and hear about all the time. I've heard stories from other fraternities about group sex and trains and stuff like that. It was just like, you know, 'So this is what I've heard about, this is what it's like, what I've heard about.' That's what it seemed like, you know." Because of that group acceptance, he readily joined in.

A few fraternities are trying to remove such mythology from their midsts. On the national level, several are beginning to address acquaintance rape, gang acquaintance rape, and sexual harassment among their members, although most are quick to note that their membership only reflects society at large. At least two organizations, the 12,000-member Sigma Alpha Epsilon and 6,000-member Pi Kappa Phi, have issued formal position statements against sexual abuse. In a 1987 article explaining why sexual abuse should be the fraternity's concern, SAE's national magazine said:

> We thought the friendly "gang bang" was O.K. After all, the woman went along with it.
>
> Wrong, brothers. Not only is the "gang bang" itself wrong by legal standards — it's rape no matter how you rationalize it — but it's an act of violence based on a perverted myth of masculinity and sexuality.

Strong stuff from a fraternity. And Pi Kappa Phi backed up its statement on sexual abuse with a poster which Scott E. Evans, the fraternity's national director of communications, says has been sent to more than 500 colleges and universities. The poster features a detail from *The Rape of the Sabine Women,* an engraving that shows a wild scene of soldiers forcing themselves on female captives. Under the picture, the caption reads:

> TODAY'S GREEKS CALL IT DATE RAPE.
> Just a reminder from Pi Kappa Phi.
> Against her will is against the law.

Athletic Teams

It was late September 1986, on a Saturday night following a University of California at Berkeley football game. Naturally, there were parties. The 18-year-old freshman woman had been drinking, as had many others in her dorm. That included four freshman football players the female student knew who also lived there.

According to the woman, late that evening, those four players held her down, ignored her protests, raped her, and forced her to have oral sex with them. According to the men, she willingly had group sex with them.

"Four large football players and one small girl is an odd definition of group sex to me," said Nancy Scheper-Hughes, an anthropology professor and dean of freshman and sophomore studies at Berkeley, after the incident became public. The county declined to prosecute the men because of what it said was insufficient evidence. The university decided that the football players should apologize to the woman, move out of the dorm, undergo counseling, and perform 40 hours of community service. Neither their academic nor athletic status would be affected by the incident.

Scheper-Hughes was in the forefront of faculty and students who protested the school's handling of the rape case. "I think there should be nothing less than dismissal from the university for all four of the men," she said, and many agreed with her. The campus was in an uproar for weeks following the university's decision. RAPE IS NOT A GAME, read signs that protestors carried at subsequent football games. After the university ruling one female student, who had helped form an anti-rape group called the Coalition to Break the Silence, received threatening phone calls, taunts, and warnings written on the front door of her home. Then, one day a man stepped from behind a truck parked near the student's house and threw two rocks at her, one of which cut her face. In addition, Scheper-Hughes told reporters that "another female student has alleged that she was raped two weeks ago but has decided not to press charges as a result of the official university response in this case."

Finally, in January 1987, Chancellor Ira Michael Heyman sent Berkeley's 31,000 students a statement decrying acquaintance rape as something which "degrades its victims, our campus community, and society at large." Included with Heyman's letter was a brochure about acquaintance rape, ways to avoid it, and where to go for help.

In recent years, several other gang acquaintance-rape cases involving collegiate athletes have reached the public eye, including:

- *University of Minnesota:* Three sophomore basketball players are accused of raping a woman in a Madison, Wisconsin, hotel room after going to a bar to celebrate a team victory. All three are acquitted on 12 counts of sexual assault. Just a few months before, one of the three athletes was tried and acquitted of raping a female student in the coed dorm where he lived. The university forfeited one basketball game after the Madison incident and dismissed all three athletes after the filing of charges. The team's coach resigned.

- *West Virginia University:* Five basketball players are accused of raping a woman in a campus dormitory. No criminal charges are filed, but two players are suspended from the team for the entire season and three receive one-semester suspensions.

- *Duquesne University:* Four basketball players are charged with raping a woman in their dormitory. All four are suspended by the university pending their trial. Three of the athletes are acquitted; charges against the fourth are dropped. After the trial, two of the suspensions are continued until the middle of basketball season and two of the athletes are expelled from school.

Moreover, many college athletes have been reported for individual rapes at schools across the country such as Kansas University, Arizona State, University of Rhode Island, Colorado University, North Carolina State, Northern Illinois University, Florida A & M, Central Connecticut State, and others.

Like fraternities, athletic teams are breeding grounds for rape, particularly gang acquaintance rape. They are organizations which pride themselves on the physical aggressiveness of their members, and which demand group loyalty and reinforce it through promoting the superiority of their members over outsiders. Athletic teams are often populated by men steeped in sexist, rape-supportive beliefs. "Locker-room talk" is well named: The locker room, center of an athlete's world, is often a place where women are discussed as little else but sex objects, fitting and deserving of degradation, humiliation, and scorn.

Sex itself is incorporated into the athlete's language of hostility and aggression. Around the time of the episode with the Berkeley football players and the female student, Berkeley football coach Joe

Kapp was asked by a reporter whether the team's coaching had anything to do with its recent losses. The *Los Angeles Times* reported that in answer to that question, Kapp unzipped his pants and said, "Do you want to see my [bleep]?"

Within such a culture, gang rape may easily be seen as "group sex"—just another way for the team members to strengthen their bonds with each other. In addition, in the college athletes' world, be it a small-town campus or Big Ten school, team members hold a special status that wins them public attention, fame, and sometimes adoration. Players, especially good players, are accustomed to having women flirt with them, even proposition them. Because of this popularity, many athletes believe that no woman is off limits and, indeed, that they don't even have to ask first before taking. If they encounter resistance from women, they know they can deal with it as successfully as they do on the field or court. "I was five foot two and weighed 110 pounds. He was six foot five and weighed 265. I didn't have any choice," says Rachel of the football player who lived down the hall from her at her Midwest school and who raped her after a party. "I was scared of him. I thought he was going to hurt me."

The adoration that college athletes receive does not come only from other students. Many athletes are wooed to attend certain schools by zealous alumni, coaches, and even administrators who provide goodies ranging from cash to "available" women when the young stars come to campus. That support may continue even after athletes are slapped with rape charges. Pressure from alumni and administrators may keep such cases out of the public view or see to it that punishment is minimal and doesn't include suspension or expulsion from the team.

In a series titled "Rape and the College Athlete," *Philadelphia Daily News* sportswriter Rich Hofmann discovered that between 1983 and 1986, a college athlete was reported for sexual assault, on the average, once every 18 days. (As with all rape and sexual assault reports, those numbers are just a small representation of actual attacks.) Hofmann found 61 incidents involving 88 athletes at 46 different schools during that period. In more than 90 percent of those cases, the victim knew her attacker or attackers. "Football and basketball players representing NCAA-affiliated schools were reported to police for sexual assault approximately 38 percent more often than the average male on a college campus," Hofmann said.

This may not mean that athletes commit more rape than other men, however, but that they may be reported more often for one of two reasons that defenders often cite: One, the athletes are famous; or, two, they are black. The first reason—fame—may explain why some men are reported, but it also explains why so many are not. ("Who would believe me? He was a really good football player," Rachel says.) As to the second reason, Hofmann says some black leaders believe "it is logical to conclude that the prejudices of the criminal justice system could account for" many of the rape charges filed against black athletes. About 90 percent of the athletes in Hofmann's study were black.

As with fraternities, there's some evidence that a few changes are taking place. Although the NCAA has no official policy governing athletes and sexual assault, some schools are trying to educate players about acquaintance rape and change the attitudes that breed it. At Washington State University, for example, in response to a challenge from the women's center, the entire football team underwent a mandatory seminar about acquaintance rape. The team participated in the program with the enthusiastic endorsement of its coach.

It would be wonderful if more schools, teams, and coaches would become involved in improving the rape-awareness education of the people who are often the most prominent undergraduates on campus. Yet even a well-meaning program may not be able to overcome the culture in which those individuals spend most of their time. Consider that sometime before September 1986, some members of one school's football team took part in a rape prevention education program.

The team? The University of California—at Berkeley.

CHAPTER 8

Teenagers and Acquaintance Rape

"I felt I couldn't go to my parents, . . . the police were out . . . and my friends would quickly disown me for having one of our own thrown in jail."
— Melissa, a high school victim raped by a friend

Although college is often seen as the environment in which acquaintance rape flourishes, high school and even junior high girls are being raped by boys they know. Perched in the emotionally shaky middle ground between childhood and adult life, teenagers are ill equipped to fend off these assaults.

Early in September of Melissa's junior year in high school, her boyfriend David told her that he wanted to start dating another girl. Melissa, then 16, begged him not to. She loved David with the intensity of teenage first love: They had been dating for more than a year and had become sexually intimate during that time.

After David told her that he was going to go out with the other girl that Saturday night, Melissa received a telephone call from Brian, David's best friend.

Brian asked me if I wanted to "get back" at David for two-timing me. He suggested we go out together, double dating with David and this woman. He assured me it was all on the up-and-up. He said he didn't like to see David treating me this way. I agreed.

The foursome went to the movies, then drove to a local beach. David and his new date went for a walk near the water. Brian suggested that he and Melissa sit on the rocks and wait for them to return.

> We sat on some huge boulders and talked about nothing in particular. After a few minutes, Brian stood up and turned toward me and started to unbuckle his pants. I asked him what he was doing. He said, "Let's really get back at David for what he did."
>
> I said, "No," but didn't think he was really serious. He continued to take off his pants. It wasn't until he reached for my belt that I believed he was serious.
>
> I told him to stop and started to move away from him. He grabbed my arms and pinned them behind me so that I was half lying and half standing against the boulder. He used one hand to hold my hands behind me and the other to undo my pants. I started screaming for David to help me, while begging Brian to stop.

Brian didn't stop. He ejaculated quickly. Melissa pulled up her pants and went back to the car. When David and his date returned, the four drove home. Melissa said nothing.

The next day, David came to her house.

> He said Brian had bragged about "screwing" me. And David wanted to know why I had "let" him. I told him how I didn't let Brian do anything, that I had screamed for him [David] to help me, how Brian had pinned me against the rock.
>
> David said he hadn't heard me. He then said that it wouldn't be the same between us anymore because he wasn't the only one to have had sex with me.
>
> I felt I couldn't go to my parents, because the fact that I was having sex with David would arise and somehow my loss of virginity would be worse than the rape in their eyes. The police were out for the same reason and my friends would quickly disown me for having one of our own thrown in jail. Who would believe me when I didn't know if I believed it myself?

Hidden Rape: A Teenage Reality

Every now and then an acquaintance rape among teenagers receives publicity. In late 1985, seven boys were expelled from the prestigious St. Mark's School in Southborough, Massachusetts, a private boarding school affiliated with the Episcopal Church, after local police received a complaint that a 15-year-old tenth-grade girl had been raped in one of the school dormitories. Eight other students who were aware of the incident received lighter punishments.

But the vast number of acquaintance rapes among teens remain hidden. Those rapes—like acquaintance rapes among adults—cut across all regional, economic, and ethnic lines. Teenage girls are being raped by classmates, boyfriends, casual friends, and, as more teens take on part-time jobs, by co-workers.

Ms. SURVEY STAT □ **38 percent of the women who had been raped were 14, 15, 16, or 17 years old at the time of their assaults.**

Jenny, a California woman, recalls her experience:

I was raped at 16 by an acquaintance from my job during a party he hosted. He was supposed to drive me home. I blacked out from drinking too much and when I woke up, we were still in his car and he was inside me. I shouted at him to get out of me, but he kept going until he climaxed.

I found out later that he [the rapist] bragged about this action to everyone else there. . . . Because the host and I and most of the guests all worked in the same large discount store, the humiliation forced me to quit.

Imani was 17 and baby-sitting for her brother and sister-in-law at their Philadelphia home when she was raped by a date, a college man.

He came over that evening and he played with my two nephews. We got them up to bed and read them a story.

We were downstairs in the living room, watching television. I had kissed him, but nothing real intense. We were just talking and he began fondling me.

When I said to him, "Stop," he was okay about that, but later on he continued. We were sitting on the floor and he got on top of me . . . I was literally pinned down on the floor and he was taking my pants off and I'm struggling against him, but I didn't want to struggle too loud 'cause I didn't want to scare my nephews.

He was about six foot three, built like a football player. He suffo-cated me. I felt like I had this creature in the house that's capable of doing anything and the fear I had was for myself and for my nephews.

Imani tried to fight, but her attacker won. After he raped her, he said he was sorry. "He had that apologetic tone, it's that tone where men can apologize but you know it's not genuine because some-where in the apology you're being blamed," she says now, recalling that moment.

I said to him, "You need to leave," and I remember that he was somewhat argumentative about leaving. As he left, he went to kiss me. I pushed him and he smiled.

That was the last time I saw him ever in my whole entire life and I was just totally freaked out.

Trisha was 17 when a friend from her Midwest high school offered to drive her home from a party. In the car, they talked about school and mutual friends.

Finally, he pulled over and said, "Guess what we're going to do?" My reply was, "You can't be serious. You said you were going to take me home."

We had both been drinking, but not enough to lose perspective on life. I was angry at first and threatened to walk home. I threatened to tell. It was late and I knew my parents would be expecting me.

He was verbally abusive and would reach for me and touch me. . . . I began to believe he was serious, and he was frightening me. Then he said that he wasn't going to argue about it anymore, and he proceeded to tear at my shirt and shorts. I hit him and kicked him, but he was so determined. I just thought to myself, "God! Why me?" I cried.

It seemed like an eternity, but finally he rolled off. We got dressed. Then he drove me home—a long, silent drive. I hated him! I wanted to do something to ruin his life . . . but what? I never wanted to see him again. I didn't want to live and I didn't want to face anybody.

I never went to anyone and talked about it. I just withdrew.

A long-term study of adolescent vulnerability to sexual assault by Suzanne S. Ageton of the Behavioral Research Institute in Boulder, Colorado, found that nearly all of the female teen victims knew their attackers:

- ☐ 56 percent had been raped by a date
- ☐ 30 percent had been raped by a friend
- ☐ 11 percent had been raped by a boyfriend

In the Ageton study, 78 percent of the victims did not tell their parents about the incident, although 71 percent confided in one or more of their own teenage friends. Only 6 percent reported the assault to police. Among those who did not, most failed to do so because they knew the attacker or had sustained no visible injuries. Like other women, these girls did not label what happened to them as a crime because it was not committed by a stranger and they had no wounds to prove they had been hurt. In other words, they believed all the myths that continue to keep such rapes a hidden phenomenon.

Teen Attitudes About Rape

Sandi, a New Hampshire woman, was 17 when she was raped by an acquaintance. She was a virgin. At the time, her view of her attack was one that many teens share today. "There was a part of me back then that thought that's the way 'it' was done. Guys pounced on you, you struggled, then forgot about the whole thing," she says.

At 17 . . . what mattered was clothes, hair, making good impressions on boys, getting and keeping a boyfriend, and drugs in any form.

> I never told anyone I was raped. I would not have thought that
> was what it was. It was unwilling sex. I just didn't want to and he did.
> Today, at 29, I know it was rape.

Walk into any junior high or high school and you're likely to meet
a lot of young people who hold the same beliefs that Sandi once did
because teens often show rigid adherence to the doctrines of hypermasculinity and female sexual socialization. A team of researchers
from the University of California at Los Angeles studied the way 432
teens aged 14 to 18 perceived male-female interactions. Concluded
Jacqueline D. Goodchild, Gail Zellman, Paula D. Johnson, and Roseann Giarrusso: "We appear to have uncovered some rather distress-
ing indications that a new generation is entering into the adult
world of relationships, especially that of sexual intimacy between a
man and a woman, carrying along shockingly outmoded baggage."

What was some of that baggage those teens carried? Survey
subjects were asked if it was ever okay for a male to force sex from
a female, given certain circumstances. The study, like many of its
kind, did not use the word "rape." Some of the findings:

CIRCUMSTANCE	PERCENTAGE OF BOYS AGREEING THAT IT'S OK TO FORCE SEX	PERCENTAGE OF GIRLS AGREEING THAT IT'S OK TO FORCE SEX
She is going to have sex with him and changes her mind.	54	31
She has "led" him on.	54	26
She gets him sexually excited.	51	42
They have dated for a long time.	43	32
She lets him touch her above the waist.	39	28

No wonder the researchers expressed such gloom. More than half
the boys and nearly half the girls thought that it was okay for a male
to force (that is, rape) a female if he was sexually aroused by her.

The Los Angeles researchers also presented their adolescent subjects with 27 vignettes of dating experiences and asked them to rate

who was responsible for the outcome of the interaction. In one group of vignettes, the boy described wants sex, the girl does not, and he forces her. The vignettes varied by the degree of the relationship between the two (just met, casual acquaintance, or dating) and the boy's action (threatens to spread rumors about her, threatens physical harm, uses physical force). In all vignettes, even the most forceful, male and female subjects attributed a significant share of responsibility for what happened to the female.

For example, if the boy and girl had just met and had sex after he threatened to spread rumors about her, teenage subjects believed that the outcome was 78 percent the boy's fault and 34 percent the girl's (proportions will not equal 100 percent due to the rating system used). In the case where the boy and girl had a dating relationship and he used physical force to obtain sex, the teens found the outcome 86 percent the boy's fault and 23 percent the girl's. Overall, for the 27 vignettes, the subjects assigned 84 percent responsibility to the male and 27 percent to the female. Those scores, said the researchers, "were rather a surprise. We had expected—hoped for—a distribution more like 100 and 0 (100 percent male responsibility/0 percent female)."

Other social forces in the teen world add more vulnerability to acquaintance rape. High school culture, like that of college students, is often alcohol or drug centered. According to the National Institute on Alcohol Abuse and Alcoholism, the average age when a child now takes a first real drink is 12. And teens drink to get drunk: 3.3 million Americans aged 14 to 17 are now considered problem drinkers. Both boys and girls are in jeopardy when drunk since many acquaintance rapists and their victims are intoxicated when the incident occurs.

How Acquaintance Rape Affects Teens

The business of being an adolescent is a difficult one. It is a time of separating emotionally from parents, developing a personal and sexual identity, building academic skills, and considering one's future direction and goals. Because teenagers are at such a critical point in their self-development, sexual victimization—especially rape by a trusted friend or acquaintance—can have devastating results. Their world often seems shaken to its core. They may suffer feelings of diminished self-worth, even to the point of considering suicide.

Kathi Vonderharr was an athletic 15-year-old who loved swimming, horseback riding, and skiing. But where she lived, in suburban St. Paul, hockey was king. So it wasn't surprising when Kathi joined a friend's family on a trip to a teen hockey tournament. Several boys she had grown up with were on one of those teams.

At the tournament, several of those boys forced their way into the motel room where Kathi and her friend were staying. Three of the boys—two 15-year-olds and one 14-year-old—grabbed away a pillow Kathi was clutching to her body, pulled her shirt up and her pants down, and fondled her breasts and vagina as other team members watched them. Then the boys left. After a few minutes, the three boys who assaulted her returned, saying they wanted to apologize. One did, but the other two attacked her again the same way.

Kathi and her friend decided not to tell anyone, but changed their minds after the boys bragged to friends that they had "screwed" her. Her family decided to press charges. The boys were suspended from the hockey team for one game. Friends, neighbors, and strangers called Kathi's family, telling them to drop the charges. Adult supporters of the youth hockey association were the most vociferous. "Boys will be boys," the family was told. At school, Kathi was harassed, called obscene names and ostracized. Four days after a hearing in the case, in what her mother said was a call for help, Kathi took 10 Tylenol. She spent two weeks in the hospital.

That September, she and the boys entered high school. Weeks later, in juvenile court, two of them pleaded guilty to sexual assault charges; the third was found guilty later. They were placed on probation until age 19, ordered to perform community service and to pay all of Kathi's medical expenses.

But her harassment continued. Two of the boys quickly became admired star hockey players on the high school team. Many of Kathi's friends stopped associating with her and one day she found a message on her locker: "Kill the bitch, she took our friends to court." As *Minneapolis Star and Tribune* reporter Doug Grow would write in July 1987, "The irony—that the assailants were heroes and the victim an outcast in many circles in her school—was constantly there for her to see."

Kathi tried to get on with her life, but there were always reminders. School and local publications featured glowing stories about the on-ice performances of the athletes who had attacked her. In May 1987, one of the boys asked that his probation be lifted. She wrote to the judge, asking that the request be denied.

The following month, Kathi had a birthday party. Afterward, she carefully wrote out her thank-you notes. They were still lying in a stack in her room several days later when she drove a car into her family's garage, closed the door, and let the motor run. When she was found dead, there was a teddy bear by her side, some tissues, and a photograph of the people she loved.

Not all sexual victimizations of teenagers end in such tragedy, of course, but the potential is there, especially when the attack comes from one or more acquaintances. Kathi was assaulted physically, and then, when she broke the social "code" among her peers (and even among her town's adults, it seems) by reporting the incident, she exposed herself to further emotional assaults. Few adults would be strong enough to withstand that kind of bombardment.

There are other effects of sexual assault on teens. Many young acquaintance-rape victims are virgins at the time of their attack. For them, the incident may distort their perceptions about sexual intercourse and radically affect their future relationships with men. Because the teen years are a time for sexual exploration and identification, the fallout from an acquaintance rape may last for years.

Even teenagers uninterested in heterosexual relations are affected. Gloria was 16 and involved in a lesbian relationship, but wanted to try to be "normal," so she accepted a date with a boy she knew. They went to the movies and then he invited her to go back to his house to meet his parents. Despite an inner feeling that told her not to go, Gloria accepted.

He walked in and, of course, the place is totally dark. He said, "Oh, they must have gone to dinner, they should be back soon." I believed

him. We sat down to watch TV and he started kissing me. It soon
progressed to him pushing me down on the couch and jumping on me.
That's when I said, "No, no, no way, "immediately. He just started
tearing my clothes off.

Gloria finally managed to get away, when the boy had to shift his
position—he had wedged them between a couch and a sideboard
credenza. "When he lifted his weight up, it gave me the opportunity
to push him off and he hit his head on the credenza," she says. She
ran outside to her car and drove off, viewing the incident as her
fault.

I had a real unclear picture about what straight people did (sexually). I
talked myself into believing that that (the rape) was normal and if I
was a normal female that that's what I would have wanted too.

Another problem for the teen victim is that she often will see her
attacker on a daily basis, in school or in her neighborhood. Many
times, the rapist will boast about the incident, describing it as a
successful sexual conquest, and the victim will often be ostracized
by those who hear about it for her "participation." Even if charges
are brought, there's no guarantee that the offender won't still return
to school, to work, or to live near the victim. Indeed, that's what
happened recently in Washington, D.C., when a 16-year-old male
student was permitted to return to his high school after being
charged with raping a classmate. In protest of that school board
decision, the school's principal asked to be reassigned, saying he
could not "in good conscience" allow the youth to stay.

Because teen victims are so unlikely to tell any adult about what
happened to them, many suffer the emotional effects of the rape
alone. "When adolescents conceal their feelings and experiences
from others, they have the difficult task of using only their own
inner resources to heal and integrate the incident," says teen victimization expert Ann Wolbert Burgess of the University of Pennsylvania School of Nursing. And because those inner resources are
weak in many teenagers, they may not be able to cope.

The adolescent male who commits acquaintance rape or other
sexual assault is likely not to be identified, and so he often goes on
to repeat his behavior. "Most have decided it wasn't harmful . . . and

won't admit that they planned the rape," says Nancy Nissen, a Seattle social worker who works with adolescent sex offenders. The average age for their first sexually aggressive behavior, says Nissen, is 10 years old.

Why Teenagers Don't Tell About Acquaintance Rape

It is difficult for parents—loving, caring parents—to imagine their child concealing something so awful as a rape from them. But for most teenagers, there's never much question about it. In the Ageton study, only one in five teen victims told their parents about being attacked. Why?

Many teenage girls, fearing parental disapproval for a behavior that may be related to the rape (drinking or taking drugs, going to a forbidden place, dating without permission) or one that may be unrelated (being sexually active), believe their parents will blame them for what happened, rather than offer support and love. Like many acquaintance-rape victims, these teens are already blaming themselves, so it's not surprising that they don't want to be subjected to more recriminations. As veterans of previous battles with their parents, they also expect to hear only unsympathetic "I-told-you-so" lectures. Victims may already have encountered a lack of sympathy from friends and peers, so why should they expect adults to be more understanding? Indeed, teenagers are often correct in their assumptions. Many parents *do* blame their daughters for acquaintance-rape incidents.

In addition, since the victim knows that what happened to her wasn't "real rape"—that is, it didn't involve a stranger jumping from the bushes and holding a knife to her throat—she may fear what her parents will think about her "giving in." And some don't tell parents because they are unwilling to prosecute the attacker out of peer loyalty, or fear, or both. Angry parents may push to press charges because of their own need for retribution, but such prosecution may not be what their child wants or needs.

A 1979 study by University of Pennsylvania researchers A. W. Burgess and L. L. Holmstrom revealed five major reasons adolescent victims cited for not telling family members about their rapes:

□ *To protect the family:* These victims believed they could handle the fact of the rape, but their families could not.

□ *Value conflicts:* Family members would not understand because of attitudes about rape, religious beliefs, or disapproval of the victim's life-style.

□ *Desire to maintain independence:* Telling family would restrict victim's independence, a major teenage battleground.

□ *Psychological distance:* Some felt emotionally distant from families and therefore would not tell.

□ *Geographic distance:* Victims away at school or in another residence felt they were too far away to involve the family.

It's sad that so many teens are unable or unwilling to report their assaults to family members, rape counselors, or police. In that, though, they are not much different from adult victims. And, as the following chapter will show, reporting an acquaintance rape does not necessarily mean that the rapist will be brought to justice.

CHAPTER 9

Police, Court, and University Responses to Acquaintance Rape

"Everybody knows that if you tell the truth, the system is supposed to work for the truth."
— Maggie, who pressed charges against the man who raped her when she was 31

Two women, two acquaintance rapes, two prosecutions, two verdicts.

Maggie was raped in Alaska, Holly in Oregon, but their stories exemplify the nationwide difficulties of criminally prosecuting acquaintance-rape cases. According to Gary D. LaFree, a sociologist and criminology researcher at the University of New Mexico in Albuquerque, convictions are most likely to occur in cases that fit society's stereotype of rape—an act committed by an armed stranger—and are less likely in cases in which the woman and her assailant know each other, especially if they were dating or had any prior sexual contact. Due to that bias, police and prosecutors are often reluctant to charge perpetrators in acquaintance-rape crimes, just as juries are often unwilling to convict. This bias is so strong on all levels of the legal system that some rape-crisis counselors now advise victims of acquaintance rape not to become involved in criminal proceedings at all.

Maggie's Rape: Verdict — Not Guilty

Maggie had been living in Alaska for several months when she met Bruce at a bar. They talked for much of the evening and although Maggie was interested in him, she found him pushy in a way that made her uncomfortable. And he certainly *was* persistent: He got Maggie's telephone number from one of the other women at the table and called several times. Maggie, who was 31 at the time, felt wary.

> I hadn't dated or done anything for ages, so there was some sort of flattery in his calling. He wanted to go to dinner, to do this and that. And yet I had this discomfort, so I kept saying, "No."

Finally, they had a date. And another. On the third date, Maggie invited Bruce to spend the night. "That evening was sort of okay," she says, but she still had mixed feelings about him. Then they didn't see each other for several weeks. Maggie decided that she really didn't want to sleep with Bruce again or go out with him anymore.

At the time, Maggie was living alone in a home she was house-sitting. Like many people in her town, she never locked the door. The night of her rape was no exception. When she walked out of the bathroom, wearing just a towel, she looked over the second-floor balcony and saw Bruce standing in the center hall.

> He said, "I just want to talk to you." I could tell he was drunk. He kept saying, "You're the best woman I ever met." And I said, "Get out of here."
>
> Before I had been ambivalent in that I was flattered by the attention and yet not liking his attitude. But after we went through that first [dating] phase . . . I felt real clear about where I was and I knew I was real clear with him.

When he wouldn't leave, Maggie went back into the bathroom to put on some clothes, but when she emerged again Bruce was up-stairs, in the bedroom. She again told him to leave. To usher him out, she started walking down the stairs.

> He grabbed me and tried to pull me back into the bedroom. I sat down at the top of the stairs so he couldn't pull me and he sort of threw himself over my back. . . . His whole chest went down on the back of my neck, there was a crunch, and I couldn't lift it up after that for a while. He threw me down on the floor and we started fighting on the balcony.
>
> We would fight and he would hurt me . . . he'd pin me down or hit me in the ribs.

The house was in an isolated spot, with a big cliff behind it. The nearest house was beyond the cliff. "I just felt like I've got to depend on myself to get out of this situation," Maggie recalls.

That would be no easy task. Her opponent was six foot two, weighed over 215 pounds, and was powerfully built. As they fought, Maggie tried to force herself to gouge his eyes, but all she could imagine was his eyes dropping onto her. At another point, while he was pounding her head on a parquet floor, she imagined her skull splitting open. But her greatest fear was that he would throw her off the balcony.

> I said, "I'm afraid you're going to hurt me." And he said, "I'm not going to kill you."
>
> He said he just wanted to go to bed with me. He was saying things like he was going to have sex with me one way or another and if that meant rape, that meant rape.

Twisting her arm painfully, Bruce steered Maggie into the bedroom. He ordered her to take her clothes off. When she refused, he pinned her on the bed and punched her in the face. He stripped her, hit her again, and then put his fist in her face and said, "If you try anything, I'll punch your lights out." At that point, Maggie was overcome with shock, fear, and pain. She had a feeling of leaving her body and floating off away from the attack.

Bruce penetrated her vaginally, then lost his erection several times before ejaculating. When he finally rolled off her, he made her promise not to call anyone after he left. Then he went downstairs, leaving her lying in bed, terrified.

> I heard the door open and shut. I didn't hear anything. I was just laying there, waiting for his car to start.

> Then I heard a cigarette lighter. He had opened the door and shut
> it and was waiting inside to see if I would move. Then he called up, "I
> know you're going to tell somebody. Come down here."

He made her sit next to him on the couch as he rambled on about
her reporting what had happened. He had been drinking and taking
drugs so, as he talked, he would nod off, then quickly awaken.
Maggie contemplated running out each time he nodded off, but she
never knew if he was asleep enough to make it safe. She kept prom-
ising him that she would not tell anyone and begged him to leave.
Finally, he did.

She sat still on the couch until she heard Bruce drive off. Then
she got down below the level of the windows and scrambled to lock
the door. She called her sister and brother-in-law. They summoned
the police and a representative from a local women's center.

From the beginning, the police thought Maggie had a good case.
They took samples from her during a rape examination at the hospital and found specimens of her blood and rug fibers from the
house on Bruce's body and clothing after they arrested him. He had
a history of aggressive behavior, dating back to his school years,
including several encounters with police. Although his family was
influential locally, the police seemed happy finally to be able to nail
him. Bruce was charged with first-degree rape, assault, and trespass
to commit a crime.

The problems with the case emerged almost immediately. There
were the photographs taken of Maggie shortly after the rape. She
hadn't bruised that badly and what bruises she had didn't show up
very well in the photos, although she says, "I felt like sombody had
run over me with a truck."

The district attorney was an older man, not known for zeal in
pursuing rape cases. He repeatedly reminded Maggie that "this is
not your usual case of rape." In questioning shortly after the rape,
he asked her whether she had ever had an abortion and she said no.
However, when she gave testimony at a later deposition, she admitted that she had had two. The district attorney, whose religion
opposed abortion, was furious. In his office he said to her, "If you'd
lie about this, what else is there that you've lied about?" With each

passing week of the investigation, he seemed to become more unsympathetic to her.

Among the personal information Maggie did share with the district attorney was the fact that she maintained a journal, a result of her interest in homeopathic medicine and astrological cycles. In her journal—really a diary of her physical and mental health—she recorded when her periods occurred, when she had headaches or felt depressed, what the weather was, and other data, including her sexual activity.

The defense wanted to see the journal. At an evidentiary hearing, the judge went through the book and only permitted the chart pertaining to the time of the rape to be put in evidence. But the damage was done. The story soon leaked out in town about the alleged rape victim's "sex diary."

The pretrial ordeal dragged on. Samples of blood taken off Bruce's body and clothes after his arrest had molded in the laboratory and could not be properly evaluated. His defense attorney filed a barrage of motions, including 45 in just one day. Meanwhile, Bruce harassed Maggie on the street, cursing at her, threatening to sue her, or simply following her in his car. A few days before the trial, the district attorney told Maggie of his plan for the prosecution: He wanted to use Bruce in a live demonstration with Maggie to show how he had choked her from behind. "I just started crying and said, 'That man is never going to touch me again,' " she recalls. The prosecutor relented on the idea.

Finally, the trial began. Maggie testified for eight hours. In the middle of the trial, she was called to the district attorney's office. He told her that cocaine metabolites had been found in the blood of a tampon that she had been wearing the night of the rape. (Bruce had pulled the tampon out before penetrating her.) Because Maggie had told the district attorney that she didn't use drugs—and she didn't—he again thought she was lying. He told her that he was thinking of withdrawing from the case. "It shook him up in terms of the confidence level he had in me which was pretty weak anyway," Maggie says. In fact, as the police explained to her, the cocaine most likely came from Bruce's hands.

Bruce's lawyer didn't have to prove that his client didn't rape

Maggie. All he had to do was create enough alternatives to cast doubt on the prosecution's case. On the stand, the defense asked Maggie about her sexual life, noting that since many women don't want sex after being raped, wasn't it unusual that she had sex several weeks later as noted in her journal? Other questions were similarly framed to cast doubts about her story in the jury's minds. There was the "sex diary" and questions about whether she preferred younger men (both Bruce and her current lover were younger). And because the police had told her to write down everything she could remember about the rape—she had filled 12 pages of notebook paper on both sides—the defense suggested she was pursuing the case only to write a book about it. They also questioned her about her previous job, working at a domestic violence shelter. "So I was crazy and I hated men, I was sexually weird, and I was writing a book," Maggie says. "All these things were possibilities."

The testimony lasted for three weeks. At one point, the chief police investigator was questioned about his "personal relationship" with the victim, questions that implied that he and Maggie were having an affair. They were not. Bruce, dressed every day in a three-piece suit, never testified in his own behalf.

The jury deliberated for a day and a half. Bruce was found not guilty of rape, not guilty of assault, but guilty on the trespass charge. However, since it was a charge of trespass to commit a crime—but the jury had found no crime—that finding was thrown out. He had beaten every charge. Again, Maggie felt like she had been hit by a truck. "I don't know what I was expecting, but I had this whole belief system that the truth will prevail," she says. "Everybody knows that if you tell the truth, the system is supposed to work for the truth."

There was fallout from the trial. The district attorney was transferred to another jurisdiction. The judge was barred from hearing future sexual assault cases. Later, Maggie talked to the chief investigator for the police, who had questioned the jurors afterward to find out why they voted the way they did.

He told me they said, "We really think something happened, but we just didn't know what." They said they wanted more pictures, some real gory pictures, something concrete that said, "Wow! There couldn't

be any other explanation!" They didn't deny they thought it had occurred, but they didn't feel like the evidence was there.

Maggie stayed in town for another 15 months. Bruce continued
to harass her. She finally decided to leave Alaska. Now, five years
after the trial, she's happily contemplating becoming a mother
for the first time. But although she's pleased that acquaintance-
rape cases in her former town are being handled with more sensitivity by new personnel, she knows who paid the price for that
advance.

"I felt like I was the fall guy," she says, "just the sacrificial
lamb."

Holly's Rape: Verdict — Guilty

Holly was sitting in a club with several female friends when an
attractive, genial guy sat down for a chat, introducing himself as
Ted. Holly, who was recently separated, was enjoying a rare night
out; at 25, she had two young children, one of whom she was still
breast-feeding. Her children so defined her reality at the time that
when Ted asked what she did, she said, without hesitation, "I'm a
mom." Ted talked to all the women at the table and then asked
Holly to dance.

Around midnight, Holly decided it was time to leave. Her roommate had gone home a short time before to relieve the baby-sitter.
Ted said he needed to go too and would walk with her. At the door
of the club, Holly paused to consider the heavy rain which had
suddenly begun, then pulled her coat up over her head to make the
cold, wet run to the far end of the parking lot where she had left
her car. Ted, whose car was parked near the club entrance, offered
to drive her to her car instead. Holly accepted.

Once inside the car, Ted and Holly sat and talked about Ted's job
with a local radio station and mutual friends they knew there. When
he suggested that they get a bite to eat, Holly reiterated that she
needed to get home and check on her children. Ted countered with
the suggestion that they stop by Holly's house, see that the kids
were okay, and then go out, leaving her roommate to baby-sit. "I

said, 'Oh, I don't know,' " Holly says, recalling that conversation. "I was so wishy-washy and so stupid."

When they arrived at her home, Holly's children were fine, but she decided that she really didn't want to go out. It had been a long night and she was tired. Her car, however, was still back at the club and she needed Ted to drive her there to get it. Leaving her wallet on a table in her house, she grabbed just her keys. As they drove back to the club, Ted asked if she minded if he stopped at his house to let his dog out. Holly agreed wearily, but said they would have to hurry. When they got to the trailer where Ted lived, he invited her inside.

> I wanted to go home. It had probably been five hours since I'd nursed the baby . . . but I thought, "Well, I'm not going to be a pig about this — let him let his damn dog out."
>
> It didn't seem like a bad idea. We walked in and I'm sitting there and he let the dog out and the next thing I know he's trying to kiss me. Well, even this seemed all right, and I kissed him a couple of times. Pretty soon he got really insistent and I started pushing back against his chest.

The trailer was tiny, containing only a bed, where Holly and Ted were sitting, and a few others pieces of furniture. As he intensified his aggression, Ted pushed Holly back onto the bed. Still, she didn't think he'd be a real problem. She had had episodes throughout her dating experience where she had said, "No," to persistent men and they had always complied with her wishes. This time, though, Ted didn't.

> He was holding me down and I was starting to get a little bit afraid . . . I said, "We can still be friends and give it another chance on another night," even though I would never have gone out with him again. He looked at me and said, "I don't care about being friends with you." And now I'm starting to get a little scared.
>
> I finally pushed up on his chest and said, "Look, if you don't cool it, I'm going to scream, so just let me up." All of a sudden, he pulled his arm up around my throat, pulled me off the bed, and held me against the bed, wrapping his arms around my neck . . . so my head

was down and I couldn't breathe. . . . I started to black out and go kind of limp.

Finally, I just started to lose consciousness and I guess he decided he better back off a little bit. I said to him, "I just want to see my babies again," and he said, "You do what I tell you, just listen up and do what I tell you and you'll see your kids again." He was real cold and real angry.

Ted then forced Holly to perform oral sex on him, tightly twisting the double strand of beads she wore against her neck. He threatened her with anal sex and then had vaginal intercourse with her. When he discovered she was wearing a tampon, he merely pulled it out and tossed it on the floor. "I just remember closing my eyes and saying to myself, 'I'm not even going to think about this whole thing happening,' " Holly says. She cried throughout the rape. After it was over, she saw that Ted was covered with her menstrual blood. Fearful that he would become angry again at the sight of it, she consolingly told him, "It's okay, it's okay. It's time for me to go home." At this point, Ted started crying and lamented what he had done to her. "It's okay," Holly lied, "I know you're a nice person."

Ted finally took her back to her car. Holly drove home, her dress ripped and stained, with bruises on her neck, wrists, and legs. She woke her roommate and told her what happened. The next day, Holly called a help line and they put her in touch with a rape-crisis center. She went to a doctor. She did not want to prosecute but did file an anonymous report about the incident through the rape center. Such reports put the perpetrator's name on file with police, but are not criminal complaints. For the next four weeks, Holly met several times with rape-crisis counselors. She tried to put her life back in order. Then, one day, one of the counselors telephoned her and said, "Are you sitting down? He's done it again."

Ted had sodomized a woman in another Oregon town. The woman had then jumped naked from his car, moving at 40 miles per hour, to escape. She lived, but was badly injured. As in Holly's case, Ted had told the woman his name. The police search stretched into California, where Ted was found in a car full of pornographic magazines, watching teenage girls at a mall through binoculars.

After his arrest, the state police came across Holly's anonymous incident report and contacted the rape center which had filed it.

When she heard the news, Holly decided she had to report her rape officially. "It was the fact that he wasn't stopping, that for all of his remorse that night, he turned around exactly four weeks later and did it again," she says. Holly felt awful that another woman had been hurt, possibly because of her original decision not to go to the police.

Ted was charged in Holly's case with first-degree rape and first-degree sodomy (for the oral sex). Holly never expected the case to go to trial; she thought Ted would plead guilty, but he didn't. Unlike many victims, though, Holly had a "warm-up" session for her own trial when she was called to be a witness in the other woman's case. "I think he was absolutely shocked to see me come in," she says of Ted's reaction to her appearance in a courtroom hundreds of miles from her hometown. "I got a taste for what it was going to be like," she says. Then the real blow hit. After being charged with assault, kidnapping, sodomy, and attempted rape in the injured woman's case, Ted was found not guilty of everything except assault. Holly was devastated.

> That sent me right into a tailspin. I mean, shit, she's got all this physical evidence 'cause she was hurt so badly and they didn't find him guilty. And I thought, "We don't have a snowball's chance in hell down here," and I was really worried about that.

The grand jury charged Ted with Holly's rape in March. The case didn't go to trial until late November. During the months of waiting, Holly endured periodic meetings at the district attorney's office to rehash the case and conferences with the local victim support agency. She repeatedly had to take time off from a job she started just days after the rape; fortunately, her boss was understanding. When she heard radio reports about her case, she became terrified that her name would be publicized, but it wasn't.

Finally, the trial came. "It was so much different than I expected," Holly says. "I had seen only horrible courtroom dramas where the victim is put on the stand and they say, 'How many men do you sleep with every night?' They didn't do that at all. There were very few personal questions."

During initial questioning by police, Holly had felt "too humiliated" to tell them about having had her period and how Ted had pulled out her tampon and flung it aside. Before going to trial, though, she told that part of the story to the district attorney and that information worked in her favor during the trial. When the defense argued that the incident between Ted and Holly was simply consensual sex, the prosecution made a strong contention that a menstruating woman was not likely to engage in casual sex with a man she had just met.

Looking back, Holly says that waiting for the trial was more painful than actually being in court. Although she testified for "what seemed like an eternity," the trial lasted only a day and a half. Holly was allowed in the courtroom only to give testimony and listen to closing arguments.

> His defense was so goddamned lame. He said that, yes, we went to his house and, yes, he choked me. There was no way he could get out of that because I had physical evidence. He said, yes, we had sex but only because after he choked me, I calmed down and I became the seducer and seduced him.
>
> It was so ludicrous. The only thing that came as a surprise, that I didn't anticipate, was that they said they found nothing but blood on my dress — meaning no semen — and their explanation for that was that I had taken off my dress because I was totally in cooperation with him.

The jury was about half male and half female. They deliberated for only an hour. When they filed back into court, Holly was there, supported by her rape-crisis counselor.

> I had prepared myself for it being a "not guilty," . . . but all I wanted was it to be "guilty" so bad. The counselor had her arm around me and when they said, "Guilty" [on the rape charge], I didn't even listen to the sodomy charge.
>
> The counselor said, "Now, do you feel better?" and I just started crying and said, "No," 'cause I really didn't. It didn't make me feel any better and that's what a lot of people don't realize. I think they thought I was going to be totally normal after this happened.

Although the jury found Ted guilty of rape, they found him not guilty of sodomy. Holly thinks that may be because she was so reluctant to give details about the forced oral sex she endured.

The following March, Holly went back into court for Ted's sentencing.

> Our side asked for seven years' minimum. Then Ted decided to get real smart and stand up and say something in his behalf.
>
> He would have been better off if he had shut up. He was sentenced to 20 years' maximum, 10 years' minimum — three more years than our side asked for.
>
> At that point, I felt good.

Now, one year after sentencing, Holly sits in the living room of her home, surrounded by children's toys, and assesses the changes in her life. Shortly after Ted began serving his sentence for raping her, she gave an interview about her case to the local newspaper. She even agreed to let them print her name.

> If we stay silent on this shit, they are just going to keep it up. I've proven that. I was quiet, I let him go. I said, "He didn't really mean to do it," and I believed all of that stupid stuff he told me, when he said that he was sorry and he had never done it before and he would never do it again.
>
> I feel good about it now. I don't feel I've anything to hide.

Making a "Good" Case in Criminal Court

Why was Holly's rapist convicted and Maggie's set free? Both cases involved physical violence, restraint of the woman, and sexual intercourse committed against her will. Both cases also involved some mistakes by the victims—in Maggie's case, it was leaving her door unlocked; in Holly's, it was agreeing to go to Ted's trailer.

Yet there was a difference between the two. Although both women knew their attackers, Holly had just met the man who raped her while Maggie had willingly gone on several dates with her attacker and had sex with him before. Because of the prior relationship she had with Bruce, both the district attorney and the jury found it hard to label Maggie's experience "rape," although it was.

Not too long ago, Holly's case might not have ended in a conviction either, but rape laws have changed recently in ways that are allowing more acquaintance-rape cases to be prosecuted successfully. By the late 1970s and early 1980s, many states had revised their rape statutes to broaden the definition of rape to include many forms of sexual assault (not just vaginal intercourse) against both men and women, to restrict use of a woman's sexual history as evidence for the defense, and to eliminate standards of resistance the victim needed to meet to "prove" she was forced to have sex. Moreover, some states have permitted the use of expert testimony stating that the victim suffered rape trauma syndrome as a way to prove that rape occurred. However, although there have been improvements in the law, there are still dramatically fewer convictions in acquaintance-rape cases than in stranger rapes. The reason lies in the concept of the "good" case.

In the prototypical "good" rape case, the victim—a virgin who lives at home with her parents—is grabbed from behind by a man she's never seen before as she's walking in broad daylight to visit her dying grandmother in the hospital. Her assailant has a knife, a gun, and brass knuckles. He breaks her jaw by punching her, so she can't scream, and stabs her at least once before forcing her into the bushes and raping her. She fights back forcefully nonetheless, and the struggle attracts the attention of a male police officer, who arrives and pulls the man off of his victim. An official examination finds the man's semen within the woman's vagina and traces of her blood and skin on his body. The bruises on her face match the pattern on his brass knuckles.

Rapes are prosecuted according to how well they fit such a "good" case standard, so it's no wonder that few acquaintance rapes come to trial. In an acquaintance rape, the woman involved is often voluntarily with the man who attacks her. He usually does not use a weapon and may not hit her; she usually doesn't scream—out of fear, not out of physical inability—and she often has few severe marks or bruises afterward. The presence of semen in or on her body simply shows that the two had sex, not that it was forced. There is rarely a witness to the rape. Because she often doesn't identify the assault as rape until days later, the woman may not report the incident promptly to police.

To Charge or Not

Decisions to classify rape complaints as "founded" (that is, valid and prosecutable) or "unfounded" (unprosecutable for some reason) often depend on factors that have nothing to do with whether the woman was forced to have sex against her will. More than anything else, those decisions have to do with whether the legal gatekeepers (first the police and then the district attorneys) find the victim acceptable and the circumstances of her rape sufficiently like a "good" case to be believed.

The number of rape cases labeled "unfounded" by police varies wildly from municipality to municipality (in one recent year, Detroit ruled that 1.3 percent of rape complaints were "unfounded," while Chicago labeled 54.1 percent that way). The existence of "unfounded" cases sparks two interpretations: Some believe the numbers prove that women lie about rape; others say the figures show that police unfairly disbelieve rape victims.

The bulk of the cases labeled "unfounded" are date rapes and acquaintance rapes. A study reviewing police files in New York showed that 24 percent of acquaintance-rape complaints were deemed "unfounded" compared with only 5 percent of stranger rapes. Cases may be designated "unfounded" because the police, for good reasons or bad, may not believe the victim, because the assault may not have occurred within that jurisdiction, or because the victim may have changed her mind about pressing charges. In acquaintance rapes, it is especially likely that myths about rape and the continuing belief that women lie about rape to "punish" men for broken relationships or win attention for themselves greatly influence police decisions to declare some cases "unfounded." Although better education about rape is changing these attitudes, old ideas still die hard.

In a study of 905 sexual assault complaints in a large midwestern city, researcher Gary LaFree found that extralegal determinants affected whether police charged a suspect with rape or not. Those factors which often resulted in the suspect's *not* being charged frequently occur in instances of acquaintance rape, including:

□ victim "misconduct"—e.g., hitchhiking, drinking, being alone
   at a bar, engaging in sex outside of marriage, or willingly entering the suspect's car, house, or apartment
□ victim delay in filing a report
□ a prior relationship between a victim and suspect
□ the absence of a weapon

While LaFree found that the best predictors of whether a suspect
would be arrested were legal determinants—the victim's ability to
identify her attacker and her willingness to prosecute—extralegal
factors had great influence on police decisions to arrest. For example, *no arrests* were made in any cases LaFree studied in which
police found victim "misconduct," such as going to the man's apartment or drinking. "Interviews with police showed that police associate victim misconduct with carelessness or outright complicity in
the incident," LaFree says.

The study also showed that gang acquaintance rapes and acquaintance rapes involving teenagers were viewed by police as less
serious than other types of rapes. LaFree found that "detectives were
suspicious of sexual assaults involving more than one offender—
particularly when these cases also involved more than one victim,
when victims and offenders were acquainted prior to the incident,
or when victims and offenders were young. Several detectives re-
ferred to cases with these characteristics as 'party rapes,' and suggested that such incidents deserved less serious attention than other
complaints."

Considering all of those attitudes, it's not surprising that a recent study in Seattle showed that having a prior relationship with
the assailant was the chief reason women cited for not reporting
their rapes to police.

There are other factors contributing to the nonreporting of acquaintance rapes. Key among these is fear. Since many women live
or work near their attackers, there's real cause for concern, especially if they believe that the police might declare their case without
merit, thus denying them the protection of having the assailant
jailed. Even when police consider an acquaintance-rape case "good,"
it is no guarantee of safety for the victim. In Philadelphia in 1987 a
man raped a 20-year-old woman after she had refused to continue

dating him, then shot and seriously wounded her when she reported the rape to the police. According to the victim's relatives, the man had threatened just after the rape to shoot the woman if she reported him.

The Difficulties of Proving Acquaintance Rape

Most criminal complaints of rape are defended by one of four arguments: The identification of the suspect is wrong; the suspect had diminished responsibility due to mental incompetence; the victim consented to have sex with the suspect; or no sexual activity occurred. While defendants in stranger-rape cases tend to build their cases around the first defense (identification), in acquaintance-rape cases, where the suspect is known, the defense usually uses the third or fourth arguments—consent or "nothing happened." Consent, as defined by one state criminal code (Minnesota's) is "a voluntary uncoerced manifestation of a present agreement to perform a particular sexual act." But how was that consent, or lack of it, expressed? The defense will often attempt to argue that consent was implied by the victim's behavior, life-style, or lack of resistance.

From a police and prosecutorial perspective, a "good" case will hinge solely on identification of the suspect along with evidentiary proof of rape. Prosecuting against a claim of consent muddies the waters considerably, so many prosecutors are disinclined to take on acquaintance-rape incidents. That's due in part to their own ignorance and prejudices about rape and rape victims and in part to their belief that jurors will hold the same antivictim views.

That belief is often correct. Several studies have shown that juries are reluctant to convict rapists if there is any hint of victim "misconduct." In addition, juries are more likely to convict if the attacker used a weapon and much less likely if lesser force was employed. They are also inclined to acquit rape defendants who have good social standing—frequently the profiles of men accused in date rapes and acquaintance rapes.

Women jurors are often especially harsh on victims who have suffered acquaintance rape. The reason may have much to do with the female jurors' need to dissociate themselves from the victim's experience. "To live with the knowledge that not only are all women vulnerable to rape, but that frequently they are raped by men they know is difficult," says researcher Pauline B. Bart. "If, however, women believe in fact that only bad women can be raped and only crazy men who are strangers are rapists, then they can feel safe."

A 1985 study of 360 jurors in rape cases was conducted by the University of New Mexico's Gary LaFree, Barbara F. Reskin of the University of Michigan, and Christy A. Visher of the National Research Council/National Academy of Sciences. It showed that in cases where the man claimed the woman had consented to sex or that no sexual activity had occurred, the jurors were more likely to believe the man if the woman had engaged in nonmarried sex, drank or took drugs, or had known the defendant even briefly before the attack. [The influence of prior acquaintance was profound on juries, the study found, even when that acquaintance was only that of a shopper (the victim) to a grocery clerk (the rapist), or a customer to a bank teller.] These considerations, the researchers noted, "may represent either a legitimate concern with a victim's credibility or an illegitimate concern with her moral character." In many cases, it is the latter.

Because of these juror biases, law-enforcement officials feel justified in pursuing only those rapes which most closely approximate "good" cases. But perpetuating that status quo is both bad ethics and bad law. "The fact that juries distinguish among rape cases based on prior relationship and force and resistance provides a powerful defense for the reliance on these factors by police and prosecutors," says Susan Estrich, a professor at Harvard Law School, in her book *Real Rape*. "But it is not necessarily determinative, if the factors are unjustifiable in their own right: That juries may consider race and class is no excuse for prosecutors to discriminate."

Juries are also sometimes reluctant to convict a man for an acquaintance rape—especially one involving little physical violence —because they consider it a "lesser" crime than a stranger rape. Some rape-victim advocates support the idea of creating another criminal classification for date rapes and acquaintance rapes, one that would encourage police to deem more cases "founded," that would cause prosecutors to pursue those cases more vigorously and juries to convict more often. However, because such a classification would carry lower penalties than for stranger rape, it would also perpetuate the notion that acquaintance rapes aren't serious crimes.

Another Path to Justice: Civil Court

In a Los Angeles park, a newly arrived young woman from Iowa meets a friendly part-time actor. They chat for a while and then he suggests that they go for a scenic ride through the Hollywood Hills. On the way, he insists on stopping at his house so he can change his shirt. Once inside the home, he locks the door, rapes the woman, and forces her to submit to oral sex.

Just another acquaintance-rape horror story? Yes, only this one has an unusual ending: Eight years after the rape, a jury awarded the woman $5 million in damages. In this case, the man was also tried and convicted in criminal court—although it took the victim nearly a year to convince prosecutors to file charges.

Taking acquaintance-rape complaints to civil court is a new approach that offers many victims a better way to fight back than they may find through criminal law channels. "When somebody's caused harm in this way, money's not going to make it all right," says Robert K. Dawson, a Seattle lawyer who has won several lawsuits against acquaintance rapists, " . . . but civil suits can help the victim and they're a deterrent to people."

In criminal trials, there are usually three factors weighing against the acquaintance-rape victim: The defendant does not have to testify (and many don't); the law demands a high burden of proof (higher than is possible to establish in many cases), and the decision to convict must be reached by a unanimous jury (many of whom are predisposed against the victim). In civil court, though, the man may be forced to testify, the burden of proof required is somewhat less (by a "preponderence of evidence" rather than "beyond a reasonable doubt"), and a decision in favor of the victim may be made with a less than unanimous jury. "It's a fair fight," Dawson says.

And it is a fight that more and more women are choosing to wage.

Dawson, for example, represented a woman who went to a party, drank heavily, and was gang-raped by four men. There was no criminal prosecution in the case. The civil case began three and a half years after the rape. Dawson argued that the rape had harmed the woman for the rest of her life. She had become quite fearful and could no longer go out at night. A jury awarded her $300,000 in damages.

To pursue a civil case, it is necessary to show that the victim suffered harm by the defendant's action (the rape). As in criminal cases, good evidence (doctors' reports, photographs of injuries, witnesses' accounts) will buttress a claim, but they aren't mandatory. All that's really needed is the victim's testimony.

Unlike criminal proceedings, the victim who chooses to file a lawsuit against her attacker is liable for the expenses of that undertaking. Such costs can range from a few thousand to many thousands of dollars, depending on the complexity of the case. As in many civil actions, most lawyers who handle such cases take them on a contingency basis. That means the lawyer advances the costs of the lawsuit plus attorney's fees and gets paid only after an award is collected. Most contingency fees are one-third of the award amount. Defendants have 10 years to pay.

It should be noted that very few of these cases actually go to trial. The majority are settled out of court, with the victim and defendant agreeing to a settlement amount. Such agreements are reached when one or both parties wants to avoid the costs or risks of a trial as well as the possible publicity. In general, civil suits take much longer to come to trial than do criminal cases.

An interesting adjunct to suing the perpetrator is suing a third party who may have had some responsibility for the circumstances in which the rape occurred. These third parties, although not *intentionally* involved in the rape, may be shown to be liable because they should have anticipated it and taken steps to prevent it. Often, women choose to sue such third parties—businesses, universities, fraternities—to prevent a similar situation from occurring again. Moreover, these third parties often have greater financial resources than the defendant does, so the possibility of collecting the full amount awarded is better. For example, a jury in Indiana awarded $800,000 to a woman who sued her employer, a large car rental firm, after being raped by a fellow employee. A second employee, also raped by the same man, received a $300,000 out-of-court settlement. Recently, the 18-year-old woman who reported she was raped by four members of a fraternity at San Diego State sued the state, the university, the fraternity, and the sorority she had been pledging at the time for $2.5 million.

Third-party cases in acquaintance rapes are still a rarity, according to Ellen Godbey Carson, a Honolulu lawyer who has won several third-party lawsuits for her clients who have been raped and who tracks legal trends of such cases nationwide. Most cases still involve the third party's responsibility to keep strangers off the premises. Acquaintance rapes, because they involve "the consent issue," are less frequently litigated, Carson says.

But the fear of becoming a target in such a case has many organizations so worried that they are starting acquaintance-rape education programs. "We made it part of a total risk management program," says Joe Langella, national alumni director for the Sigma Phi Epsilon fraternity. Langella describes the program as being "designed to instruct our chapters in ways to minimize liability lawsuits and the types of activity that would bring about a situation like that, such as date rape and acquaintance rape." Although making fraternity men sensitive to acquaintance rape so as to minimize the potential for financial loss is certainly not the motivation most women would prefer, it's better than no motivation at all.

Victims, however, aren't the only ones turning to the civil courts. In a case filed in mid-1987, a fraternity member at the University of Michigan sued a female student whose complaint led to his arrest on rape charges following a frat party. "Nobody had ever heard of this tactic before," says Julie Steiner, director of the university's Sexual Assault Prevention and Awareness Center. Steiner and others who support the victim believe the lawsuit was meant to intimidate the woman into dropping criminal charges. The lawsuit, which claims that the woman libeled the man, has yet to be decided. But several months after it was filed, the male student was acquitted of the criminal charges. That acquittal sparked a spontaneous protest on campus, marked by a candlelight vigil involving more than 300 students and protests outside the fraternity house where the attack was alleged to have occurred.

Steiner speaks grimly about the influence such a lawsuit can have on rape victims. "It's had a chilling effect," she says. "Since the trial, the impact on our clients [raped women] has been incredible. For those who decided not to report their rapes, it's convinced them all the more that their decision was correct. Even the police are upset because they know what an impact it's going to have on reports."

Seattle lawyer Dawson has had several female clients countersued for malicious prosecution after they filed civil claims against rapists, but all of those countersuits were dismissed. "There's never been a successful malicious prosecution suit against a sexual assault victim in this state," he says.

The Collegiate Alternative: University Judicial Boards

Donna, who was raped off campus by a fellow student, decided not to press criminal charges against the man who raped her. Instead she chose to take the case before the judicial board at her Illinois college.

Many schools and universities have such boards to enforce behavioral codes and mete out punishment to those who break the rules. These boards are perhaps the last vestige of the days when universities functioned in parental roles, although the membership of most boards usually includes students as well as faculty and staff. Concerned mainly with cases involving plagiarism, vandalism, and alcohol abuse, these boards are often ill prepared to handle the complexities of acquaintance rapes.

Indeed, not one of the women interviewed for this book who had taken her case before a university judicial board felt satisfied with the result. Although on Donna's campus the behavioral code calls for suspension after a first rape offense and expulsion after a second, her attacker—who admitted to the board that he had forced Donna to have sex—received only probation and was required to write a paper on sexual assault. "I was given a copy of it," Donna says, "and

I think it was written out of a book. I think he really didn't learn anything." Angered by the college ruling, Donna then decided to press criminal charges, but the state prosecutor advised her that she had waited too long to make a "good" case.

Jocelyn, now a junior at a college in Michigan, was raped in the first semester of her sophomore year by another student who served as a tutor in one of her classes. "I pursued litigation through the college system, mostly out of a need to get the blame away from myself," she says. "I figured that if I never tried to get him punished, I would never forgive myself. So I tried it the college's way, which failed miserably. The statement (issued by the university judicial board) said things like 'no evidence given' because there were no witnesses and 'the college should not interfere in the sexual activities of its students'—as if to say that if we insist upon sexual freedom, we must take *all* the consequences of what could happen." In addition, the board's statement apologized to the male student "for any trauma or inconvenience this has brought you."

Despite that ruling, Jocelyn came back to campus after summer break. "I returned to school in part to prove how much power I have now," she says, "and to continue to hold the college responsible for what I see as its grave injustice. If I had just disappeared from campus, they would be free to continue this; already they have had to strengthen services for women. Thank God."

Sometimes university boards refuse even to hear a case. Beth met the man who would rape her at a campus fraternity house, then went with him to a nearby apartment where friends of his from the fraternity lived. Beth says she was drunk, but still able to refuse the man's sexual advances. He ignored her refusal, held her down, and raped her. Beth was a freshman; the man who raped her had just graduated from the same New York school. "I reported the rape to the administration," she says. "I wanted to press charges and keep him from coming back to campus while I was still here." The university denied her request, contending that since the man had already graduated, there was nothing it could do. "I didn't report it to the police because I was afraid I wouldn't be believed," Beth says. "Acquaintance rapes are very common at our college, but the administration is unwilling to believe it and many women are afraid to tell."

University boards are also concerned with the public perception of their campuses. If an acquaintance-rape complaint should be investigated and the rapist punished by the university—thereby verifying that the attack occurred—such notoriety could hurt the school's reputation (and enrollment). Judicial board members may try to impose a lesser charge that won't carry the stigma for the university that a rape finding would.

Even highly publicized cases which result in criminal punishments may not be sufficient to persuade a university judicial board to take action. When a Syracuse University football player pleaded guilty in criminal court in July 1986 to sexual misconduct for forcing a first-year student to have intercourse against her will, he was sentenced to serve three years' probation and perform community service. However, two weeks later, a college hearing board decided that the athlete had not violated any university regulations. He was permitted to remain in school, keep his scholarship, and continue to play football.

The victim left Syracuse three days after the rape and has since transferred to another school. In an interview with the Syracuse *Post-Standard* shortly after the university board's decision, she said: "I went into the [college] hearing believing that its purpose was to see what punishment they were going to give him for being convicted of the crime he pleaded guilty to. It turned out that the panel judged my accusations against him and found him innocent of those accusations. I couldn't believe it. By the way they ruled, they have called me a liar and have slandered my name."

There are those who feel that university judicial boards are doing the best they can, given the circumstances. "Date and acquaintance rapes are the most difficult cases to handle in a disciplinary hearing just as they are in a court of law, for the same reasons," says Thomas R. Dougan, director of student life at the University of Rhode Island. "It's her word versus his word." At his school, Dougan says, if the man is deemed a "clear and present danger," he may be removed from the residence halls and suspended briefly pending a college investigation. Victims may also file reports of incidents without pressing charges.

Do college judicial boards serve a useful function in combating acquaintance rape? Dougan says that being brought before a hearing board has an effect on the accused male students.

"Do they take it seriously? You betcha," he says. "Does it have an impact on them? No question."

Then, after a thoughtful pause, he adds, "Will they ever do it again? I don't know."

CHAPTER 10

For Women: How to Prevent Acquaintance Rape

"The thing I learned from that terrible night was to trust my inner self."

— Meryl, raped on a first date

Every day, women are being raped by men they know. Many of those rapes are unpredictable and unavoidable. But many acquaintance rapes *can* be stopped before they occur.

The average woman is at a distinct disadvantage when an acquaintance begins to escalate his actions toward rape: She is less quick to identify in a friend behavior that she might instantly recognize as rape-threatening from a stranger. Likewise, because the man is an acquaintance, she may not think of screaming for help, hitting him, or even running away—actions she might be able to take when assaulted by a stranger.

To combat date rape and acquaintance rape, it's necessary for women to understand what is happening, to avoid the situations and people that hold the potential for rape, and to learn the methods to follow when confronted. Once armed with such knowledge, it may be possible for a woman to avoid or thwart an attack.

The Wrong Kind of Men

Avoiding acquaintance rape means avoiding acquaintance rapists. But identifying these men is no easy task; some are even attractive and desirable. However, many of these men do give off clues about themselves, danger signals that women must learn to read.

Rape counselors and women who have been raped by acquaintances recommend that you run, do not walk, from any man who displays any of these characteristics:

- Emotionally abuses you (through insults, belittling comments, ignoring your opinion, or by acting sulky or angry when you initiate an action or idea)
- Tells you who you may may be friends with, how you should dress, or tries to control other elements of your life or relationship (he insists on picking the movie you'll see, the restaurant where you'll eat, and so on)
- Talks negatively about women in general
- Gets jealous when there's no reason
- Drinks heavily or uses drugs or tries to get you intoxicated
- Berates you for not wanting to get drunk, get high, have sex, or go with him to an isolated or personal place (his room, your apartment, or the like)
- Refuses to let you share any of the expenses of a date and gets angry when you offer to pay
- Is physically violent to you or others, even if it's "just" grabbing and pushing to get his way
- Acts in an intimidating way toward you (sits too close, uses his body to block your way, speaks as if he knows you much better than he does, touches you when you tell him not to)
- Is unable to handle sexual and emotional frustrations without becoming angry
- Doesn't view you as an equal, either because he's older or because he sees himself as smarter or socially superior
- Has a fascination with weapons
- Enjoys being cruel to animals, children, or people he can bully

The Wrong Kind of Places

Where you are is often as important as whom you are with. Men who rape women they know need the right opportunity to attack.

An assault is most likely to happen in an isolated spot. Parked cars, nighttime beaches, the "upstairs" rooms in a fraternity house—all are good places for the acquaintance rapist to take his victim because he can be sure that they will be left alone and undisturbed, possibly for hours. Often the man will drive himself and his victim to the rape site, leaving her with no way to get home except by first giving him what he demands.

Such isolated places are as likely to be in the heart of big cities as in remote country areas. Sheryl was raped in a car by a man she met at a friend's party. "I was too afraid to run out of the car because it was a 'bad neighborhood,' " she says. "He kept threatening to beat me up, while I kept fighting him off. I was too afraid [of the neighborhood] to jump out or draw attention to us." Vivian, on the other hand, was raped by a family friend who took her to a cabin in the woods.

> We arrived at the chain that blocked off the driveway and we parked there for a very long time. I refused to go in — not violently, but silently.
>
> I was thinking that this was not like any of the rapes I'd ever heard about. I was alone in a car with a man I knew. What were my options? I could, it seemed to me, walk through the woods in my pumps and skirt, make it to the highway, only to flag down a truck, where another man — a stranger at that — would carry me to safety? No thanks.

Especially with recent acquaintances, women should insist on going only to public places such as restaurants and movie theaters.

Don't Set Yourself Up

Women do not cause acquaintance rape; acquaintance rapists do. However, there are things women can do to reduce their risks of being victimized. Gleaned from anti-rape counselors and experts, here are several guidelines for beliefs and behaviors women should adopt:

1. *You have the right to set sexual limits and to communicate those limits.* Know what your limits are before engaging in sexual

activity and tell your partner clearly. Indeed, you *must* communicate those limits—most men are not psychic. If you let them guess what you want, you may get hurt.

Talk with your partner about sex to establish that any sexual activity will be a mutual decision. It is not unfeminine to express your interest in sex, just as it is not uncool to make your lack of interest clear. It is perfectly all right to want to just kiss, or just kiss and let him touch your breasts, or whatever—without having intercourse.

2. *Be assertive.* Forget the cultural training that taught you to be coy. Being feminine does not mean being passive. State what you really want and what you're really feeling. When you say "no," be sure that you mean "no." When you say, "yes," be sure you first know what you're agreeing to.

When you set limits on sexual activity, but the man ignores them, act immediately. Tell him exactly what you object to. You can be friendly but forceful. If he continues to ignore your wishes, get angry. Don't worry about being polite. If you need to yell or hurt him to attract help or get away, do it. Forget about being "a nice girl." Don't worry about his feelings. Make a scene.

That's the advice that Myra gave her stepdaughter before the young woman went off to college. It's advice that Myra learned from her own experience when she was 18 and went to visit a friend who was in college. Myra's friend fixed her up with a date for "a real college beach party with a bonfire and beer." Her date was genial and good-looking. "A lot of fantasies started—he could fall in love with me, etc., etc.," Myra says. They kissed once and then her date suggested that they walk down the beach to look at the sky. Myra agreed.

> As soon as we were out of range, he threw me down and said if I tried to stop him he would "leave it in" and I'd get pregnant. I am pretty strong and tried to get away. I even tried looking for a piece of wood to hit him with.
>
> But my overall feeling was embarrassment. What would everybody think if I yelled out or hurt him? I might spoil everybody's time if I made a scene.

> I didn't want to make trouble. I was raised very other oriented and I know this was part of it. . . . I wish I could have been the me that I am now — it [the rape] never would have happened.

3. *Stay sober.* Your best chance for staying in control is not to lose touch with what's happening around you. Too many acquaintance rapes happen to women who are drunk or stoned.

If you like to drink, drink in moderation. A man who is planning to rape a woman he knows (even though he may conceptualize it as "seduction") will often feed her beer, liquor, or drugs to cloud her perceptions and reduce her resistance. And don't help rapists by getting drunk on your own. Men looking for targets pick out such women.

"I did not have much experience with alcohol, so did not realize the effect a few Singapore Slings (gin, cherry-flavored brandy, and lime juice) would have on me. I experienced my first blackout," says Irene, who was raped at 18 by her New Year's Eve blind date. "When I came to, I was getting fucked by this man [her date] in a bedroom somewhere in Chicago. To this day, I have no idea where I was, what happened to my girlfriend [who had been with her], or even what time it was."

At 24, Pam was a more experienced drinker than Irene, but suffered the same fate.

> I got drunk and asked to be taken home, more than once.
> I was carried upstairs like a sack of potatoes. I said, "no," several times and was ignored. I don't remember much of the actual rape, except that it happened.

Drugs are illegal and difficult to use moderately: When you take them, the point is to become high. Moreover, due to the cutting and mixing of drugs that goes on during their illegal manufacture, their effect on an individual may vary wildly from one time to the next. And experience with one drug is no preparation for experience with another.

The guy who would rape Emma lived on her dormitory floor. "He brought in some opiated hashish," she says. "I had smoked marijuana two or three times before. I had never gotten high, so I was sure that drugs just didn't work on me and I wasn't particularly worried." She should have been. The man used her intoxication to overpower her.

4. *Find out about a new date.* Double-date with friends the first few times to learn more about the man in a safe way. Talk over the exact plans for the date beforehand. Don't leave a party, bar, or anywhere else with a man you don't know very well. Ask around to find out about him from other women who may have dated him.

5. *Remain in control.* On a date, pay your own way (or let your date buy the movie tickets and you pay for pizza afterward) so that the date is not interpreted as a transaction in which you "owe" the man something. On a first date, consider taking your own car and meeting the man at your destination.

Set up a system with a friend or relative in which you can telephone for a ride, even late at night, if you need one. Carry a telephone credit card, so you won't need change to make a call. Always carry enough money to take a cab home by yourself. Don't accept rides from men you have just met.

6. *Take care of yourself.* Do not assume other people will take care of you or protect you from harm. Take a self-defense course *before* you need it. You can find programs in most communities that will help you develop the ability to read dangerous situations, act assertively, evade assault, and attack forcefully. (For organizations that offer programs, see the Resources section.)

7. *Trust your feelings.* On her first date with a new guy, Meryl noticed things about the man's behavior that she did not like—he was aggressively "macho" and treated her like his personal possession—but she shrugged them off. When they returned to her home from their date, he threatened to hurt her and then raped her. "The thing I learned from that terrible night,"she says now, "was to trust my inner self. I learned to be very careful of whom I went out with, and if I have any suspicions about someone, I turn and run as fast as possible."

If you're getting "bad vibes" about a guy, don't assume that there's something wrong with you. Believe your inner warning signals when you get a bad feeling about a person or a situation. Stay away.

"You have to learn to trust that little voice," says Paula. "Instead of giving him the benefit of the doubt, get out, get the heck out of the situation. That warning voice is trying to tell you that it's getting real dangerous. I have learned to trust that voice in me. Probably at times I'm a little overcautious, but I prefer to be that way than to risk being vulnerable again."

8. *Students should take special precautions.* For first-year college women, the Red Zone of danger is the period of time between move-in day and the first holiday break. Again and again, women are raped during these weeks by men they meet on campus. Why? These young women are good targets because they don't know campus routines or geography, they're feeling insecure and alone, yet may be eager to test the limits of a parentless society by drinking heavily and partying enthusiastically—behavior that will win them social approval. Because the Red Zone is also the time when fraternities and sororities "rush" for new members, there may be parties every night of the weekend (and some during the week as well). Those parties are likely to bring first-year women in contact with upperclass men, some of whom delight in "scoring" with the naive newcomers.

In addition, exchange students (and women tourists) from the United States are also often raped by men they meet in foreign countries. These women may be targets simply because they are strangers in unfamiliar places or because American women are often perceived as being promiscuous and therefore easy marks.

What to Do When Confronted with Acquaintance Rape

Data from the *Ms.* study helps point to ways to successfully fend off an acquaintance-rape assault. Survey responses show that the women who avoided being raped had a lower emotional response to the initial attack—that is, they felt less fear, self-blame, helplessness, and shock when accosted than did the women who were raped. These women also more often ran away and screamed for help.

What didn't seem to work against an acquaintance-rape attack? Quarreling with the rapist often led to completed rape, although crying and reasoning had some effect on some men. However, crying and reasoning were greatly inferior to active strategies such as screaming or running away. (Other studies have shown that crying, reasoning, pleading, or turning cold are ineffective in stranger rapes.)

Although each rape-threatening situation is different, there are actions that rape experts advise women to follow that may help stop an assault before it's completed:

1. *Stay calm.* You're going to need all your wits about you, so try not to give in to fear. Concentrate on being assertive.

2. *Appraise your situation, then act quickly.* Try to evaluate how much danger you are in. If you run, can you get to an area where there are other people? If you yell, will someone hear you and come to your assistance? How violent is the man who is threatening you? Is he more likely to try to bully you verbally than to use physical force or a weapon against you?

Once you've decided on your best course of action, act immediately. Your attacker won't stand around waiting for you to decide what to do.

3. *Try to get away.* Running away may catch an attacker off guard. Run toward lights, buildings, the street—anywhere you're likely to find other people. Don't worry about embarrassing yourself by running into a crowded restaurant or theater. You need help and you need it fast.

If you're in a car, get out. If you can't get out, try to use the horn.

4. *Yell for help.* Running away may not be practical, but yelling can instantly let people nearby know that you're in trouble. "Help, I'm being attacked on the parking lot!" or "Help, police!" or even "Fire!" are all effective phrases to use.

If you can, start running after you yell; your attacker may be frightened off by your noise and you'll be able to get to safety.

5. *When necessary, attack forcefully.* It's likely that you're not going to win in hand-to-hand combat with your assailant, so if you

decide to fight, do it dirty but decisively. Your goal is to incapacitate him long enough for you to get away. Do not worry about hurting him. Remember, it's harder for most women to use physical strategies in acquaintance rape than in stranger rape. Think through exactly what you are going to do and get ready for the fact that you're going to cause him pain. Realize, too, that your fighting back might also cause him to become violent. Consult a book on self-defense (see Resources) or take a class to learn such tactics.

6. *Buy time with talk.* If you can't get away, try talking. Don't attempt to argue the rapist out of his attack, but simply stall him with conversation. Some women tell the man that they find him attractive and ask him about himself. When he thinks he no longer needs to use force, he may ease up on his guard. That's a good time to make a break for the door.

Or, tell him you really like him but need to go to the bathroom first. Once inside, you may be able to get out the window. Even if you can't get out the window, the bathroom may have a lock on the door. Use it. Then start screaming out the window.

7. *Destroy his idea of a "seduction."* Tonya was raped by a stranger when she was 20 and remembered the feelings of power, control, and "meanness" her attacker had exuded. So, at 23, when she found herself in a deserted parking lot with a first-time date who had been belittling her all night, keeping her wineglass filled, and now was not taking "no" for an answer, she knew better than many women do what was about to happen. She foiled his rape attempt by feigning an attack of hysterics, complete with phony hallucinations that the trees nearby were coming to get her. After about 15 minutes of her performance, her date started the car and drove her home. "He was visibly disgusted at the way the evening turned out," Tonya says. "He couldn't drop me off quick enough."

There are other such possibilities for foiling an assault. Try telling your attacker that you have a sexually transmitted disease. If you actually have your period, tell him so; it might turn him off. So might telling him that you're pregnant. You might try to do physical things to turn him off: Urinate on the floor, pick your nose, belch, pass gas, even vomit—anything to break his perception that what is happening is a "seduction." Before trying any of these tactics, however, realize that they might not work.

Giving in Is Not Consent

Giving in to an acquaintance rapist *is not* something to be ashamed of. He may threaten you. He may be physically violent. He may terrify you so much that you cannot respond effectively. Going along with him is often the only smart thing to do.

Giving in is a survival strategy. It is not consent if his actions force you to consent. Consenting to sex is a mutual decision, freely reached, without any hint of force or coercion.

Do not berate yourself that you "let" him rape you. A rape-threatening situation is also a life-threatening situation. Your only responsibility as a victim is to yourself. You do not need to sustain injury or death to "prove" you were raped. Stay alive.

CHAPTER 11

For Men: The Benefits of Change

□ ———————————————————————————— □

"It is men who rape and men who collectively have the power to end rape."

— author Timothy Beneke

There are those who argue that men should be concerned about acquaintance rape because it could happen to those they love—daughters, sisters, wives, mothers, girlfriends. But the truth is that *all* men are hurt deeply by acquaintance rape, not just the ones whose daughters or girlfriends are attacked. Men are hurt, just as our whole society is hurt, by behavior that catastrophically affects so many women and reduces so many "regular guys" to sexual, social, and moral hooligans.

Guidelines for Change

Acquaintance rape—indeed, all forms of rape—has to be understood by men as their problem too. "It is men who rape and men who collectively have the power to end rape," writes Timothy Beneke in *Men On Rape.*

To harness that power, many men will have to rethink their beliefs about women and sex and change their behaviors. The following 11 points are guidelines suggested by rape-awareness advocates to help men achieve that goal:

1. *Never force a woman to have sex* —even if she has "led" you on, even if she has slept with your friends, even if she at first said

"yes" and then changed her mind before having sex, even if she had sex with you before. This includes *all* unwanted sexual contact—from kissing to "copping a feel" to forcing intercourse on her against her will.

Women have the right to set limits on sexual behavior—just as you do. As a sexual *partner,* you must understand and respect those limits. When partners' desires conflict, the one who wants more activity has to yield to the one who wants less (either male or female).

2. *Don't pressure a woman to have sex.* Men often see their verbal pressuring as being less forceful than women do. Even when the words you use are not threatening, the woman may feel that she is in danger. Just the fact that you are a man can be intimidating. Your size, strength, social role, and age are all factors that can contribute to her feeling powerless against your pressure for sex. Don't lie to a woman in order to con her into agreeing to have sex either.

3. *Stay sober.* Right. This is exactly the same advice given women earlier. In many individual acquaintance rapes and nearly all gang acquaintance rapes, the men involved had been drinking, taking drugs, or both, and were often intoxicated. Social groups that emphasize heavy drinking and drug taking are often those whose members condone acquaintance rape.

When you're drunk or high on drugs, your decision-making abilities are crippled, your aggression level may rise, and your ability to control your impulses may disappear. Adopt this rule: *If you get drunk or stoned, don't have sex.* Your intoxicated perception may be that you are seducing a willing woman when in fact you are forcing her to have sex against her will.

Being drunk is no legal defense against committing rape or any other sexual assault. You will still be charged with rape, regardless of your blood-alcohol content. And that's a sobering thought.

4. *Don't buy the myth that a drunk woman "deserves" to be raped.* Of course no woman does. But men often think it's not rape if the woman was too drunk or stoned to know what was going on, or if she had passed out from using drugs and alcohol. In fact, an

intoxicated woman cannot give intelligent consent about sexual activity; therefore the likelihood is even greater that what went on was rape.

5. *Do not "join in" if a friend invites you to participate in sexual behavior.* Do not have intercourse or other sexual contact with a woman who is having sex with a group of men, particularly if she is drunk or stoned. This is gang rape. Any other possibility exists almost exclusively in the fantasy world of X-rated movies and magazines. A drunken or intimidated woman being assaulted by a group of men is not enjoying a fantasy come true. Instead of contributing to her attack, you should try to stop the assault or call police.

6. *Do not confuse "scoring" with having a successful social encounter.* Sex is not a payback for a pleasant evening. You can have intercourse with 100 women and still not know anything about good sex or love or what it means to be a "real" man. Ejaculating is no big deal; having a mutually agreed-upon and sustained relationship is.

If your friends think keeping count of the number of times you've had intercourse is important, tell them that you don't agree. If they continue to demand "body counts" from you and to brag about their own sexual "victories," find new friends.

7. *Don't assume that you know what a woman wants and vice versa.* Ask her. Give her an unpressured atmosphere in which to answer. If she doesn't know how involved she wants to be with you sexually, then back off.

Just because a woman wants affection (hugging, kissing, sitting close) or sex play (sexual fondling) doesn't mean that she wants sexual intercourse. Again, ask her. You deserve a clear, definitive response. If you don't get one, do not assume that intercourse is okay.

8. *"No" means "no."* Forget all the times your friends told you that all women say "no" when they mean "yes." It's not true.

When a woman says "no" that means "no." Stop. She does not want to go further. Do not try to cajole her or argue with her. And do not ignore her. If you think she's saying "no" to protect her "reputation" (even though you know she *really* wants to have sex with you), so what? When (and if) she's ready to have sex with you, let it be her choice to make.

If a woman says "no" and really means "yes, but you have to convince me," then you don't want to be with her anyway. She's playing a game and it's a game that nobody wins. Forget about "losing an opportunity." Just walk away.

9. *Speak up if you feel you're getting a double message from a woman.* Ask her directly what she wants. Again, if she can't tell you, don't have sex with her.

10. *Communicate with women.* Try talking to women, lots of different women, not just the ones you date or want to date. By talking with women about their lives and feelings, you can develop understanding that will benefit you in all of your relationships.

11. *Communicate with other men.* Talk about sex, dating, and acquaintance rape with your male friends. Let them know you dislike behavior and talk that are hostile, abusive, and even rape threatening toward women. Step in if you think a friend is about to cross the line between sexual interest and sexual assault.

If you live in a dorm, belong to a fraternity, or play on an athletic team, find out what acquaintance-rape awareness programs are available for your group. Support and participate in such programs.

Men Changing Men

Acquaintance rape is a subject guaranteed to make most men feel defensive. Nowhere is that more evident than when one or more women stands before a group of dating-age people (both sexes or all-male) and tries to conduct an acquaintance-rape education workshop. Fortunately, across the country, men are now beginning to stand in front of those groups too. Some of them are peers of the men in the audience (fellow students, fraternity brothers, co-workers); others are psychologists, religious and community leaders, school officials, or law-enforcement specialists. With men conducting such sessions, information about date rape and acquaintance rape that some men might resist accepting from women is often more successfully transmitted and believed.

That's not surprising, since most men feel that another man better understands where they're coming from than a woman. Ron Campbell, director of housing and residential life at Drew University in Madison, New Jersey, saw the need for men to work with other men after reading an article that addressed the issue. "It [the article] said that men need to start taking responsibility for their own lives," Campbell says. "Who better understands the mythology and everything else that we're all about and who better to approach men? When I went to my first acquaintance-rape workshop, as a man I felt very angry because there was all negatives, nothing positive. I talked to other men who had gone and were feeling the same way."

So Campbell set out to change that situation and improve men's acceptance of such workshops. But first he says, "I did some personal looking."

What he found, he now shares publicly. "I identified myself as an acquaintance rapist," he says. "I didn't knock anybody down, I didn't say. 'If you don't do this, I'll twist your arm,' . . . but I can remember perfectly overpowering people in that persuasive way that we [men] do: We lay on top of you (the woman) and you can't move. I can remember lying and creating all kinds of scenarios and never asking for consensual sex. You know, not caring what happens the next day or having that person feel uncomfortable or unsettled about what had happened."

Campbell now shares these recollections with groups of men he speaks to on various college campuses. In the workshops, he talks about male sexual socialization and attacks the forces it breeds that promote acquaintance rape. But, he admits, awareness levels among college men are still low. "I still think it [men's concern about acquaintance rape] is more, 'How can I avoid going to jail?' rather than, 'How can I be a better sex partner?' "

Men's Programs That Work

When *Ms.* magazine published an article on acquaintance rape in October 1985, the editors received phone calls from men on campuses across the country who wanted to start rape-awareness programs. Now such programs are catching on. Mark Willmarth, a career counselor at the College of Great Falls in Great Falls, Montana, has created a workshop for men that has been used by administrators, educators, and men's groups. He advocates men talking to men in all-male settings. "I presented the workshop recently to a group of basketball players and they really opened up," Willmarth says. "Then I did one to a mixed (male/female) audience and it bombed. There was no male participation." Another program just for men called, "I Know She Said, 'No,' But Thought She Said, 'Maybe,' " is offered by psychologist Mark Stevens, a counselor at the University of Southern California in Los Angeles. Stevens presents his workshops at campuses nationwide.

At Cornell University in Ithaca, New York, male students rather than adult counselors deliver the message. They are peer educators in a program on acquaintance rape and sex roles aimed at other male students. Titled "How to Be a Better Lover," the program is sponsored by Cornell's health education unit.

Men are being reached by men in other ways as well. At the University of Arizona, for example, the Interfraternity Council educates members and pledges about sexual assault. Says the communications director of one national fraternity, Pi Kappa Phi: "There's not many people who want to belong to an Animal House anymore." That may be an overly optimistic view, but members of a few fraternities *are* taking leadership roles in fostering acquaintance-rape understanding among their own. At the University of Florida at Gainesville, for example, a group called SAGA (Sexual Awareness Greek Association) conducts programs on sex roles and rape education in fraternity and sorority houses (called "Greeks" for short, because most group names are comprised of Greek letters). Those programs are run by fraternity and sorority members.

"The first thing we say to them when we stand in front of them is that we're Greeks, talking to Greeks," says Paul Carland, a junior and Beta Theta Pi fraternity member who volunteers his time to SAGA. "We say, 'We understand exactly what you're going through because we've been through it ourselves. I can sit here and talk about what happens in the socials 'cause I know, I've been to the socials, I've been to the happy hours. I know what possibly can go wrong.' " Carland feels the SAGA programs are having an effect on Fraternity Row. "It's a tough topic and there are still a lot of people in the [fraternity] system who don't understand it or don't think we need it, they think we're wasting their time, . . . but I know in my fraternity, the attitudes really have changed."

The greatest active participation and response nationwide against acquaintance rape, however, has come from men who don't belong to traditional all-male groups. In Madison, Wisconsin, a group called Men Stopping Rape, comprised both of students and nonstudents, provides community educational programs about rape. The organization has been active on the University of Wisconsin campus for several years and is now taking its programming into high schools and middle schools. "We think it's necessary to reach men at a younger age," says group member George Marx.

At Haverford College near Philadelphia, students from a men's group called Dialogue About Men joined with female students to form Awareness, an organization that presents programs on acquaintance rape. However, Awareness members recognize the limitations to a program in which attendance is voluntary and whose subject matter makes many men uncomfortable. Sometimes, says Haverford graduate Erik Johnke, he felt as though he was preaching to the converted and missing the real target audience. "I think it reaches men who are predisposed to a feminist perspective," Johnke says. "We used to joke that we always wanted to get the rugby players [to attend a program] and we did get one guy. But it's difficult to get men to come to a discussion that's so threatening to them."

On occasion, men come to workshops and then become active in acquaintance-rape prevention groups when they recognize their own behavior being described. That's what happened to one man, a junior at the University of Southern California. "I want other people to be aware that this sort of thing can happen and that it happens a lot more than most people ever imagine," he told *Newsweek* magazine. "It just has to stop."

CHAPTER 12

Whose Responsibility Is It? Parents, Schools, Lawmakers, and Acquaintance Rape

"You have a responsibility to teach behavior to people."
— Father Randolph Chew, University of Rhode Island

The leading cause of acquaintance rape is blindness—obstinate blindness—to the forces that create the social acceptance of men raping women they know. The cure: educating boys and girls *before* they reach dating age and then reinforcing that education throughout the most rape-endangered years, ages 14 to 24.

But whose responsibility is it to provide that education? The two most likely candidates, families and schools, have repeatedly ducked the issue.

Parents, when they hear reports of date rape, acquaintance rape, and gang "party" rape, often react by saying:

- "Thank God I only have sons!"
- "My kid's friends would never do anything like that."
- "I know that my daughter is too smart to get raped."

Few recognize that acquaintance rape is as much a concern for the parents of boys as it is for those of girls, because it is boys who are doing the raping. (Moreover, parents of boys involved in acquaintance rape may be held partially liable in civil suits resulting from such attacks.) As to the other common parental reactions: People from all economic and cultural backgrounds commit acquaintance rape and are victims of it, and no female, however smart, is immune to being raped by someone she knows.

Educators show the same blindness. They will often say:

- "That's not a problem at our school."
- "We don't discuss it because it's bad for public relations."
- "We think that's a subject best dealt with by parents."

Educators choose to ignore the reality that acquaintance rape happens in junior highs, senior highs, and colleges across the country. Moreover, some school officials find it easier to punt the problem back to uninformed parents rather than risk calling attention to a possible negative situation in their own institutions. (Schools and colleges, like parents, may find themselves the targets of lawsuits stemming from acquaintance rapes [see Chapter 9, page 127]).

What Parents Can Do

Parents need to talk about sexual rights and responsibilities with their children, starting at an early age. These conversations should be buttressed with age-appropriate resource materials. (See Resources section, page 217.) In addition, according to researcher Andrea Parrot of Cornell University in Ithaca, New York, parents can help their children avoid involvement in acquaintance rape by attacking some of the contributing forces. She recommends that mothers behave assertively and fathers support that assertive behavior, that parents foster the child's positive self-image and encourage open communication about sex. By taking on nontraditional roles and jointly sharing household and child-care duties, parents can teach their children that every individual—female or male—is of equal importance and worth.

As children move into adolescence, parents should push for programming in junior high and high school sex education classes that addresses the problems of dating, encourages healthier sex roles, offers information about sexual violence, and teaches about date rape and acquaintance rape. Rape educators agree that parents need to talk about acquaintance rape in specific terms with teens. One good way to do this might be to share this book's information and true-life stories, as well as the prevention ideas found in Chapters 10 and 11. Single mothers may want the help of an adult male in talking about these issues with their sons (and vice versa for single fathers). Some parents may want to role-play with each other before talking to their teens. Parents who themselves were the victims of acquaintance rape may also want to talk to a counselor about their experiences before approaching their children.

Parents of every young person entering college need to talk with their child about the many new social choices and pressures the student will face. Drinking, drugs, sexual aggression, and rape are all problems young people may encounter. Parents and their children need to find out about the on-campus support services available should a potential problem or actual incident occur.

Parents of students mulling over which college to attend may also want to investigate what each school is doing to educate its students about rape and to keep them safe while on campus. In the wake of the 1986 rape and murder of their daughter, Jeanne Ann, by a fellow student in her Lehigh University dormitory room, Howard and Constance Clery of Bryn Mawr, Pennsylvania, have launched a campaign to make parents more aware of crimes committed on college campuses. The couple has created a security questionnaire parents can send to administrators of schools their children are considering (see Resources).

Ultimately, to help protect young people from acquaintance rape, parents must do nothing less than promote a new ideal of sex, says Py Bateman, a Seattle acquaintance-rape expert. That ideal is built on the concept of both people participating equally, freely, and with respect for each other. "If we achieve that mutuality of desire and eagerness, don't we derive great joy?" she says. "If we can promote this, not just at the level of intercourse, but also at the level of holding hands, mightn't we begin to tear down the preconditions [to acquaintance rape]? Mightn't it then become a totally incomprehensible idea that one person would force any kind of a sexual touch or a sexual activity on another?"

Why College Officials Resist Acquaintance-Rape Education

Although it's understandable that school authorities in some communities might be nervous about introducing acquaintance-rape awareness programs in junior high schools, it's downright mystifying why there should be so much administrative resistance at colleges and universities.

To begin with, most college administrators *know* that rape is a fact of campus life—at their schools and elsewhere. For proof, they need look no farther than the annual FBI Uniform Crime Reports, one section of which details crimes reported to police at 118 U.S. colleges and universities. At those schools in 1986, there were 246 reported rapes. Assuming conservatively that 75 percent of those rapes were acquaintance rapes, that means 185 acquaintance rapes were reported in that one year at those campuses.

However, the *Ms.* college-based study shows that only 5 percent of acquaintance rapes are reported—meaning that those 185 rapes represent only 5 percent of the real total. In other words, 3,700 acquaintance rapes *actually* occurred in 1986 at those 118 schools —an average of 31 per college.

Many believe that school administrators must accept their role in combating rape on campus. "I think any university, any college, has a responsibility to teach sexual responsibility to their students. You have a responsibility to teach behavior to people," says Father Randolph Chew, director of the Catholic Center at the University of Rhode Island. Susan Ervin-Tripp, a psychology professor at the University of California at Berkeley, agrees. "Colleges are the last chance that we have to educate young men and women about human relations, living together, competition, and fair play," she says.

Problems that surfaced as part of the *Ms.* national campus survey illustrate how resistant many college officials are even to an assessment of the problem on their campuses. More than 60 colleges, selected to span the nation, rejected requests to conduct the survey at their schools, despite the fact that anonymity for both the institutions and their students was guaranteed. Reasons for turning down the survey ranged from concerns about objections from parents, taxpayers, and "religious" students to one school's contention that its male students were highly intelligent and therefore not as likely to commit acquaintance rape as students of lesser ability at less prestigious schools. But behind much of the college administrators' concern was quite simply a fear of publicity.

Many colleges, fearing just such attention, won't allow acquaintance-rape workshops on campus, or limit the money and staffing for such programs, making them infrequent, toothless symposia that few students participate in. "To discuss sexual assault is to send a message to your potential student cohort that it is an unsafe campus, and therefore institutions tend to play that down," Henry Johnson, a vice-president for student services at the University of Michigan in Ann Arbor, told reporter Helen Zia of *Metropolitan Detroit* magazine in January 1985. "Rape is a red flag word—in many people's minds it conjures up something that's unsafe, that's to be suspect at best—a very bad environment to be in."

What Schools Can Do

"The problem on this campus is not rape in the dark. It's what's happening in the dorms and at fraternity parties," says Jan Harrow, coordinator of a commission on the status of women at the University of New Hampshire in Durham. "We've been lulled into complacency at this small, pastoral university." The school was shaken out of that complacency by a 1987 student gang rape, which resulted in two male students pleading guilty to sexual assault and being sentenced to 60 days in jail.

UNH took action about the rape following protests by angry students, faculty, and staff. Since then, according to Harrow, an administrative advisory board on sexual assault and rape has been established, an antirape staff member and a coordinator of Greek-system affairs have been hired, and a task force has been looking at how the university judicial board should deal with possibly criminal cases. In addition, the university president publicly condemned violence against women and a men's group began conducting programming to build rape awareness among male students. "Out of a really horrible crisis, we're trying to heal," Harrow says.

School administrators can learn from the UNH experience that it's better to take comprehensive action against acquaintance rape before it becomes a "horrible crisis" on their campuses too. Here is a checklist of things to do suggested by rape-awareness educators.

1. *Implement programs in junior and senior high schools.* Explore possible programs with rape-crisis centers, Planned Parenthood chapters, and adolescent counseling specialists. One example: A workshop on sexual assault protection/prevention is provided to students in junior high and senior high schools in Santa Barbara County, California, by the Santa Barbara Rape Crisis Center. The program emphasizes date rape and acquaintance rape. In just three years, more than 4,000 teens took part in the program, which is team-taught by male and female staff members and funded by the California Office of Criminal Justice. A similar program was recently developed by the Cleveland Rape Crisis Center. It includes exercises on sexual development, communication, and assertiveness.

2. *Improve college programs.* Even on campuses that have presented acquaintance-rape awareness programming at some time, the job is far from over. Each September, a new wave of first-year students arrives, bringing in a new load of myths about sex and rape, providing a fresh batch of candidates for the roles of victims and aggressors. And students who received rape education as freshmen need to have that information reinforced each year.

Education programs should be incorporated into freshman orientation workshops, with additional sessions for *all* students during the school year, particularly during the most dangerous period—from the first day of classes to Thanksgiving break.

3. *Establish an on-campus rape counseling and education group and finance it generously.* Encourage the group to use male and female students as well as staff members to lead workshops. Have the group train workshop leaders who are members of fraternities, sororities, and athletic teams. To get a successful program going, "you need a strong women's center and then you need faculty and staff who are going to fight for the bucks," says Mark Stevens, a psychologist who helped organize an acquaintance-rape program for men at Ohio State University and who now conducts workshops at the University of Southern California and elsewhere.

Put money into programs that are related to acquaintance-rape problems as well. For example, Lorraine Huckel, of the Counseling Center at the University of Rhode Island, suggests that workshops aimed at reducing underage drinking and alcohol abuse on campuses will also help reduce acquaintance rape.

4. *Distribute information on rape, rape treatment, and university procedures for dealing with offenders.* The University of Pennsylvania in Philadelphia publishes a 44-page "Safer Living Guide" that discusses acquaintance rape, provides safety tips for on and off campus, and explains how victims can get help. Vanderbilt University issues students at its Nashville campus a 20-page booklet, "Rape and Sexual Abuse: Prevention, Intervention, Resolution." And Baylor University in Waco, Texas, distributes a flier about acquaintance rape which details causes, risky situations, avoidance techniques, and what to do if attacked.

5. *Mandate acquaintance-rape programming for social clubs and athletic teams.* Fraternities, sororities, and other groups operating on campus should undergo rape-awareness training each year before being allowed to hold parties on college grounds.

6. *Establish university control of fraternities and sororities.* Outlaw "little sister" programs at fraternities because they offer too great a risk for exploitation. Consider reestablishing the requirement of having a "house parent" living on the premises in every fraternity and sorority house. Appoint a college administrator to watchdog the campus Greek system.

7. *Rethink dorm safety.* Many date rapes and acquaintance rapes have occurred in coed dorms. Campuses should provide at least the option of single-sex dormitories to their students. Coed dorms are best when organized by single-sex floors or halls, not when male and female students are placed in alternating rooms. (In the UNH gang rape, the men and woman involved all lived on the same dorm floor.) All dorms should have live-in supervision, residence-hall assistants should receive acquaintance-rape training every semester, and dorm residents should receive such training early in the school year. Take quick action against sexual offenders.

8. *Take a strong institutional stand against acquaintance rape, sexual assault, and harrassment.* Administrators need to make their views about acquaintance rape known—and forcefully. "Colleges should not just do the minimum necessary to avoid a lawsuit in these kinds of cases," says Berkeley's Ervin-Tripp. "To deal effectively with the problem, university officials must make clear that they are concerned about the moral environment on campus, that there are regulations governing student behavior, and that those regulations will be stringently enforced."

9. *Analyze college judicial board and police contact procedures.* Investigate how well the college judicial board can respond to cases of acquaintance rape and, if necessary, make reforms *before* the next attack is reported. Provide campus security personnel with acquaintance-rape awareness training. Determine how local police should be involved in crimes occurring on campus.

10. *Make self-defense and assertiveness training classes available on campus each semester.* Work with the college's rape counseling and education group to find courses that teach defense against both stranger rape and acquaintance rape.

College Programs That Work

Student actors dramatize dating conflicts before audiences of newly arrived freshmen at Glassboro State College in New Jersey; male basketball players sit around discussing myths about rape and sex at the College of Great Falls in Montana. Such programs aimed at reducing acquaintance rape are happening across the country. There are still not enough, but each year more schools and organizations are getting involved.

Many follow basic ground rules, such as those used at a session at the University of Pennsylvania: confidentiality (what is said in the workshop stays in the workshop) with an attack-free environment (respect for opinions, no interrupting). Then one of the group leaders (staff members from the housing office and counseling and women's centers) reads a series of statements and, after each one, the audience moves to stand in zones delineated as "agree," "disagree," or "don't know," according to their reactions. The statements range from, "If a man doesn't take advantage of the opportunity to have sex, he is a fool or a wimp," to, "If a woman allows herself to get high on alcohol or drugs or if she goes out with an 'animal,' she's setting herself up and deserves whatever she gets." Students then discuss why they picked the zones they are standing in. That exercise is followed by a student-made film about acquaintance rape, after which the audience breaks up into small discussion groups.

One of the nation's most comprehensive programs is found at the University of Florida in Gainesville. There, a group called Campus Organized Against Rape presents programs during classes as well as after hours. A key element to COAR's success is the involvement of male and female students as group leaders. "It requires real training," says Claire Walsh, program director of UF's Sexual Assault Recovery Service, which oversees COAR. Student volunteers receive 20 hours of training before they can lead a workshop. And Walsh insists that a professional counselor be present at every workshop session because "you're gonna have some victims in your audience." One workshop aimed at new students features the student-made film "Casting Shadows," which depicts an acquaintance-rape situation that could occur in the normal course of college life, followed by a discussion about some of the issues the movie raises. Other programs use a rape-myth quiz, a slide show of media images that contribute to sexual stereotypes, and discussions of body language and assertiveness in dating.

At Cornell University, acquaintance-rape expert Andrea Parrot and a male colleague conduct standing-room-only sessions to male and female students after dinner in large rooms near the college dining halls. "We market it very cleverly," Parrot says. "We don't call it an acquaintance-rape program. We call it 'Sex at 7:00—How to Get What You Want But Not More Than You Bargained For.' "

Featured in the Cornell program are student actors who portray "Mary" and "Dave," a couple who, after an expensive restaurant meal, return to Dave's fraternity house where Dave rapes Mary. Then the actors leave the stage and the audience discusses what has taken place. The actors are then brought back, staying in character, for the audience to ask them questions and make suggestions as to what could have been done to prevent the rape. ("The more conservative the group, the more often they give suggestions to Mary," Parrot says. "The more liberal, the more often to Dave.") Then the actors replay the same date scenario, but integrating the students' suggestions. "Mary" and "Dave" end up becoming friends and liking each other at the evening's end. "It models behavior for the audience that they can employ," Parrot says.

Students at Swarthmore College filmed two potential acquaintance-rape situations which are shown in sessions led by trained junior and senior students at the Swarthmore, Pennsylvania, school. Attendance at the workshops is mandatory for all first-year students and sessions are held in the first three weeks of the academic year. The Swarthmore-produced films are also used at the University of Michigan, where coed student teams lead workshops in dorms and classes. Before they take charge, the student leaders receive 40 hours of training.

The campus police department at Washington State University in Pullman, Washington, has successfully conducted a program titled, "When Sex Becomes a Crime," for several years now. The response to the program was so positive that the school's football coach decided to make it mandatory for his players.

Role playing is the main feature of the date-rape awareness workshops all freshmen must attend at Wesleyan University in Middletown, Connecticut. The workshops, conducted by the college's Sexual Assault Education Project, are also presented to fraternities and other groups. Wes*Safe, another campus organization, provides trained student sexual-assault counselors for education projects as well as for peer counseling.

The Rape Education and Prevention Program (REPP) at the Ohio State University in Columbus offers five-week self-defense programs that feature confrontational techniques to use in rape-threatening dating or party situations. REPP also presents about 160 rape-prevention workshops each year, mostly in residence halls. A special men's task force put together a program for men that looks at male socialization, expectations, and behaviors that support rape. REPP is also developing a program to focus on black women and their experiences with rape.

Sometimes schools get in gear only after an incident happens.

After a sophomore male at Dartmouth College in Hanover, New Hampshire, was charged in 1986 with raping a nonstudent visiting a female friend in a campus dormitory, more than 900 students gathered at a forum on rape awareness sponsored by the school's Women's Issues League and the Sexual Assault Coordinating Committee. During the year that followed, more than 30 workshops on acquaintance rape were held. Interest has been high. "We've gotten to the point where some of the workshops have more men than women. That's very unusual," says Diane Farley, Dartmouth's coordinator of sexual abuse awareness programs. "I'm used to having victims come up afterward, but now I'm also hearing a lot more from people who know offenders."

The University of Minnesota in Minneapolis is another campus where an alleged acquaintance-rape incident led to increased awareness education. After a highly publicized episode involving UM basketball players (see Chapter 7), the university set up a Sexual Violence Program that includes, among its services, one-hour mandatory lectures during freshman orientation. In the first year of operation, more than 6,200 students attended program workshops.

What Legislators Can Do

Lawmakers concerned about acquaintance rape can also help build awareness. They might follow the lead of California Assemblyman Tom Hayden, who recently proposed a state law requiring colleges and universities to establish clearly worded codes prohibiting rape and other forms of sexual battery by students, faculty, or staff. Hayden's bill requires the schools to set up penalties for rapists, to provide mandatory rape-awareness workshops for students, to maintain counseling centers on campuses, and to release data on all rapes to the public.

According to Hayden's administrative assistant, Judy Corbett, the legislator's concern was sparked in part by the 1986 gang acquaintance rape at Berkeley and was heightened by the findings of the *Ms.* survey. "It was clear that morally and legally the universities and colleges needed to do something," Corbett says. "University administrators have been very quiet." Several other lawmakers co-sponsored Hayden's bill, including many with University of California campuses in their districts.

The bill includes a section on establishing a college disciplinary process "based on the principles of due process and sensitivity and respect for the rights of the victims." Those rights include equal rights, with the man, in deciding whether hearings should be open or closed; the right to have a support person present; the right to be present for the entire hearing; the right to privacy about past sexual history; the right to an immediate hearing when the victim and accused live in the same dorm and the prompt relocation of either person.

Moreover, the bill charges university chief administrative officers to pursue disciplinary action even if the victim fails to file a formal complaint with the school or police. It also stipulates that anyone committing rape or standing by while it happens would forfeit scholarships or state funds.

Another state considering legislation is New York, where State Senator Kenneth P. LaValle is pushing for a law that would require colleges to educate students about rape, enforce sexual assault policies, and punish offenders. In Pennsylvania, legislators are also concerned. A law proposed there by Representative Richard A. McClatchy, Jr. (sparked by the anti-campus-crime crusade of parents Howard and Connie Clery) would require the state's colleges to provide prospective students with a brochure detailing campus crime statistics for the previous three years.

The Effects of Institutional Responsibility

Acquaintance rape is wrong and it is time for parents, educators, and lawmakers to combine their voices to get that message across.

By joining together some of the strongest forces our society has for setting and approving behavior, we can make it clear that sex and violence do not belong together, that sexual assault will not be condoned, that acquaintance-rape victims will receive help from their community, and that their attackers will be punished.

Through just such a united effort, acquaintance rape can end.

CHAPTER 13

Helping the Acquaintance-Rape Survivor

□ ───────────────────────────────── □

"Knowing how to help a person who's been raped is as important as knowing how to help a choking victim or someone who's drowning. It's basic first aid."

— rape counselor Cindi Kammer

She may be your roommate, friend, daughter, co-worker, lover, or student. Whatever your relationship, if you are the one a rape victim turns to, you should consider yourself lucky.

After a rape, there are few better sources of solace for the victim than good friends. In the stories women told about their experiences for this book, some friends—female and male—shone through. These friends provided immediate comfort and relief, ranging from holding the woman and letting her cry to giving her a safe place to sleep or taking her to a hospital emergency room and standing by during an examination for evidence of the assault. Later, some friends encouraged the women to seek counseling for the emotional aftereffects troubling them.

Perhaps the best support friends can provide in acquaintance-rape cases is the ability to help the woman correctly identify what has happened to her so she may take the first step toward recovery.

During the time just after her rape, when her family was being unsupportive, Vera called an old friend.

She was part of the same group of black kids who grew up together — the same group that both Steven and I were in. I broke down and began to tell her what happened. As soon as I said that Steven had taken me to his apartment, my friend said, "And he raped you. You are about the sixth girl that I know of that he's raped. He needs to have his pecker cut off."

Learning that information both helped and angered me. At least I knew I wasn't losing my mind and hadn't imagined being raped. She was the first person to offer any really tangible sympathy.

As the *Ms.* survey showed, nearly half of all females raped by men they knew told no one about the incident—not a friend, relative, or counselor. Only 5 perent reported the rape to police or college authorities. Instead, these women endured the aftereffects of rape in silence and attempted to rebuild their lives and psyches on their own. Those attempts, as seen in Chapter 5, are never easy and often not successful.

That's why understanding acquaintance rape and responding to a woman who has experienced it is so important. The reactions of the people around her and the support she receives soon after the assault may be critical to the woman's survival and recovery. "Knowing how to help a person who's been raped is as important as knowing how to help a choking victim or someone who's drowning," says Cindi Kammer, a rape counselor at Glassboro State College in New Jersey. "It's basic first aid." Yet most people are ill prepared to handle such a situation, despite the likelihood that one in four women they know will be attacked.

What to Do

Here are 14 guidelines that counseling experts advise for helping someone you know recover from acquaintance rape.

1. *Believe her.* The greatest fear of acquaintance-rape survivors is that they will not be believed, or that their experience will be minimized as "not important." If you've read the rest of this book, you know that women are raped by men they know *four times more often* than they are by strangers. Accept what you are hearing—

even if the man involved is a popular, desirable guy, even if the woman appears confused and unable to put her thoughts together clearly. She is in shock. She may also seem calm and collected, behavior that may seem inappropriate in someone who has just been raped. Both extremes are possible (and normal) reactions.

Attempted rape is often as traumatic as completed rape. Although the woman may have foiled the rape or the man may have been unable to penetrate her, the aftereffects of the experience may be severe. Treat the victim of attempted rape with the same care as the victim of completed rape.

2. *Listen.* Find somewhere to be alone with the woman and just let her talk. She may not begin in a rush of words, so be patient. Let her know that listening to her is more important than anything else she may think you want to do. Let her tell the story at her own speed.

3. *Comfort her.* Try to calm her down if she's agitated, but do so in a soothing—not disapproving—way. She may want to be held while she cries or may not want to be touched. Offer tea, cocoa, soup, a blanket, a stuffed animal. One date-rape victim recalls her friend giving her a flannel nightgown. These suggestions all give the woman a warm, secure feeling in sharp contrast to what she has just experienced.

4. *Reinforce that the rape was not her fault.* Avoid questions that seem to blame her for her actions, such as, "Why didn't you scream?" and "Why did you go to his room?" Allow her to talk out her feelings of self-blame if she wants to, but make her see that the rapist caused the rape, not her.

5. *Provide protection.* Give her a secure place to sleep and companionship once she returns to her own living quarters. If she lives alone, strongly recommend that you stay with her for at least one night.

6. *Suggest calling a rape-crisis center.* This does not mean that the woman must report the rape to police. A rape-crisis center will provide a trained worker to guide the survivor (and her friend) through the next critical hours. All calls to rape-crisis hot lines are

confidential. To find one in your community, look under "Rape" in the white pages of the telephone directory. This is an important step to take even if the woman has not yet attached the word "rape" to her experience.

7. *Encourage her to preserve evidence.* The sooner an acquaintance rape is reported, the better the likelihood of charges being filed and the offender being convicted. However, because so many women fail to recognize their experience as rape until days, weeks, months, and even years later, vital evidence is lost. Call a rape-crisis hot line and get information about having the woman undergo a post-rape examination *before* she washes her hands, face, and body or brushes her teeth. During an official rape exam in a hospital, specimens will be taken from her to find traces of blood, hair, saliva, and semen from the rapist, so it's important that nothing be washed away. The woman may change her clothes if she puts all the clothing she was wearing during the assault in paper bags (a separate bag for each article so specimens don't become contaminated).

8. *Treat her medical needs.* She may have bruises, cuts, or other injuries. Even if she appears unhurt, encourage her to get medical attention. She should receive treatment because the rapist may have had a sexually transmitted disease or she might become pregnant from the rape. Go with her to the hospital, clinic, or doctor's office and stay during the examination if she wants.

9. *Help her organize her thoughts, but let her make decisions about how to proceed.* The acquaintance-rape survivor needs to regain the feeling of being in control. Allow her to do that. Parents of a raped teenager may want to press charges, but that might not be the best choice for their child. Likewise, friends of an older woman might want to arrest the man involved. Try to separate how you feel about what has happened from what is best for the woman's recovery. If she decides not to report it and you disagree with that, let her know that you support her decision nonetheless.

10. *If you are her lover, with her approval, use appropriate touching and language to reestablish her feelings of worth.* Gentle touching will help her understand that your connection with her is unbroken, that you do not consider her "dirty." Let her decide when

sexual activity and intercourse should begin again. Don't pressure her out of the belief that you need to prove everything is "normal" between you. Some victims have sex again before they're ready just to allay partners' fears about becoming sexual again.

11. *Help her get psychological and legal help.* In the immediate aftermath of acquaintance rape, the survivor may not be able to seek out sources for help. Do the legwork for her. Drive her to appointments or baby-sit or provide other help so she can meet with lawyers, police, and counselors.

12. *Be available.* In the weeks and months following the rape, reassure the woman that she can turn to you whenever she needs to. Then, when she does, give her your time and attention.

13. *Learn about rape-trauma syndrome.* Your friend's recovery period will last a long time, during which her moods and reactions may change radically from one day to the next. Read Chapter 5 of this book and other material about rape recovery so that you'll know what to expect. Share this material with the woman who has been raped.

14. *Get help for yourself.* You need to talk with someone other than the acquaintance-rape survivor to discuss your feelings about the attack and its aftermath. A rape-crisis center, women's center, or university counseling center will be able to suggest someone who can help you.

CHAPTER 14

What to Do if Acquaintance Rape Happens to You

Most women know what to do after they've been raped by a stranger—they call for help immediately. Yet when women are raped by a man they know, they often cannot react as clearly.

The following are suggestions from rape counselors and recovered women about how to proceed after you have survived a date-rape or acquaintance-rape attack.

1. *Believe in yourself.* If you were forced to have sexual intercourse against your will, what happened to you was wrong, regardless of whether you were dating the man who attacked you or you were former lovers, longtime friends, casual acquaintances, or strangers to each other. It was rape even if he didn't use a weapon and you weren't physically hurt.

You may be blaming yourself for what happened, thinking the rape was your fault. It was not. Your rape happened because the man who attacked you decided to do so. Even if you did something you now consider foolish (got drunk, accepted a ride, went to a man's apartment), that action does not mean you deserved to be raped. *No one* deserves to be raped.

185

2. *Tell someone.* You may want to hide the whole episode as deep inside as possible in an attempt to forget it. Don't. Call someone immediately whom you trust—a close friend, a sister or parent, a counselor or adviser—and go to that person's home. Tell them what happened. Before you change your clothes or wash, call your local rape-crisis hot line or women's center (look under "Rape" in the telephone directory). They will send someone to talk with you and help you through the difficult hours ahead. If you must change your clothing, put each piece in a separate paper bag for possible later use as evidence.

3. *Get medical help.* You should be checked by a doctor immediately following your rape. Have your friend or other support person go with you to the hospital, student health center, or doctor's office and stay with you during the examination. You need to be checked for the possibility of pregnancy or sexually transmitted diseases as well as receive treatment for any injuries you may have suffered. You also might agree to be examined for rape evidence.

4. *Decide whether you want to report the rape to police or other authorities.* Reporting any rape to police or university security personnel can be a frightening ordeal. Usually, you will have to recount what happened, often in graphic detail, and undergo a medical exam that looks for rape evidence (semen, saliva, blood, hair) in, among other places, your genital area, anus, and mouth.

Police and prosecutors may question you closely about the rape and they may be openly skeptical of what you say (see Chapter 8). Should they decide to press criminal charges against the man who raped you, you will have to repeat your testimony several times, including in court. The defense will probably argue that you willingly agreed to have sex with the rapist. He may be found not guilty, he may plea-bargain to a lesser charge, or he may receive a sentence that to you seems inadequate for the crime: All of these are possibilities. Of course, he may also be judged guilty and handed an appropriate punishment.

If so many negatives could happen, why should you report an acquaintance rape? It is a decision only you can make. However, there are some good arguments in favor of reporting: to bring your attacker to justice, to punish him, to stop him from attacking again.

Filing criminal charges gives some women a sense of empowerment in a situation in which they have felt helpless. Some feel avenged by the man's arrest and conviction. But arresting a rapist can also provide you (and other women) with immediate protection. Since legal precedent is still being set in acquaintance-rape cases, you may also be helping women in future cases by prosecuting your own. In addition, in states which offer financial restitution and compensation to crime victims, you must file criminal charges to be eligible for those payments.

It's possible to report an acquaintance rape without pressing charges. In many communities, this is done by filing an incident report through the local rape-crisis center. This information goes into a general police data clearinghouse. The victim usually remains anonymous in these reports, but the rapist is named. If he is picked up later on another charge, the police then know a prior complaint has been made against him and it can help buttress their case. Colleges and universities often have their own version of this system, which allows the woman to report the man without filing formal charges.

5. *Take time to recover.* Find a place to stay for a few days where you feel secure. Take several days off from your job or school. Returning to "normal" activities as quickly as possible may be comforting, but realize that you will probably have a wide range of emotions—from fear to anger to depression to guilt—over the next few weeks and months, so proceed cautiously.

6. *Get counseling.* The process of recovering from rape takes time and you can help that process by receiving good mental health support. You need to talk with a trained counselor about what happened and how it affects your life. Inquire through a rape-crisis group, campus counseling center, or your doctor about finding someone to talk to. As Georgette said about the counseling that helped her recovery: "All the space that guilt occupied has been filled with anger and outrage. I know it wasn't my fault, but his. I also know I'll never be able to completely let go of my experience. It touched me too deeply and changed me too much."

You may also want to join a group counseling session with other rape survivors. "I was in a support group," says Donna, who also survived acquaintance rape, "and that was a positive for me. I'm at a point now where I'm doing very, very well."

7. *Learn more about acquaintance rape.* When the immediacy of your situation has passed, you may want to read the rest of this book to gain a fuller understanding of the phenomenon of acquaintance rape. There are also other good materials listed in the Resources section. The more you know about date rape and acquaintance rape, the better you'll be able to deal with your own experience.

8. *Strengthen yourself.* Study the avoidance strategies detailed in Chapter 10. Sign up for a self-defense or assertiveness training course in your hometown. These classes are offered by a wide range of groups, from antirape organizations to YWCAs to police departments.

9. *Talk with other women.* You can help get the word out about acquaintance rape by talking one to one with your friends, by advocating rape education programs in your school or through your club, and by building awareness among women who influence young people (mothers, teachers, coaches, social workers, organization sponsors, religious and community leaders). And you can help by talking with other women who have been raped by an acquaintance—help them to understand what happened, what to do, and how to carry on.

AFTERWORD

The Methods Used in the *Ms.* Project on Campus Sexual Assault

Mary P. Koss, Ph.D.

The study described in this book, known as the *Ms.* Magazine Campus Project on Sexual Assault, was funded by the Center for Antisocial and Violent Behavior of the National Institute of Mental Health. Conceived and conducted as a scientific study, the project completed data collection in 1985. Technically trained readers will want to consult the citations to the professional literature given at the end of this section for detailed descriptions of methodology, data analysis, and results.

Why Was the Study Done?

In 1976 when I started my research career, I chose the words "hidden rape" to describe what I wanted to study. In those days the expression "date rape" had not been invented nor was there any convincing evidence that rape or rapelike behavior occurred among "normal" people. However, many justice authorities believed that rapes, particularly those involving intimate acquaintances, were the most underreported of major crimes. Official crime statistics do not adequately reflect rape among intimates, rapes not labeled by the victim as crime, and lesser but still upsetting forms of sexual victimization. College students were selected to be the focus of my work simply because "they were there." As it turns out, this "decision" to use college students was fortuitous because the college years happen to coincide with the greatest period of risk for rape.

I first obtained federal funding in 1978 to attempt a scientific survey of sexual aggression and victimization among 4,000 students at Kent State University in Ohio. The project was finished in 1982 (see Koss and Oros, 1982; Koss, 1985) and was described in a *Ms.* article on date rape among college students, the first national magazine article to address this issue. *Ms.* was convinced that date rape existed and was a serious problem. To ensure that results similar to the Ohio data would be obtained in other parts of the country, however, a national study was needed. The idea of working together was raised by the *Ms.* editors and grew out of their interest in the subject, their contacts on college campuses, and their commitment to change. Planning for the national study occurred during most of 1983 at the *Ms.* offices in New York City, and it was there that a team of experts from the National Institute of Mental Health made a site visit to review the ideas and people who would work on the proposed survey. Their major concerns were that the conduct of the survey be scientific, not politicized or sensational; and that respondents be a representative sample of *all* students, not just of students at schools where *Ms.* personnel had connections (which could tend to be liberal or elite East Coast schools).

To overcome these concerns, a division of labor was created. A private company, Clark/Jones, Inc., of Columbus, Ohio, was hired to design a plan for choosing a group of schools that would fairly represent the diversity of higher education settings and students. *Ms.* personnel took over all administrative work such as making contact with the schools, persuading them to give us permission to collect data, and facilitating the on-campus arrangements for the data collectors. I was responsible for all scientific decisions including the questions to ask, procedures to use to collect the information, and the analysis and interpretation of the results. Based upon these plans, $267,500 was awarded to carry out the survey. Although this sounds like a lot of money, it is actually rock-bottom for a project that took three years to complete, was nationwide in scope, involved 22 technically trained personnel, reached 32 different locations from coast to coast, and obtained 71 pages of information from 6,159 participants.

The Methods Used in the Study

The goals of the *Ms.* Project on Campus Sexual Assault were the following: (1) to learn how much sexual aggression and victimization, up to and including acts of rape, is occurring among college students today; (2) to gather details about actual incidents; (3) to describe the men who commit sexually aggressive acts; (4) to study the women who have been victimized; and (5) to measure the psychological difficulties, if any, that result from sexual victimization. Although five papers describing the results of the project have been published in professional journals, work is still ongoing.

Initial Decisions

In this study women were only looked at as victims and men as perpetrators of violence. This was done for a number of reasons. The FBI definition of rape limits the crime of rape to female victims by stating, "rape is carnal knowledge of a *female*. . . ." Virtually 100 percent of reported rapes involve female victims. Many of the definitions of rape used by the states are sex neutral. For example, Ohio's definition begins, "Rape is penetration of the victim by the offender. . . ." (Ohio Revised Code, 1980). However, this neutrality was introduced to allow prosecution as rape of forced anal penetration of one man by another man. Under a sex neutral definition of rape, a woman could rape a man but this would involve acts such as a group of women forcibly holding a man down while they use carrots to penetrate him anally. This is not usually what people have in mind. Rather, they think that it would be rape if a woman told a man, "Have sex with me or I'll spread it around that you're impotent." Such conduct is not very ethical no matter whether a woman or a man does it. But it is not rape because it doesn't involve force or threat of bodily harm and because it doesn't involve penetration of the victim by the offender. Such an act would be penetration of the offender by the victim!

Another decision involved which students to include in the survey. Ideally I sought a scientifically representative sample of the higher education student population in the United States in all its diversity—males, females, technical schools, community colleges, Ivy League schools, state universities, and so forth. This decision meant using as potential sites all the institutions of academic post-secondary education in the United States and administrating the survey in person. People who respond to sex surveys through the mail may not be typical. On-site administration in classrooms produces higher participation rates among those students asked to complete the survey. It also allows for a trained person to mediate if a student becomes upset by the questions. Finally, the sample had to be drawn from the diversity of offerings within each institution to ensure that certain instructors would not prefer (or ignore) us and bias the findings. These requirements dictated that the sample be selected in stages. The first stage was the selection of schools. The second stage was the selection of classes within schools.

How the Schools Were Chosen

The United States Department of Education (Office of Civil Rights) maintains records of the enrollment characteristics from 3,269 institutions of higher education in the United States. This office provided a copy of their data for 1980 (the latest available at the time) on computer tape to the survey consultants, Clark/Jones, Inc., of Columbus, Ohio. Using this information, schools were sorted into groups that consisted only of those schools similar to each other in five ways:

1. Location in or outside of a Standard Metropolitan Statistical Area (SMSA) of a certain size. Schools were classified according to whether they were in a city or its surrounding area with more than one million people, in a city and its surrounding area of less than one million people, or whether the school was located in a rural area.

2. Enrollment above or below the national average for percentage of minority students.

3. Control of the institution by private but not religious authority, private religious authority, or public authority.

4. Type of institution including university, other four-year college, and two-year institutions.

5. Location in one of the 10 U.S. Department of Education regions of the United States.

6. Total enrollment within three levels of approximately equal numbers of students The sizes we used were 1,000–2,499 students, 2,500–9,999 students, and schools larger than 10,000 students.

Using these criteria, the schools of the entire nation were divided by region into small groups. Each small group consisted only of schools with similar locations, minority percentage, type of control, level of study, and size. The schools that were asked to participate in the study were selected "randomly" from among the small groups. Think of each of these groups as a separate jar of lottery numbers. "Random" selection is like reaching into each jar while blindfolded. The number of schools that were taken from each small group depended on the total number of students who attended that particular type of school as a proportion of the entire national enrollment. If the original school proved uncooperative, replacements were selected from the same small group. Thus, the final schools that participated were the result of an interplay of scientific selection and head-to-head negotiation but within the limits of substitution rules requiring replacement from a homogeneous group.

Several exceptions to the sampling rules were made for the sake of reasonableness and cost constraint. First, military schools were omitted because it was felt that the type of information sought might place students in conflict with their military code. Also, previous experience had suggested that permission to do research perceived as sexual was very difficult or impossible to obtain from military personnel. Second, schools with enrollments under 1,000 were eliminated. There are approximately 1,000 such schools in the United States and I could not afford the expense of traveling to them for only a small number of survey responses. Third, schools in Alaska, Hawaii, and Puerto Rico were also eliminated because of budget limitations. Finally, graduate schools were eliminated because postgraduate students were not the focus of the project.

Why It Took Three Years to Finish

To obtain permission to administer the survey at a particular school, members of the *Ms.* staff began by identifying the responsible individual in the central administration, often the Dean of Student Affairs. This individual was first contacted by telephone and the initial call was followed up with a package of information sent through the mail. Most administrators were unwilling to make a personal decision about participation. In virtually every case, the proposed project was placed before committees for decision. To enhance cooperation, letters of support were obtained from the directors of education of the major religious denominations and from women clergy who work in the area of sexual abuse. In addition, personal campus visits were made by the staff of *Ms.* magazine, and members of the *Ms.* board of consultants intervened personally when possible. When a campus had a women's studies program, the assistance of the director was solicited. If and when the administrator said yes, a signed "permission for institutional access" form was obtained.

Documents were then submitted to each school's human subjects review board. Scientific research that involves people cannot be conducted without a thorough review to insure that participation will be voluntary and that every possible precaution has been taken to protect people from unnecessary suffering or harm. Most insitutions felt that the subject matter of this survey was controversial and required a full review. Often two or more meetings of the board were required to satisfy all objections. A number of schools flatly refused because of beliefs, which no amount of evidence from past experience with studies of college students could shake, that participants would be harmed psychologically by responding to the survey. In addition to these problems, the large number of vacation breaks in the academic calendar meant that almost one and a half years was the amount of time required to obtain a decision from some of the institutions.

In all, 93 schools were contacted and 32 agreed to allow the survey. Nineteen of the institutions were first choices; the remaining 13 were solicited from among 60 replacements. The actual institutional participants cannot be listed because they were guaranteed anonymity. However, the number of schools within each region was as follows: New England 2; Mideast, 5; Great Lakes, 7; Plains, 3; Southeast, 7; Southwest, 4; Rocky Mountains, 1; West, 3. It might be argued that the resulting sample would be biased toward those schools with a "liberal" administration. However, this did not prove to be the case. Some schools with the most liberal reputations in the nation refused while others with a presumed conservative bias cooperated. The excuses given by the 61 administrators for refusing to participate were the following (the number of times each excuse was used is indicated in parentheses): religious objections (11); concerns about subject anonymity (2); concerns about sensationalization of the results (3); concerns that people would be harmed by participation (10); lack of interest in the topic (13); no research allowed in classes (6); doing their own survey (3); would not give a reason (13). The final sample was as scientific a sample of postsecondary institutions in the United States as it was possible to obtain within time and budgetary limitations and given the nature of the inquiry.

Choosing the Classes

From each participating school a class schedule was obtained. From that class schedule, a random selection process was used to choose the classes to be visited and alternates in the case of schedule conflicts or refusals. The only limitations on class selection were that classes under 30 students and large lecture sections were eliminated. These limitations were necessary to insure that one experimenter's time on a campus was used efficiently while avoiding classes that were too large for one person to handle. The actual number of classes visited was 7 at smaller and medium-sized schools and 12 at major universities. Instructors of the targeted classes were contacted by telephone and were mailed information about the survey in advance. Instructors were asked for permission to administer the survey during a specific class period. They were further requested to tell the students nothing about the project and not to be present during the administration. We preferred to have our trained data collectors give all participants the same description of the survey rather than have instructors explain it in their individual ways. Furthermore, the instructor's presence might have made students feel that they had to participate.

How the Survey Was Distributed

The survey was administered in classroom settings by 1 of 7 clinical psychologists who participated in the project, including 2 men and 5 women. These people traveled around the country administering the surveys between November 1984 and March 1985. All the data collectors were trained to follow the same procedures, to anticipate potential problems that might arise, and to assist students who became upset while answering the questions. Surveys were distributed to students who were asked not to open them until the directions were given. Data collectors had memorized a prepared script so that they could give directions to everyone in the same way.

The first page of the survey contained all the information necessary to insure that people were participating voluntarily and understood the risks and benefits of answering the questions. Thus students read (and were told orally by the data collector) that they did not have to fill out the survey if they did not want to, that they could skip questions, that the language was explicit and would possibly offend some people, and that the focus of the questions was intimate sexual experiences involving coercion. Students were not asked to sign their names on the survey to ensure anonymity. Surveys from each school were kept in a separate box with no identifying code marks.

Students who did not wish to participate in the survey were asked to remain at their desks and do other work. This step was taken so that people who objected to the survey would not be embarrassed by having to stand up and walk out of the room. Virtually all the students in the selected classes were willing to complete the survey. Only 91 persons (1.5 percent) declined, making the participation rate 98.5 percent.

After all students had completed the survey, the data collector explained its purpose and offered to answer any questions. All students were also given a sheet that indicated where the experimenter would be available for a private conference and contained phone numbers of local agencies who had agreed to answer questions or to offer services to participants. The college counseling center of every campus was informed of the project and invited to list a sexual assault specialist on the sheet and/or to send observers to the classes if desired. Very few problems with participants were encountered and only a handful of students showed up to ask questions privately.

The Students Who Participated

The *Ms.* Project on Campus Sexual Assault had 6,159 responses, including 3,187 women and 2,972 men students. The women participants were characterized as follows: Their average age was 21.4 years old; 85 percent were single, 11 percent were married, and 4 percent were divorced; 86 percent were white, 7 percent were black, 3 percent were Hispanic, 3 percent were Asian, and 1 percent were Native American; and 39 percent were Catholic, 38 percent were Protestant, 4 percent were Jewish, and 20 percent belonged to a religion that was not listed or had no religious affiliation. The 2,972 male participants were characterized as follows: Their average age was 21.0 years old; 87 percent were single, 9 percent were married, 1 percent were divorced; 86 percent were white, 6 percent were black, 3 percent were Hispanic, 4 percent were Asian, and 1 percent were Native American; and 40 percent were Catholic, 34 percent were Protestant, 5 percent were Jewish, and 22 percent belonged to a religion that was not listed or had no religious affiliation. For both male and female students, the typical family income was between $25,000 and $35,000

How do they compare to all of the students in the United States? Four characteristics were looked at: institution location, institution region, student ethnicity, and student family income. Because of the assumptions on which the sampling plan was based and hesitancy on the part of some schools to participate, the sample is not absolutely representative. However, within the limitations of our assumptions, it is a close approximation of the higher education enrollment (see Koss, Gidycz, & Wisniewski, 1987). As is true of this enrollment for the entire United States, a large proportion of participants were 18 to 24 years old, white, and from middle-class homes.

The region in which the institutions were located was the only variable on which significant discrepancy was noted. The present sample somewhat overrepresented the proportion of students enrolled in the Northeast and Southwest and underrepresented students enrolled in the West. These discrepancies reflected irremediable difficulties in obtaining cooperation in some locations. For example, in the West, 12 institutions were approached and a personal visit was made by a member of the *Ms.* staff, the efforts of the affirmative action director of the California State University System were enlisted, a prominent member of the clergy made personal calls to several private schools, calls were made by the principal investigator to the women's studies directors at target schools, and special re-reviews were obtained at two major California universities. In spite of these efforts, only 3 institutions agreed to allow data collection. In order that the success of the entire project not be jeopardized, I decided to proceed with data collection without full representation from West Coast schools. The regional disproportion is unimportant in many respects since even without extensive sampling in the West, the individual participants in the sample were still reflective of national enrollment in terms of ethnicity and family income. Nevertheless, weighting factors were developed, but comparison of weighted and unweighted data indicated that the effect of weighting was small (see Koss, Gidycz, & Wisniewski, 1987).

Did People Tell the Truth on the Survey?

Some scientists question the truthfulness of people's descriptions of their own sexual behavior. Perhaps some persons exaggerate their sexual experience to enjoy a "fantasy trip." Other people may deny acts they have done but realize are wrong. Thus, there are concerns that some people would overstate and some people understate the truth. It is hard to think of a method to obtain objective information about people's sexual lives. A major alternative to getting information by self-report is to use a private interview. But this method, too, depends on truthfulness of the respondent. Serious problems have been encountered in studies employing an interview format for studies of sexual behavior among high school and college students. Typical problems have been that people refused to be interviewed or, once present, were reluctant to talk about sexual behavior. If people's own descriptions of their sexual behavior could be shown to be truthful and accurate, then it might be a better approach than interviews on sexual topics.

I have done several studies to examine the truthfulness of self-reported sexual behavior. In one study about sexual aggression and victimization, ten questions about sexual behavior involving coercion and force were administered to people on two separate occasions one week apart. Virtually all responses were identical on the two occasions. In a second study, these same questions were given to several classes of Kent State University students. Then, 1 to 4 months later, the questions were re-administered to each student privately by an interviewer of the same sex as the respondent. Among the 68 rape victims who were studied, only 2 changed their responses or were believed to have misunderstood the question (see Koss & Gidycz, 1985). In a third study, a male interviewer recruited 15 male students with demographic characteristics similar to the makeup of the national sample. All of these men responded to a survey about their sexual experiences first. Then they were interviewed individually. The interview questions included items pertaining to participants' sexual history both before and after the age of 14. The intent of these questions was to match the participants' verbal responses with their survey responses. It was found that 14 of the participants (93 percent) gave the same responses about their adult sexual behavior on self-report and in interview. The one inconsistency involved an individual who admitted a behavior on self-report which he later denied to the interviewer. The same rate of agreement (93 percent) was found between interview and self-report of sexual experiences before the age of 14. The one instance of inconsistency involved a different man who indicated on self-report that he had had intercourse before the age of 14, whereas in his conversations with the interviewer he indicated that he had not achieved full penetration. On average, subjects rated their honesty as 95 percent and indicated that the reason for lack of full honesty was time pressures getting through the questionnaire (see Risin & Koss, 1987). Thus, the accuracy and truthfulness of responses to the survey probably are not markedly different from the accuracy that would have been obtained if the same questions had been administered by an interviewer.

How Were the Questions Chosen?

The five goals of the *Ms.* project required the review of a large number and range of questions. Some were chosen to uncover the amount of sexual aggression and to obtain concrete details about the incidents. Other questions were directed at understanding "why" such things happen. Three bodies of writing were reviewed to guide the selecton of "why" questions.

People who write surveys use the questions they think are the most important to know. Since time is nearly always limited, one has to make decisions and leave some desirable questions out. You simply can't make up a survey that's neutral. A judgment that a certain question is important can usually be traced back to the theory the researcher has about why certain people do various things.

CAUSES OF SEXUAL AGGRESSION: Until recently, research on rapists was guided by a confusing array of theories with different focuses. For example, some researchers held theories that rape was caused by some form of mental illness, others believed that rapists were hostile toward women, while a third group assumed that rapists had deviant sexual arousal because they derived sexual pleasure in spite of another person resisting and suffering. Now papers are beginning to appear that attempt to integrate various sources of information (see Malamuth, 1986; Koss & Dinero, in press).

Integrative models of rape have been stimulated by Finkelhor's (1979) thoughts about the causes of child abuse. He suggests that before a man will commit sexual violence: (1) Rape must be consistent with the perpetrator's beliefs about right and wrong; (2) sexual arousal must occur even though the woman is saying no, struggling and resisting; (3) obstacles must exist that make the man feel deprived of the number of sexual outlets he believes he needs; (4) something must happen that allows behavior that is typically kept in check to come out such as occurs when people drink alcohol; and (5) a private setting must be found and the victim's resistance must be overcome. This is the set of beliefs about sexual aggression that guided the selection of the questions that were given to men.

RISK FACTORS FOR RAPE: Many researchers mention at least briefly the possibility that there may be victim variables that heighten particular women's vulnerability to rape (e.g., Amir, 1971; Selkin, 1978; Myers, Templer, & Brown, 1984) or diminish the ability of some women to resist effectively (e.g., Russell, 1984). Some of these studies, particularly in the former group, have provoked published charges of scientific inadequacy and insensitivity to the potential harm of reinforcing already existing predispositions to blame the victim (e.g., Wieder, 1985). Although it is tempting to spend a lot of time criticizing these ideas, the best revenge is to make the ideas prove themselves.

The choice of questions about risk factors that could increase vulnerability to rape was guided by three different sets of ideas that are evident in professional writing on rape victims. The first idea, called *psychological vulnerability* (e.g., Meyers, Templer, & Brown, 1984) suggests that rape victims may have certain personality characteristics such as passivity that knowingly or unknowingly raise their chances of being selected as a rape victim or lower their chances of resisting effectively. Women who oversubscribe to traditional notions of femininity and accept common myths about rape are uniquely vulnerable to victimization (e.g., Weis & Borges, 1973). These women are predicted to act passively toward men, to expect men to be dominant and forceful, and to be slow to realize that an interaction is progressing toward rape. The second idea, which is called *traumatic experiences,* suggests that women who have been victimized during an earlier life period may be at greater risk for rape. Finally, certain environments, called *risky situations,* have been viewed as increasing the likelihood that a rape could occur. These are the ideas that guided selection of questions regarding risk factors for rape.

THE IMPACT OF RAPE: Four categories of posttraumatic symptoms have been explored in published research on reactions to rape: anxiety/fears, depression, social adjustment, and sexual functioning. (For extensive reviews of this information, see Holmes & St. Lawrence, 1983; Ellis, 1983.) A number of things may heighten or lessen the symptomatic response to rape including crime characteristics such as the nature of the sex acts involved, whether a weapon was used, and relationship between victim and offender. The amount of support and help provided by friends and family and the psychological health of the victim before the rape may also have an impact on the severity of post-rape experiences. Thus, questions and standard psychological tests relevant to each of these influences and mitigating circumstances were included in the national survey.

The Contents of the Survey

The survey was titled, "National Survey of Inter-Gender Relationships," a title intentionally selected to be neutral and to avoid the word "sex" so that participants did not prejudge the content of the survey before explanations were given. The 71-page survey consisted of over 300 questions divided into eight sections. However, not everyone filled out all the sections. Those people who have *not* been involved in any degree of sexual aggression or victimization skipped the sections about those experiences. The specific content of the questionnaire was as follows.

SECTION A: This section contained questions regarding the participant's demographic characteristics such as age, ethnic group, family income, and religious affiliation.

SECTION B: This section contained questions regarding the participant's upbringing and current values and habits. Included were questions regarding early family stability, parental strictness, family violence, delinquent involvements, history of psychological disturbance as reflected by suicide attempts and psychotherapeutic treatment, drinking and other drug use habits, magazine readership including pornographic magazines, participation in sexually oriented discussions of women, sexual values, number of sexual partners, current satisfaction with several forms of sexual intimacy, and the perceived quality of the respondent's relationships with people.

SECTION C: This section contained the ten-question Sexual Experiences Survey used in much of my earlier research on college students (see Koss & Oros, 1982; Koss & Gidycz, 1985; Koss, Gidycz, & Wisniewski, 1987). These questions inquire about various degrees of sexual aggression and victimization obtained by the offender against the consent of the victim through the use of coercion, threats of bodily harm, and actual violence.

SECTION D: This section contained questions that explore the most serious level of sexual aggression the individual reported. If more than one instance of sexual violence had occurred, the respondent was asked to focus on the one that is best remembered. Questions included the number of perpetrators, relationship between victim and offender, degree of acquaintance, prior intimacy they had shared, location of the assault, drinking or drugs involved, the social situation surrounding the assault, the emotions experienced at the time, the types of force used by the man, forms of resistance used by the woman, and what happened afterward including who was told, how they reacted, how they labeled the experience, and whether it is expected to happen again.

SECTION E: This section contained different psychological measures for men and women. For men, the primary goal was to include psychological measures to predict sexual aggression. Thus, male respondents were administered the 28 items of the short form MMPI Psychopathic Deviate Scale (Graham, 1977, p. 247). In addition, male respondents were asked to answer the 30-item Hostility Toward Woman Scale (Check, 1984; Check & Malamuth, 1983).

For female participants, the major goal toward which standardized psychological tests were directed was to examine the impact of sexual victimization. Because depression and rape-related anxiety are two major aftereffects of sexual victimization (Ellis, 1983), women were asked to respond to the Beck Depression Inventory (Beck, Ward, Mendelson, Mock, & Erbaugh, 1961) and the State-Trait Anxiety Inventory (Spielberger, Gorsuch, & Luschene, 1970). The Beck Depression Inventory consists of 21 items which are believed to reflect symptoms and attitudes of depression. The Trait Anxiety Scale consists of 20 items. Trait anxiety refers to relatively stable differences between people in the extent to which they experience symptoms related to anxiety.

SECTION F: This section contained questions about sexually abusive experiences before the age of 14. The questions were slightly modified from Finkelhor's (1979) survey of college students. Typical of the questions is the following: "Have you had any of the following experiences before age 14? You touched or stroked another person's sex organs at his or her request?" The remaining items in the section request more detailed information about the childhood sexual experience. If they had more than one experience, respondents were asked to refer to the most serious one in answering the questions. The questions covered the age of victim, age of perpetrator, relationship between victim and perpetrator, how many times the sexual act occurred, the reason the victim participated, who was told, how they reacted, emotions the victim experienced at the time, and the degree to which the person felt victimized by the experience.

SECTION G: This section contained the 36 items developed by Burt (1980) to measure the extent to which an individual endorses a set of beliefs that could increase the likelihood of sexual violence. Included in these beliefs are false ideas about rape that could allow sexual violence to occur and to be rationalized away as seduction afterward.

SECTION H: Section H contained two standard psychological measures. The first was the Extended Personal Attributes Scale (Spence,

Helmreich, & Holahan, 1979). Earlier I mentioned that differences between people in how traditionally masculine or femininine they act could be important in understanding why some men rape and some women become victims.

Finally, this section contained the Conflict Tactics Scale (Strauss, 1979). The questions in this scale describe various strategies that can be used to express anger and resolve arguments with significant others including verbal behaviors (calm discussion, yelling or insults), withdrawal, noncontact physical aggression, and physical aggression.

How the Survey Was Scored

Statistical analysis is based on probability. Say I am comparing the drinking of five levels of sexually aggressive men and I have found that on average my group of 10 nonaggressive men drink one drink per day while my group of 10 sexually aggressive men drink 2 drinks per day. Is this difference important? Although it may look important, I need to know how likely it is that this difference could have occurred just by chance among the 20 people from whom I got information. If the differences were just chance, then I would not get the same results if I asked the question again but used a new sample of men. Usually, I will be unwilling to consider as important any difference that had more than 5 chances in 100 of being due simply to chance. Determination of the likelihood a difference is due to chance involves calculations that involve both how much each person's score differs from the group average and how many people were studied.

Now, the analysis of over 300 questions presents problems. With such a large number of questions, I am likely to come up with some differences—maybe 15 or so—that have attained statistical significance but are really just due to chance. Ideally, I should be careful to conduct as few separate comparisons as possible because the more I do, the greater the risk I take that some seemingly important differences will really be due to chance.

The second issue that is problematic with large surveys is the true size of the differences. When analyzing the responses of more than 6,000 people, some comparisons attain statistical significance just because there are so many people who each differ from each other by just a minuscule amount. When added together, these differences attain statistical significance but they are of little practical importance. Thus, what are known as "effect size" calculations were used to determine whether differences that attained statistical significance were truly important, real differences. I have followed the procedures described by Cohen [1977] in his book on power analysis and I have followed his guidelines for interpretation of the effect size which is called w for chi-square and the f for analysis of variance.

Getting to a Manageable Number of Characteristics

To reduce as much as possible the likelihood of chance findings as opposed to systematic differences, I limited the number of characteristics that I analyzed. The technical expression for getting your characteristics down to a manageable number is "reducing the data." Except for descriptive purposes, I have used summed variables, 16 for men and 13 for women. These variables were created by procedures and are beyond the scope of this appendix, but they are described in my articles (see Koss & Dinero, 1987, and Koss & Dinero, in press).

Determining a Person's Degree of Sexual Aggression and Sexual Victimization

Most of the data analyses utilized "factorial designs." Factorial means that several different degrees of a characteristic were studied. A comparison of drinking habits among men who differ in their degree of sexual aggression would be a factorial design. Five classes of sexual aggression and sexual victimization were developed including no sexual aggression or victimization, sexual contact, sexual coercion, attempted rape, and rape. The groups labeled "rape" and "attempted rape" included women who had experienced and men who had perpetrated acts that met legal definitions of these crimes. The typical definition of rape is the following: ". . . vaginal intercourse between male and female, and anal intercourse, fellatio, and cunnilingus . . . Penetration, however slight, is sufficient to complete vaginal or anal intercourse. . . . No person shall engage in sexual conduct with another person . . . when any of the following apply: (1)the offender purposely compels the other person to submit by force or threat of force, (2) for the purpose of preventing resistance the offender substantially impairs the other person's judgment or control by administering any drug or intoxicant to the other person. . . ." (Ohio Revised Code, 1980). I have used this strict, narrow definition of rape and have tried to stay in line with legal requirements. The people labeled "rape" victims or perpetrators all experienced acts that involved oral, anal, or vaginal penetration or penetration by objects against consent through the use of force or threat of bodily harm, or intentional incapacitation of the victim.

The group labeled "sexual coercion" included women who had experienced and men who had performed sexual intercourse subsequent to the use of menacing verbal pressure or misuse of authority over the victim. No threats of force or direct physical force were used. The group labeled "sexual contact" consisted of women who had experienced and men who had perpetrated sexual play such as fondling or kissing subsequent to the use of menacing verbal pressure, misuse of authority, threats of physical force, or actual physical force. None of these acts involved attempts by the offender to penetrate the victim. Few of these acts of coercion or contact would qualify as crimes. Persons who responded no to all 10 sexual experience items were labeled "sexually nonvictimized" or "sexually nonaggressive."

How the Conclusions were Reached

The project had five goals and to get information for each one, different kinds of statistical analyses had to be performed.

TO DETERMINE HOW MUCH SEXUAL AGGRESSION AND VICTIMIZATION IS OCCURRING AMONG COLLEGE STUDENTS TODAY: This goal was really the simplest mathematically. First, the percentage of women and men who said yes to each question about various types of sexual behavior was determined. Then the scoring rules were used to place each person into a level of sexual aggression or victimization and the percentage of people who ended up in each level was obtained. These rates were calculated both with and without weighting factors to allow estimation of the severity of the regional disproportion.

Finally, the number of people who reported that they had experienced or perpetrated a rape or attempted rape during the previous 12 months was counted. These rates were then divided by two to make them equivalent to a 6-month rate. Next, they were set to a base of 1,000 people rather than the 6,159 who were studied. Thus victimization and perpetration rates were calculated that could be compared to government crime rates (with appropriate recognition of the limits of generalization of the present sample, of course).

TO DESCRIBE THE TYPICAL INCIDENTS: The second aim was addressed through inferential statistical procedures used descriptively. If the characteristic of interest is something continuous like age, the appropriate statistical technique is called analysis of variance—ANOVA for short. When the characteristic of interest is discrete such as black, white, Hispanic, Asian, or Native American, the appropriate statistical technique is called chi-square—x^2 for short. No weights were used in any of the descriptive analyses. These analyses allow one to determine if two or more groups differ significantly on the particular characteristic of interest.

TO PREDICT SEXUAL AGGRESSION: For this goal, a statistical procedure called discriminant function analysis was used. Let's say that the characteristics that were measured about each man are like secret markings on the back of cards. On the face of the cards—where the pictures of spades, hearts, and clubs are—is each person's true confession about his sexual aggression. Lets say that "clubs" stand for sexually aggressive men. Discriminant analysis allows me to sort the cards into stacks of different suits by using only the secret markings, that is, the characteristics I've measured about the men. Then, by looking at the face of the cards, I can determine how accurate the predictions are. If nearly all the cards are sorted into the correct suits by using the secret markings, then the characteristics that were measured are important, powerful predictors. On the other hand, if lots of mistakes are made, then the characteristics that were measured aren't very good predictors of sexual aggression. The analyses are described in Koss & Dinero (in press).

EVALUATING RISK FACTORS FOR RAPE: Discriminant function analysis, as described above, was also used to reach conclusions about the risk factors for rape among college women. The analyses are described in Koss & Dinero, 1987.

THE IMPACT OF RAPE: The aftereffects of rape have been examined in a comparison between stranger and acquaintance-rape victims. Then victims of acquaintance rape were subdivided into women raped by nonromantic acquaintances, casual dates, steady dates, and spouses or family members. The analyses are described in Koss, Dinero, Seibel, & Cox, 1987.

How the Study Shaped the Book

A recent article about date rape in a national magazine began with a case history of a victim's experience which involved being raped repeatedly with a Coke bottle by her former boyfriend over the course of several hours. The incident succeeded in doing what the writer wanted: to draw readers to the article. Yet, the article was disturbing because this degree of violence is not typical and the case history presents a misleading picture of date rape.

First-person experiences are not "scientific" in the sense that they are based on only one person whose experiences may have been unusual. On the other hand, case histories are a vivid and effective communication tool. In the development of this book, the findings of the *Ms.* study have been used to guide selection of the real-life experiences so that these personal incidents illuminate the major trends that characterized respondents in the national survey. On the other hand, there is a lot of material in the book that is not drawn from results of the survey but instead is the work of other respected clinicians and researchers. Without this material, the book would not have given readers a full of range of views on the subject of acquaintance rape.

SELECTED BIBLIOGRAPHY

Ageton, Suzanne S. "Sexual assault among adolescents." Lexington, MA: D. C. Heath & Company, 1983.

Amir, Menachem. *Patterns in Forcible Rape.* Chicago: University of Chicago Press, 1971.

Barnett, Nona J., and Feild, Hubert S. "Sex Differences in University Students' Attitudes Toward Rape." *Journal of College Student Personnel* (1977): 93–96.

Bart, Pauline B. "Rape as a Paradigm of Sexism in Society—Victimization and Its Discontents." *Women's Studies International Quarterly* 2 (1979): 347–57.

Beck, A. T.; Ward, C. H.; Mendelson, M.; Mock, J.; and Erbaugh, J. "An Inventory for Measuring Depression." *Archives of General Psychiatry* 4 (1961): 561–71.

Bureau of Justice Statistics. *Criminal Victimization in the United States, 1982.* Washington, D.C.: U.S. Department of Justice, 1984.

Burgess, Ann W., and Holmstrom, Lynda L. "Rape Trauma Syndrome." *American Journal of Psychiatry* 131 (1974): 981–86.

Burkhart, Barry R., and Stanton, Annette L. "Sexual Aggression in Acquaintance Relationships." In *Violence in Intimate Relationships,* edited by Gordon Russell. Spectrum Press, 1985.

Burt, Martha R. "Cultural Myths and Support for Rape." *Journal of Personality and Social Psychology* 38 (1980): 217–30.

Check, James V. P. "The Hostility Toward Women Scale." Unpublished doctoral dissertation. Manitoba, Can.: University of Manitoba, 1984.

——— and Malamuth, Neil M. "Sex Role Stereotyping and Reactions to Depictions of Stranger and Acquaintance Rape." *Journal of Personality and Social Psychology* 45 (1983): 344–56.

Clark, L., and Lewis, D. *Rape: The Price of Coercive Sexuality.* Toronto: Women's Press, 1977.

Cohen, J. *Statistical Power Analysis for the Behavioral Sciences.* (Rev. ed.) New York: Academic Press, 1977.

211

Ellis, Elizabeth M. "A Review of Empirical Rape Research: Victim Reactions and Response to Treatment." *Clinical Psychology Review* 3 (1983): 473–90.

Federal Bureau of Investigation. *Uniform Crime Reports.* Washington, D.C.: U.S. Department of Justice, 1987.

Feild, Hubert S. "Attitudes Toward Rape: A Comparative Analysis of Police, Rapists, Crisis Counselors, and Citizens." *Journal of Personality and Social Psychology* 36 (1978): 156–79.

Finkelhor, David. *Sexually Victimized Children.* New York: The Free Press, 1979.

Giarrusso, Roseann; Johnson, Paula B.; Goodchilds, Jacqueline; and Zellman, Gail. "Adolescents' Cues and Signals: Sex and Assault." Paper presented at the Western Psychological Association meeting, April 1979, San Diego.

Goodchilds, Jacqueline D.; Zellman, Gail; Johnson, Paula B.; and Giarrusso, Roseann. "Adolescent and the Perceptions of Sexual Interactions Outcomes." In Burgess, A. W. (ed.), *Sexual Assault*, Vol. II. New York: Garland Publishing Company, 1988.

Graham, John R. *The MMPI: A Practical Guide.* New York: Oxford University Press, 1977.

Greendlinger, Virginia, and Byrne, Donn. "Coercive Sexual Fantasies of College Man as Predictors of Self-Reported Likelihood to Rape and Overt Sexual Aggression." *Journal of Sex Research* 23 (1987): 1–11.

Heilbrun, Alfred B., Jr., and Loftus, Maura P. "The Role of Sadism and Peer Pressure in the Sexual Aggression of Male College Students." *Journal of Sex Research* 22 (1986): 320–32.

Holmes, M. R., and St. Lawrence, J. "Treatment of Rape-Induced Trauma: Proposed Behavioral Conceptualization and Review of the Literature." *Clinical Psychological Review* 3 (1983): 417–33.

Kanin, Eugene J. "Male Aggression in Dating-Courtship Relations." *American Journal of Sociology* 63 (1957): 197–204.

––––––. "Date Rape: Unofficial Criminals and Victims." *Victimology: An International Journal* 9 (1984): 93–108.

Kilpatrick, Dean G. "Rape Victims: Detection, Assessment, and Treatment." *The Clinical Psychologist* 36 (1983): 88–101.

Koss, Mary P. "Discriminant Analysis of Risk Factors for Sexual Victimization Among a National Sample of College Women." Manuscript under review, 1987.

––––––. "Hidden Rape: Incidence, Prevalence, and Descriptive Characteristics of Sexual Aggression and Victimization in a National Sample of

College Students." In Burgess, A. W. (ed), *Sexual Assault,* vol. II. New York: Garland Publishing Company, 1988.

————. "The Hidden Rape Victim: Personality, Attitudinal, and Situational Characteristics." *Psychology of Women Quarterly* 9 (1985): 193–212.

———— and Dinero, Thomas E. "Predictors of Sexual Aggression Among a National Sample of Male College Students." In *Human Sexual Aggression,* edited by V. E. Quinsey and R. Pretky. New York: New York Academy of Sciences, forthcoming.

———— and Gidycz, Christine A. "Sexual Experiences Survey: Reliability and Validity." *Journal of Consulting and Clinical Psychology* 53 (1985).

———— and Harvey, M. R. *The Rape Victim: Clinical and Community Approaches to Treatment.* Lexington, MA: Stephen Green Press, 1987. 422–23.

———— and Oros, Cheryl J. "Sexual Experiences Survey: A Research Instrument Investigating Sexual Aggression and Victimization. *Journal of Consulting and Clinical Psychology* 50 (1982): 455–57.

————; Dinero, Thomas E.; Seibel, Cynthia A.; and Cox, Susan L. "Stranger and Acquaintance Rape: Are There Differences in the Victim's Experience?" *Psychology of Women Quarterly* 12, 1988, 1–23.

————; Gidycz, Christine A.; and Wisniewski, Nadine. "The Scope of Rape: Incidence and Prevalence of Sexual Aggression and Victimization in a National Sample of Higher Education Students." *Journal of Consulting and Clinical Psychology* 55 (1987): 162–70.

————; Leonard, Kenneth E.; Oros, Cheryl J.; and Beezley, Dana A. "Nonstranger Sexual Aggression: A Discriminant Analysis of the Psychological Characteristics of Undetected Offenders." *Sex Roles* 12 (1985): 981–92.

LaFree, Gary D. "Variables Affecting Guilty Pleas and Convictions in Rape Cases." *Social Forces* 58 (1980): 833–50.

————. "Official Reactions to Social Problems: Police Decisions in Sexual Assault Cases." *Social Problems* 28 (1981): 582–94.

————; Reskin, Barbara F.; and Visher, Christy A. "Jurors' Responses to Victims' Behavior and Legal Issues in Sexual Assault Trials." *Social Problems* 32 (1985): 389–407.

Levine-MacCombie, Joyce, and Koss, Mary P. "Acquaintance Rape: Effective Avoidance Strategies." *Psychology of Women Quarterly* 10 (1986): 311–20.

Makepeace, James M. "Courtship Violence Among College Students." *Family Relations* 30 (1981): 97–102.

Malamuth, Neil M. "Predictors of Naturalistic Sexual Aggression." *Journal of Personality and Social Psychology* 50 (1986): 953–62.

Muehlenhard, Charlene L.; Friedman, Debra E.; and Thomas, Celeste M. "Is Date Rape Justifiable?" *Psychology of Women Quarterly* 9 (1985): 297–310.

———; Linton, Melaney A.; Felts, Albert S.; and Andrews, Sandra L. "Men's Attitudes Toward the Justifiability of Date Rape." Presented at the midcontinent meeting of the Society for the Scientific Study of Sex, June 1985.

Myers, Mary Beth; Templar, Donald I.; and Brown, Ric. "Coping Ability of Women Who Became Rape Victims." *Journal of Consulting and Clinical Psychology* 52 (1984): 73–8.

Office of Civil Rights. *"Fall Enrollment and Compliance Report of Institutions of Higher Education."*(DHEW Publication No. NCES 76–135). Washington, DC: U.S. Department of Education, 1980.

Ohio Revised Code (1980). 2907.01A, 2907.02.

Parrot, Andrea. "Strategies Parents May Employ to Help Their Children Avoid Involvement in Acquaintance-Rape Situations." Paper presented at the New York State Federation of Professional Health Educators convention, November 1983, Binghamton, New York.

Rapaport, Karen, and Burkhart, Barry R. "Personality and Attitudinal Characteristics of Sexually Coercive College Males." *Journal of Abnormal Psychology* 93 (1984): 216–21.

Risin, Leslie I., and Koss, Mary P. "The Sexual Abuse of Boys: Prevalence and Descriptive Characteristics of the Childhood Victimizations." *Journal of Interpersonal Violence* 3 (1986): 309–23.

Rozee-Koker, Patricia, and Polk, Glenda C. "The Social Psychology of Group Rape." *Sexual Coercion & Assault* 1 (1986): 57–65.

Russell, Diana E. H. *Sexual Exploitation.* Beverly Hills: Sage, 1984.

Sanday, Peggy R. "The Socio-cultural Context of Rape." *Journal of Social Issues* 37 (1981): 5–27.

Spence, J. T.; Helmreich, R. L.; and Holahan, C. K. "Negative and Positive Components of Psychological Masculinity and Femininity and Their Relationships to Self-Reports of Neurotic and Acting-Out Behaviors." *Journal of Personality and Social Psychology* 37 (1979): 1673–82.

Speilberger, C. D.; Gorsuch, R. L.; and Luschene, R. E. *The State Trait Anxiety Inventory Manual.* Palo Alto: Consulting Psychologists Press, 1970.

Strauss, Murray A. "Measuring Intrafamily Conflict and Violence: The Conflicts Tactics (CT) Scales." *Journal of Marriage and the Family* 41 (1979): 75–88.

Weis, Kurt, and Borges, Sandra S. "Victimology and Rape: The Case of the Legitimate Victim." *Issues in Criminology* 8 (1973): 71–115.

Wieder, G. B. "Coping Ability of Rape Victims: Comment on Myers, Templar, and Brown." *Journal of Consulting and Clinical Psychology* 53 (1985): 429–30.

RESOURCES

BOOKS, BOOKLETS, PAMPHLETS, POSTERS

Acquaintance Rape: Awareness and Prevention for Teenagers by Py Bateman, director of Alternatives to Fear. Booklet with practical exercises for teens to help them avoid sexual violence from friends and dates. 16 pages. $4 plus $.75 postage/handling; bulk prices available. Alternatives to Fear, 1605 17th Ave., Seattle, WA 98122.

Against Our Will: Men, Women and Rape by Susan Brownmiller. The landmark book that raised America's consciousness about rape. 541 pages. $4.95. 1976. Bantam Books, New York.

Avoiding Rape on and off Campus by Carol Pritchard, rape referral counselor at Glassboro State College in Glassboro, New Jersey. 60-page booklet examining realities of acquaintance rape and stranger rape for college students. $3.95 plus $1 postage/handling; bulk prices available. 1987. State College Publishing Co., P.O. Box 209, Wenonah, NJ 08090-9990.

Campus Gang Rape: Party Games? by Julie K. Ehrhart and Bernice R. Sandler of the Project on the Status and Education of Women, Association of American Colleges. A look at college gang acquaintance rape and its causes; includes section for educators on how institutions should respond to rapes on their campuses. $3; bulk prices available. PSEW/AAC, 1818 R St., N.W., Washington, D.C. 20009.

Campus Violence: A National Concern edited by Jan Sherrill. Book for administrators examining collegiate violence. 1988. $11.95. Jossey-Bass, San Francisco.

College Security Questionnaire. For parents and prospective students to use in evaluating campus choices. Send stamped, self-addressed, legal-sized envelope to Connie and Howard Clery, P.O. Box 1518, Bryn Mawr, PA 19010.

Coping with Date Rape and Acquaintance Rape by Andrea Parrot. For adolescents and teens, a book about dealing with acquaintance rape for female and male survivors. Also includes a section for boys who now recognize that they have committed rape. 150 pages. $12.95. 1988. Rosen Publishing Group, New York.

Date Rape! A pamphlet for teens; includes guidelines for girls and boys. 50 pamphlets for $11; discounts for larger quantities available. Network Publications, P.O. Box 1830, Santa Cruz, CA 95061-1830. [For all Network Publications material, add 15% postage and handling; CA residents add 6% sales tax. $10.00 minimum order.]

Ending Men's Violence National Referral Directory. Resource listing 146 groups working with men to end violence against women. $8. 1986. RAVEN (Rape and Violence End Now), P.O. Box 24159, St. Louis, MO 63130.

"Friends" Raping Friends: Could It Happen to You? by Julie K. Ehrhart and Bernice R. Sandler. Date rape informational pamphlet aimed at college students. Contains prevention advice for women and men. 8 pages. $2; bulk prices available. PSEW/AAC, 1818 R St., N.W., Washington, DC 20009.

Her Wits About Her: Self-Defense Success Stories by Women edited by Denise Caignon and Gail Groves. 54 women tell how they effectively fought off rapists. Includes information on women's self-defense programs in the United States and Canada. 303 pages. $9.95. 1987. Harper & Row, New York.

Macho: Is That What I Really Want? by Py Bateman and Bill Mahoney. For teen boys, a 48-page booklet about dealing responsibly with social and sexual issues. $4 plus $.75 postage/handling; bulk prices available. 1986; published by Youth Education Systems, Scarborough, NY. Order from Alternatives to Fear, 1605 17th Ave., Seattle, WA 98122.

Men on Rape by Timothy Beneke. Interviews with men from various backgrounds about sexual violence. 174 pages. $5.95. 1982. St. Martin's Press, New York.

No Is Not Enough by Caren Adams, Jennifer Fay, and Jan Loreen-Martin. A guide for parents who want to help teens avoid sexual victimization. 190 pages. 1984. $6.95 plus $1.25 shipping and handling. Impact Publishers, P.O. Box 1094, San Luis Obispo, CA 93406.

Nobody Told Me It Was Rape by Caren Adams and Jennifer Fay. Guide for parents to help in talking with teens about acquaintance rape and sexual exploitation. 25 pages. $3.95; bulk prices available. 1984. Network Publications, P.O. Box 1830, Santa Cruz, CA 95061-1830.

Real Rape by Susan Estrich, professor at Harvard Law School. A legal history of acquaintance-rape cases in the United States, with suggestions for ways to make courts more responsive. 160 pages. 1987. $15.95, Harvard University Press, Cambridge, MA.

Recovering from Rape by Linda E. Ledray, director of the Minneapolis Sexual Assault Resource Service. A handbook for rape survivors and the people who love them. Includes directory of more than 275 rape-crisis centers nationwide. 258 pages. 1986. $9.95. Henry Holt and Co., New York.

Recovery: How to Survive Sexual Assault for Women, Men, Teenagers, and Their Friends and Families by Helen Benedict. Guide to physical, emotional, and social healing from rape. 293 pages. 1985. $15.95. Doubleday, New York.

Safe, Strong and Streetwise: The Teenagers' Guide to Preventing Sexual Assault by Helen Benedict. Sexual assault prevention for adolescents and teens. 192 pages. 1986. $14.95. Little, Brown & Co., Boston.

Sexual Abuse Prevention by Marie M. Fortune. 1984. $3.95. Pilgrim Press, New York.

Sexual Violence: The Unmentionable Sin by Marie M. Fortune. 240 pages. 1983. $9.95. Pilgrim Press, New York.

Stopping Rape: Successful Survival Strategies by Pauline B. Bart and Patricia H. O'Brien. A look at a variety of ways women have resisted being raped. 216 pages. 1985. $11.95 (paper); $27.50 (cloth). Pergamon Press. Elmsford, New York.

Today's Greeks Call It Date Rape. Poster distributed by Pi Kappa Phi national fraternity. $2.50. Pi Kappa Phi, P.O. Box 240526, Charlotte, NC 28224.

Top Secret: Sexual Assault Information for Teenagers Only by Jennifer Fay, Billie Jo Flerchinger, and the staff of King County (WA) Rape Relief. Booklet for teens, with handwritten "journal" entries, a question-and-answer advice column, and the voices of teen victims. Discusses everything from why a boy might rape his date to what a hospital rape exam is like. 32 pages. $3.95; bulk prices available. Network Publications, P.O. Box 1830, Santa Cruz, CA 95061-1830.

Where Do I Start? A Parents' Guide to Talking to Teens by Py Bateman and Gayle Stringer. Ways for parents to open discussions about acquaintance rape with their children, offer support and advice for protection. $4 plus

$.75 postage/handling; bulk prices available. 1984; published by Kendall/ Hunt Publishing Co., Dubuque, IA. Order from Alternatives to Fear, 1605 17th Ave., Seattle, WA 98122.

For further reading on current research, see the selected bibliography following the Afterword.

VIDEOTAPES, FILMS, AND FILMSTRIPS

A Question of Consent—Rape. Set in a courtroom, this film looks at the legal complexities of an acquaintance-rape case. 20 mins.; color. 16mm ($370); VHS videocassette ($330); 3-day rental ($60); preview available. Coronet/MTI Film and Video, 108 Wilmot Rd., Deerfield, IL 60015. Toll-free ordering: (800) 621-2131.

Acquaintance Rape Prevention Series. Four films examining date rape, group rape, and acquaintance rape for use with teens and young adults. Study guide included. 12 to 15 mins. each (47 mins. total). 16mm ($595); 3/4-inch U-matic or VHS videocassette ($535); one-week rental (all four, $125); preview available. O.D.N. Productions, Inc., 74 Varick St. #304, New York, NY 10013.

It Still Hurts, produced by the Auburn University Rape Awareness Committee. Student actors portray a classic campus date rape; tape may be paused for discussion as the scenario progresses. Includes a brief interview with a victim by acquaintance-rape expert Barry Burkhart. Available in VHS, Beta I or Beta II videocassette formats ($195), or 3/4-inch U-matic ($215). Campus Crime Prevention Programs, P.O. Box 204, Goshen, KY 40026.

Not Only Strangers. Explores emotional aftereffects of college-campus acquaintance rape. Contains explicit language. 23 mins.; color. 16mm ($515); VHS videocassette ($300); 3-day rental ($70); preview available. Coronet/ MTI Film and Video, 108 Wilmot Rd., Deerfield, IL 60015.

Rape Culture. Film exploring movies, ads, and music to show connections between violence and sexual behavior. With commentary from rape-crisis counselors and prisoners working against rape. 35 mins.; color. 16mm film, 3/4-inch U-matic videocassette ($402, single institution price); one-day rental ($46), one-week rental ($106); $6 postage. Cambridge Documentary Films, Inc., P.O. Box 385, Cambridge, MA 02139.

Rethinking Rape: A Film on Acquaintance Rape and Its Causes, directed by Jeanne Le Page. Developed with help of student-run Rape Education

Project at Stanford University, this film opens with a description of a stranger rape but moves on to acquaintance rape. Contains pornographic images in section on cultural values toward women. 26 mins. 16mm film ($425), 3/4-inch U-matic or VHS videocassettes ($275); one-day rental ($45). Film Distribution Center, 13500 N.E. 124th St., Suite 2, Kirkland, WA 98034.

Setting Limits, a series of three videotapes about preventing date rape performed entirely in sign language. Captioned version also available. 7 to 22 mins. each (57 mins. total). 3/4-inch U-matic or VHS videocassette ($500); one-week rental ($125); preview available. O.D.N. Productions, Inc., 74 Varick St., #304, New York, NY 10013.

Sexual Assault: A Chance to Think. Uses student actors from the University of Maryland to show four types of sexual assault, including acquaintance rape, that can occur on a college campus. Includes moderator's guide. 3/4-inch U-matic, VHS or Beta videocassettes ($150); two-week rental ($60). Cathy Atwell, Police Community Relations Officer, University of Maryland Police, College Park, MD 20742.

Sexual Assault Crimes: What Teens Should Know. Defines all types of sexual assault teenagers might encounter, with discussion on date rape and acquaintance rape. Includes prevention advice, psychological effects of rape, and how to get help. 30 mins. Filmstrip on VHS videocassette ($139) or two-part filmstrip ($115). Human Relations Media, 175 Tompkins Ave., Pleasantville, NY 10570.

Someone You Know: Acquaintance Rape. Examination of acquaintance rape in television documentary style, including interviews with survivors and experts. 29 mins.; color. 16mm ($520); VHS videocassette ($470); 3-day rental ($85). Preview available. 1986. Coronet/MTI Film and Video, 108 Wilmot Rd., Deerfield, IL 60015.

Still Killing Us Softly: Advertising's Image of Women by Jean Kilbourne. Film about how ads from magazines, newspapers, album covers, and billboards affect sexual roles, expression, and violence, including rape. 30 mins. 16mm film, 3/4-inch U-matic videocassette ($450, single institution price); one-day rental ($46); one-week rental ($106). $6 postage. Cambridge Documentary Films, Inc., P.O. Box 385, Cambridge, MA 02139.

Stop Date Rape! Student actors from Cornell University portray an acquaintance-rape situation in the first half of the film; in the second half, the same scenario is presented but rape is avoided due to the changed behaviors of the actors. Includes 75-page manual for leading discussion in conjunction with film. 23 mins.; color. VHS videocassette ($225); 3-day rental ($50). Cornell University Audiovisual Center, Media Services, 8 Research Park, Ithaca, NY 14850.

The Confrontation: Latinas Fight Back Against Rape, produced and directed by Anne Irving. A docudrama about a Chicana woman raped by a white man who has driven her home from a party. When the police are unable to help her, the woman decides to confront the rapist. Based on the nonviolent confrontational technique developed by Santa Cruz Women Against Rape. 37 mins.; black-and-white. 16mm, 3/4-inch U-matic and VHS videocassette ($400; one-day rental, $65) 1983. Women Make Movies, 225 Lafayette Street, Suite 212, New York, NY 10012.

The Party/The Dorm, conceived, scripted, and filmed by students at Swarthmore College. Dramatization of two situations with the potential for acquaintance rape. Includes discussion guide and informational leaflet. 16 mins. VHS videocassette ($200). Available for preview ($25). Cigus Vanni, Assistant Dean of Students, Swarthmore College, Swarthmore, PA 19081.

Waking Up to Rape, produced and directed by Meri Weingarten. Three acquaintance-rape victims talk about the long-term effects of rape, with input from rape-crisis counselors. Includes information on self-defense. 35 mins.; color. 16mm film, 3/4-inch U-matic, VHS videocassette ($500; one-day rental, $60). Women Make Movies, 225 Lafayette Street, Suite 212, New York, NY 10012.

PROGRAM GUIDES

Acquaintance Rape and Sexual Assault Prevention Training Manual by Andrea Parrot. 2nd edition. A 110-page guidebook for workshop leaders, containing general information, exercises, techniques for discussing acquaintance rape with various groups, and more. $8.50. 1987. Andrea Parrot, Dept. of Human Service Studies, N134 M.V.R. Hall, Cornell University, Ithaca, NY 14853.

Date Rape: A Basic Guide for Developing a Community Program by Randolph A. Gonzalez. Written by a security planner, this outlines how to set up a local program. 37 pages. $8.95, plus $1 shipping/handling. 1985. Eurich, Gonzalez & Associates, Inc., P.O. Box 260501, Tampa, FL 33685.

"I Know She Said, 'No,' but Thought She Said, 'Maybe'" by Mark Stevens. Outline and description of workshop. No charge. Mark Stevens, Student Counseling Center, University of Southern California, 857 West 36th Pl., Los Angeles, CA 90089.

Making It Work: A Community Action Plan for the Prevention of Teen Acquaintance Rape. Guide for individuals and organizations wanting to build community involvement in preventing acquaintance rape among teens. $3.50. Alternatives to Fear, 1605 17th Ave., Seattle, WA 98122.

Men's Curriculum of the Rape Education and Prevention Program at Ohio State University. Guide for building a men's program. No charge. REPP, 408 Ohio Union, 1739 N. High St., Columbus, OH 43210.

No Easy Answers by Cordelia Anderson Kent of Illusion Theater in Minneapolis. 20-lesson curriculum on sexual abuse for use in junior and senior high schools, includes material on sex and rape myths, acquaintance rape, and prevention. 218 pages. $29.95. 1982. Network Publications, P.O. Box 1830, Santa Cruz, CA 95061-1830.

Not for Women Only by Mark Willmarth. Guidelines for setting up a 90-minute rape-awareness program for men. $2.50. Mark Willmarth, Career/Placement Director, College of Great Falls, 1301 20th St. South, Great Falls, MT 59405.

Sex-Linked Assault Prevention/Protection Curriculum for high school population. Program for use by community-based organizations to build sexual responsibility, empathy, and conflict resolution skills. Emphasizes issues involved in date rape and acquaintance rape. Modular structure may be adapted for one-day to five-day program. $50. Marcie Servedio, Director, Adolescent Education Outreach, Santa Barbara Rape Crisis Center, 700 N. Milpas St., Santa Barbara, CA 93103.

This Is It! Teen Acquaintance Rape Information and Prevention Activities for Groups. Includes information on sexual harassment, assertiveness, and responses to rape for teens, with background information for teachers and group leaders. 200 pages. $35, $2.50 postage/handling; bulk discounts available. Alternatives to Fear, 1605 17th Ave., Seattle, WA 98122.

CONFERENCES

"Acquaintance Rape and Rape Prevention on Campus," coordinated by Daniel P. Keller, public safety director, University of Louisville. Three-day program for student leaders, college administrators, residence-hall staff, security personnel, faculty, and counselors. Held annually, usually in October, in Louisville, KY. Campus Crime Prevention Programs, P.O. Box 204, Goshen, KY 40026.

Conference on Campus Violence for administrators, counselors, residence-hall staff, faculty, and police. Held annually, usually in January, in Towson, MD. Conference on Campus Violence, Student Services, AD 100, Towson State University, Towson, MD 21204. (Also operates informational clearing-house on campus violence.)

National Conference to End Violence on Campus to be held Oct. 27–29, 1988, for students, faculty, staff, legislators, and community members. Contact: Penn Women's Center, University of Pennsylvania, 119 Houston Hall, 3417 Spruce St., Philadelphia, PA 19104-6306.

ORGANIZATIONS

Include self-addressed, stamped envelope for information.

Alternatives to Fear, 1605 17th Ave., Seattle, WA 98122. Acquaintance-rape education for adults and teens; self-defense.

Chimera, 59 E. Van Buren Ave., #714, Chicago, IL 60605. Self-defense programs for women of all ages, taught by women. Classes in eight states: IL, MA, OH, NJ, NY, NC, SD, WI.

Men's Anti-Rape Resource Center, P.O. Box 497, Madison, WI 53701-0497.

Index

Abbey, Antonia, 41
Abortion, 72–73
Acquaintance rape. *See also specific topics*
   definition of, 20–21
   extent of, 11–14, 48, 171
   identifying, 3, 4, 6–8, 23, 26, 32, 49, 50, 63, 110, 119–20
   myths about, 18–20, 25, 42–43, 45–46, 109–10, 161–63, 165
   use of term, 2–3
Acquaintance rape education, 164–67, 171–79
   fraternities and, 166–67
   parents and, 168–71
   resistance to, 171–72
   survivors and, 188
   teenagers and, 169–70
Aftereffects, 65–82, 185–88. *See also* Reactions of victims
   emotional, 67–71
   fantasies, 79–81
   friendships and family relations, 77–79, 180–84, 186
   medical examination and, 186
   physical, 71–73
   posttraumatic stress disorder, 68
   for the rapist, 90–92
   recovery and, 81–82
   sexual, 73–75
   teenagers and, 121–25
   telling boyfriends and husbands, 75–77, 183–84
Against Our Will: Men, Women, and Rape (Brownmiller), 21, 101

Ageton, Suzanne S., 119
AIDS, 72
Alcohol, 24, 43–45, 155, 162
   fraternities and, 105, 106, 108, 109
   teenagers and, 121
Anti-rape legislation, 178–79
Athletes (athletic teams), 110–14, 122–23
   sexist language and, 112–13
Awareness (organization), 167

Barnett, Nona J., 46
Bateman, Py, 23, 92, 95, 170
Benedict, Helen, 102
Beneke, Timothy, 93–94, 161
Blaming the victim, 18–23, 42–43, 45–46, 78–79
Blaming yourself, 56–58
Borges, Sandra S., 24, 63
Bowden, Mark, 109
Boyfriends, telling, 75–77
Brownmiller, Susan, 21, 101
Burgess, Ann Wolbert, 124, 125
Burkhart, Barry R., 13, 14, 60, 96
Burt, Martha R., 45, 47, 65
Byrne, Donn, 93

Cagney and Lacey (TV show), 96
Campbell, Ron, 165
Campus Organized Against Rape (COAR), 176
Carland, Paul, 166–67
Carson, Ellen Godbey, 146
Chew, Father Randolph, 168, 171
Civil court, 144–47

Clery family, 170, 179
College (college environment), 18–20, 23–25, 29–31. *See also specific topics*
   acquaintance rape education and, 164–67, 171–79
   athletic teams and, 110–14
   fraternities and, 104–10
   parents and, 170
   preventing rape and, 157
   university judicial boards and, 148–50
Communication, male-female, 41, 43
Confronting the rapist, 79–80
Corbett, Judy, 178
Cornell University, 166, 176–77
Counseling, 187–88
Criminal court system, 127, 130–33, 136–44
   difficulties of proving rape and, 142–44
   "good" cases and, 138–41
   juries and, 142–43

Dartmouth College,178
Dating (dating relationships)
   communication and, 41–42
   dating rituals and, 38–40
   interpersonal violence and, 40–41
Dawson, Robert K., 144–45
Denial, 54–55
Disassociation, 55–56
Dougan, Thomas R., 149, 150
Drew University, 165
Drug use, 24, 31–32, 43–45, 155–56, 162

Education. *See* Acquaintance rape education
Ehrhart, Julie K., 105
Emotional consequences of acquaintance rape, 67–71
Ervin-Tripp, Susan, 171, 175
Estrich, Susan, 143
Evans, Scott E., 110

Family relationships, 75–79
   husbands and, 75–77
Fantasies, postrape, 79–81
Farley, Diane, 178
Feild, Hubert S., 46

Fighting back, 158–59
   fear of, 60–62, 160
Florida, University of (Gainesville), 166–67, 176
Fraternities, 104–10
   acquaintance rape education and, 166–67
   gang rapes and, 104–10
   identifying acquaintance rape and, 110
   lawsuits and, 146
   sexist language and, 108–9
   university control of, 174
Friends, telling, 77–78, 180–84, 186

Gang rape(s), 99–114
   athletic teams and, 110–14
   dynamics of, 101–4
   fraternities and, 104–10
   group culture and, 103–14
   male bonding and, 101–3
   myth of, 109–10
   police and, 141
   victims of, 103
Giarrusso, Roseann, 120
Giving in, 160
Gone With the Wind (film), 95
Goodchild, Jacqueline D., 120
Great Falls, College of, 166
Greendlinger, Virginia, 93
Group culture, gang rape and, 103–14
Grow, Doug, 122–23

Harrow, Jan, 172
Hayden, Tom, 178–79
Heyman, Ira Michael, 111
Hielbrun, Alfred B., Jr., 97
Hofman, Rich, 113–14
Holmstrom, L. L., 125
Huckel, Lorraine, 174
Husbands, telling, 75–77
Hypermasculinity, 92–97

Identifying acquaintance rape, 3, 4, 6–8, 23, 25, 32, 49, 50
   fraternities and, 110
   revictimization and, 63
   teenagers and, 119–20
Inner signals, listening to, 58–60, 156–57
Interpersonal violence, 40–41

Johnke, Erik, 39, 167
Johnson, Henry, 172
Johnson, Paula D., 120
"Justifiable" rape, 42–43, 45–46

Kammer, Cindi, 180, 181
Kanin, Eugene J., 13, 43, 86–87
Kapp, Joe, 112–13
Katz, Bonnie L., 65
Krueger, Fred, 98

LaFree, Gary D., 127, 140–41
Landers, Ann, 22–23
Langella, Joe, 146
Language, sexist, 93–95
    athletes and, 112–13
    fraternities and, 108–9
LaValle, Kenneth P., 179
Lawsuits
    against rapist, 144–46
    against victim, 146–47
Legal system. *See also specific topics*
    bias of, 127
    civil court and, 144–47
    criminal court, 130–33, 136–44
    difficulties of proving rape and, 142–44
    "good" cases and, 138–41
    juries and, 142–43
    police attitudes and, 140–41
    third-party cases, 145–46
Legislation, anti-rape, 178–79
Loftus, Maura, 97

McClatchy, Richard A., Jr., 179
Makepeace, James M., 40–41
Malamuth, Neil, 97
Marx, George, 167
Media, the, 95–96
Medical examination, 186
Men
    acquaintance rape education for, 164–67, 171–79
    advice for, 161–64
    as victims, 3, 97–98
Men on Rape (Beneke), 93–94, 161
Men Stopping Rape, 167
Merton, Andrew, 107, 109
Minnesota, University of (Minneapolis), 178

Moonlighting (TV show), 95–96
Ms. Project on Campus Sexual Assault, 189–210
Muehlenhard, Charlene L., 41–43

New Hampshire, University of (Durham), 172–73

Ohio State University (Columbus), 177
Older victims, 26, 33–34

Parents, 25, 168–72
Parrot, Andrea, 65, 169, 176, 177
"Party" rapes. *See* Gang rape(s)
Physical consequences of acquaintance rape, 71–73
Police attitudes, 140–41
Polk, Glenda C., 102
Postrape fantasies, 79–81
Posttraumatic stress disorder, 68
Pregnancy, 71–72
Pressing charges, 20, 30, 127–47, 186–87
    advising against, 127
    civil court and, 144–47
    criminal court system and, 127, 130–33, 136–44
    fear of, 141–42
    police attitudes and, 140–41
    university judicial boards and, 148–50
Preventing acquaintance rape
    alcohol and drugs and, 155–56
    attacks in progress, 157–59
    college environment and, 157
    educational programs and, 164–67, 171–79
    fraternities and, 157
    identifying potential rapists, 151–52
    isolated places and, 152–53
    legislation and, 178–79
    men and, 161–64
    setting limits and, 153–55
    sex-role stereotypes and, 47
    by women and, 151–60

Rapaport, Karen, 96
Rape
    definition of, 20–21
    "justifiable," 42–43, 45–46

Rape-crisis hot lines, 182–83
Rape Education and Prevention Program (REPP), 176, 177
Rape-supportive attitudes, 45–46
Rape-trauma syndrome, 68–70
Rapist(s), 83–97. *See also specific topics*
  athletes, 110–14
  confronting, 79–80
  fraternity members, 104–10
  identifying potential, 151–52
  lawsuits filed by, 146–47
  methods used by, 87–90
  postrape behavior of, 90–92
  profiles of, 83–87
  socialization and, 87, 92–97
  teenage, 124–25
Reactions of victims, 54–64. *See also specific topics*
  denial, 54–55
  dissociation, 55–56
  fighting back and, 60–62
  inner signals and, 58–60
  reporting the attack and, 62
  revictimization, 62–64
  self-blame, 56–58
Real Rape (Estrich), 143
Recovery, 81–82
Recovery: How to Survive Sexual Assault for Women, Men, Teenagers, and Their Friends and Families (Benedict), 102
Reporting the attack, 62, 186–87
  rape by athletes and, 113–14
  teenagers and, 119, 124–26
Revictimization, 62–64
Rozee-Koker, Patricia, 102
Russell, Diana, 14

Sadism, 97
"Safe" victims, 50–54
Sanday, Peggy Reeves, 46
Sandler, Bernice R., 105
Saturday Night Fever (film), 95
Saying "no," 42, 154, 163–64
Scheper-Hughes, Nancy, 103, 111
Self-blame, 56–58
Sex-role socialization, 21, 23–24, 45–47, 92–97, 142–43, 154, 165. *See also* Athletes; Fraternities
  dating rituals and, 38–40

Sex-role socialization *(cont.)*
  the media and, 95–96
  men and, 87, 92–97
  parents and, 169
  teenagers and, 120
  victims and, 52
Sexual Awareness Greek Association (SAGA), 166–67
Sexual consequences of acquaintance rape, 73–75
Sexually transmitted disease, 72
Skolnick, Jerome H., 103
Southern California, University of (Los Angeles), 166
Steiner, Julie, 146, 147
Stevens, Mark, 166, 173
Stewart, David, 106
Survivors
  advice for, 185–88
  helping, 180–84
Swarthmore College, 177
Sweet, Ellen, 7

Teenagers, 115–26
  acquaintance rape education and, 169–70
  aftereffects of rape and, 121–25
  alcohol and, 121
  identifying acquaintance rape and, 119–20
  police and, 141
  as rapists, 124–25
  sexual socialization and, 119–21
  as victims, 25–29
"Trains." *See* Gang rape(s)

"Unfounded" rape cases, 140–41
Universities. *See* College
University judicial boards, 148–50

Victim(s). *See also specific topics*
  advice for, 185–88
  aftereffects of rape and, 121–25
  background of, 49, 51
  blaming the, 18–23, 42–43, 45–46, 78–79
  college students, 23–25, 29–31, 104–14, 157
  gang rapes and, 103
  helping, 180–84

Victim(s) *(cont.)*
   male, 3, 97–98
   "misconduct" of, 141–43
   older, 26, 33–34
   reactions of, 54–64
   revictimization of, 62–64
   "safe," 50–54
   socialization and, 52
   teenage, 25, 27–29, 115–26
   young single working women, 31–
     33
Violence, 40–41, 47, 61–62

Vonderharr, Kathi, 122

Walsh, Claire P., 25, 176
Washington State University (Pullman),
   177
Weis, Kurt, 24, 63
Wesleyan University, 177
Willmarth, Mark, 166
Wisconsin, University of (Madison), 167

Zellman, Gail, 120
Zia, Helen, 172